GENDER-BASED VIOLENCE IN ARTS AND CULTURE

Gender-Based Violence in Arts and Culture

Perspectives on Education and Work

Edited by Marie Buscatto, Sari Karttunen and Mathilde Provansal

OpenBook Publishers

ISBN Paperback 978-1-80511-448-2
ISBN Hardback 978-1-80511-449-9
ISBN PDF 978-1-80511-450-5
ISBN HTML 978-1-80511-452-9
ISBN EPUB 978-1-80511-451-2
DOI: 10.11647/OBP.0436

Cover image by Stefania Infante, CC BY-NC
Cover design by Jeevanjot Kaur Nagpal

Contents

Contributor Biographies

Dr Anna Bull is a Senior Lecturer (Associate Professor) in Education and Social Justice at the University of York, and co-director of The 1752 Group,[1] a research and campaigning organisation working to address sexual misconduct in higher education. As well as multiple academic and public-facing publications on sexual misconduct in higher education, Anna was an academic advisor to the National Union of Students for their report *Power in the Academy: Staff Sexual Misconduct in UK Higher Education*.[2] She sits on national advisory boards to address gender-based violence in higher education in the UK and Ireland. She has also carried out research into inequalities in classical music education and her monograph on this topic, *Class, Control, and Classical Music*, won the British Sociological Association's 2020 Philip Abrams Prize. Her research into sexual harassment in the film and television industry was published in 2023 in the report *Safe to Speak Up? Sexual Harassment in the UK Film and Television Industry since #MeToo*.[3]

Marie Buscatto is a Full Professor of Sociology at the University of Paris 1 Panthéon-Sorbonne and a researcher at IDHE.S (Paris 1—CNRS). She is a sociologist of work, gender and the arts, and a specialist in qualitative methods. Her current work focuses on gender inequalities in art worlds and prestigious professions, gender-based violence in the arts and the paradoxes of artistic work in Europe, North America and Japan. Her most recent publications in English include *Women in Jazz. Musicality, Femininity, Marginalization* (Routledge, 2021) and 'Getting Old in Art. Revisiting the Trajectories of 'Modest' Artists' (*Recherches*

---

1   See https://1752group.com/
2   See https://1752group.com/wp-content/uploads/2021/09/4f9f6-nus_staff-student_misconduct_report.pdf
3   See https://screen-network.org.uk/publication/safe-to-speak-up-sexual-harassment-in-the-uk-film-tv-industry/

sociologiques et anthropologiques, 2019). To find out more about her (more than) 160 publications, go to https://www.researchgate.net/profile/Marie-Buscatto

Having spent her post-doctoral years at Institut National des Langues et Civilisations Orientales (INALCO) and Tokyo University of Foreign Studies (Japan), **Chiharu Chujo** is currently Associate Professor at the University Jean Moulin Lyon 3 (France). Her dissertation, which she defended in 2018, focuses on committed Japanese women musicians from the 1970s to the present. She is currently pursuing her research on gender issues in the Japanese music industry, particularly in the world of hip-hop and electronic music. She has translated numerous books on the subject, including *Femmes du jazz* (Marie Buscatto, 2007) and *Be Creative* (Angela McRobbie, 2016). She is the author of several articles, including 'Chanter l'écologisme dans le Japon de l'après-Fukushima: l'ambivalence de la musique écoféministe chez UA' (*Itinéraires,* 2021) and 'Representing Love among Female Rappers: Transgressing, Poaching and Dialoguing' (in Japanese, *Eureka,* 2023).

Soline Helbert is a French lyric singer. A graduate of the universities Paris 1 and Paris 2, she is interested in the place of women in the world of opera.

Sari Karttunen, DSocSc, is a Senior Researcher at the Center for Cultural Policy Research CUPORE in Helsinki. She is also a Visiting Researcher at the University of the Arts Helsinki and holds the title of Adjunct Professor in cultural policy at the University of Jyväskylä. Her expertise lies in the sociology of artistic occupations and the analysis and critique of cultural statistics and other knowledge bases used in cultural policy. Currently, her research interests focus on diversity issues within cultural policy. Sari is an active member of the Research Network on Sociology of the Arts of the European Sociological Association, having served as co-coordinator from 2017 to 2019 and coordinator from 2019 to 2021.

Alice Laurent-Camena is currently completing a PhD in sociology at the University Rennes 2 and member of Arènes (CNRS social science research unit), France. Her thesis focuses on the feminisation of the French electronic dance music world and the ways in which this process interacts with the gendered organisation of this art world.

Bleuwenn Lechaux is Associate Professor of political science at Rennes 2 University and member of Arènes (CNRS social science research unit). Her work focuses on collective action and gender and racial discrimination, particularly in the artistic professions. She has conducted extensive fieldwork on these topics in both France and the United States. Her publications include, among others: (with Christine Guionnet), *L'ordinaire des rapports au genre* (Villeneuve-d'Ascq: Presses universitaires du Septentrion, 2025); 'Distinguer sans discriminer? Lutter contre les discriminations dans le monde du théâtre à New York' (*Critique internationale*, 2021); (with Christine Guionnet), *Rapports au genre en politique. Petits accommodements du quotidien* (Peter Lang, 2020); 'How Activist Plays Do Politics', in *How to Do Politics with Art*, ed. by Anurima Banerji and Violaine Roussel (Routledge, 2017), pp. 65–88; (with Violaine Roussel), *Voicing Dissent. American Artists and the War on Iraq* (Routledge, 2010).

Mathilde Provansal is a postdoctoral fellow in the Department of Sociology of Ludwig-Maximilians-Universität München (Germany). Her research concerns gender inequality and gender-based violence in art schools and contemporary art. She published the monograph *Artistes mais femmes. Une enquête sociologique dans l'art contemporain* (ENS Éditions, 2023), based on her dissertation on gender inequality in contemporary art, which was awarded two prizes: the Valois prize 2020 from the French Ministry of Culture, and the Louis Gruel prize from the Observatoire National de la Vie Étudiante (National Student Life Observatory). She has also published several articles, including 'Precarious Professional Identities. Women Artists and Gender Inequality within Contemporary Art' (*L'Année Sociologique*, 2024).

Ionela Roharik is a sociologist and research engineer at the research center CESPRA, École des Hautes Études en Sciences Sociales—CNRS (France). She has worked on the evolution of temporary artistic labour market sectors, on gender inequalities in the arts, and together with Janine Rannou, has published a book on the profession and careers of dancers: *Les Danseurs: Un métier d'engagement* (La Documentation Française, 2006).

Leena-Maija Rossi, PhD, works as Professor of Gender Studies at the University of Lapland (Finland). She is an expert in queer theory, intersectionality and visual culture. Her research interests also include critical studies on whiteness and posthumanist perspectives on gender. She holds the positions of Adjunct Professor in Visual Culture at the University of Turku, and in Art History and Gender Studies at the University of Helsinki. In addition to her academic career, she has served as the Executive Director of the Finnish Cultural Institute in New York, and worked as a freelance curator, collaborating with the major art museums in Helsinki, Finland.

Paula-Irene Villa is Full Professor for General Sociology and Gender Studies at LMU Munich (Germany). From 2021–2025, she served as President Elect of the German Sociological Association. Her research has been funded by several agencies such as the German Science Foundation or Volkswagen Stiftung, and focuses on biopolitics/embodiment (cosmetic surgery or food and fitness), on care and family, on gender in authoritarian politics, and most recently on academic freedom. She is the author and co-editor of twelve books and over sixty academic papers or book chapters; some of her (German and English) publications have been translated to Spanish and French. Paula Villa appears regularly on all sorts of media, and organises public science formats such as the 'Gender Salon' in Munich which has been running since 2009. She has two children and lives in Munich.

1. Introduction: A Comprehensive Understanding of Gender-Based Violence in Artistic and Cultural Worlds

Marie Buscatto, Sari Karttunen and Mathilde Provansal

Denouncing Sexual Violence in the Arts: A Loud Social Phenomenon

In October 2017, dozens of women made accusations of sexual violence against the cinema producer Harvey Weinstein (Kantor & Twohey, 2017; Farrow, 2017). Shortly after, upon the invitation of the actor Alyssa Milano, thousands of women shared their experiences of gender-based violence on social media under the hashtag #MeToo, using the name of the movement against sexual violence experienced by women of colour founded by the African American activist Tarana Burke. Sexual violence in the arts is far from being a 'red-carpet issue' involving only renowned male film directors and famous actors and actresses (Alcalde & Villa, 2022). In many locations all over the world, the past eight years have been marked by numerous denunciations of cases of sexual harassment, sexual assault and rape, mainly committed by men against women, in a large range of artistic and cultural work and education contexts. To name a few examples among many others, the website 'Paye ta note'[1] as well as the French collectives 'metoothéâtre'

---

1   See https://payetanote.com/

(Haymann & Brzezowska-Dudek, 2022) and 'metooartcontemporain'[2] have shared testimonies of sexism and sexual violence affecting female artists and 'support personnel' in these 'art worlds' (Becker, 1982). Whether in cinema, live performance arts, music, visual arts or dance, no artistic or cultural milieu has escaped this phenomenon, not even the most feminised ones.

Breaking the code of silence has unsettled the image of artistic and cultural circles as being open, egalitarian and avant-garde. In reaction to this, several actions and movements, sometimes involving renowned artists, have contested the politicisation and feminist analysis of these forms of violence against women. For example, shortly after the Weinstein affair, a hundred women mainly working in cultural and artistic spheres signed a manifesto in the French newspaper *Le Monde* defending 'a freedom to bother, indispensable to sexual freedom'[3] (Le Monde, 2018). Fortunately, these denunciations were also accompanied by the creation of feminist collectives and tools to fight gender-based violence in the arts and culture, such as the artist-led movement ENGAGEMENT fighting 'sexual harassment, sexism and abuse of power in the Belgian arts field'.[4]

Gender-based violence affects all kinds of artistic and cultural workplaces and educational institutions across many countries, which suggests that they are neither isolated incidents nor the consequences of a few individual deviant men. Instead, it reveals the systemic character of gender-based violence (Walby, 2013) in artistic and cultural worlds.

The #MeToo movement highlighted pervasive issues of sexual harassment, gender inequality and power dynamics in the artistic and cultural sectors, promising a significant reshaping of gender relations. However, the rise of 'anti-woke' sentiment casts doubt on #MeToo's lasting impact, and critical research is needed to assess the extent of changes in the gendered order. Overall, more studies are needed to approach gender-based violence as a systemic issue in the art worlds. While gender

---

2   These testimonies are published daily on the Instagram account 'metoo.art contemporain': see https://www.instagram.com/metoo.artcontemporain/
3   Our translation.
4   See https://engagementarts.be/en/about

inequalities in art worlds are well documented by academic research, the identification and explanation of gender-based violence in artistic and cultural sectors remain underexplored. Based on ambitious case studies in several artistic and cultural domains—opera, popular and electronic music, visual arts, screen industries, photography and theatre—and across a wide range of countries—Finland, France, Japan, the United Kingdom and the United States—this book aims to fill this gap.

In this introductory chapter, we first examine the current state of the art in the analysis of gender inequalities and gender-based violence in artistic and cultural work and education before presenting the key contributions of this book to a comprehensive understanding of gender-based violence in artistic and cultural work and education.

Gender Inequalities in Art Worlds: A Well-Researched Field

In the past twenty years, multiple researchers in sociology, historical and cultural studies have examined how certain artistic and cultural art worlds are feminised while others remain masculine (Buscatto, 2021; Flinn, 2024; Harris & Giuffre, 2015; Hatzipetrou-Andronikou, 2018; Ravet, 2011; Steedman, 2024). They have explored the main social processes maintaining male privileges and women's subordination in artistic and cultural worlds (Bielby, 2009; Brook et al., 2020; Buscatto, 2018; Gill, 2014; Hesmondhalgh & Baker, 2015; Provansal, 2023, 2024; Ramstedt, 2024; Stokes, 2015; Wreyford, 2018) and how these hierarchies are being obscured, naturalised and legitimised (Banks & Milestone, 2011; Buscatto, 2021; Gill, 2011; Jones & Pringles, 2015; Miller, 2016). They have also studied how gender inequality regimes intersect with other systems of inequality related to class, race, sexuality and age to stratify artists and cultural workers and their artistic and cultural production (Bull, 2019; Bull & Scharff, 2023; Buscatto et al, 2020; Provansal, 2020; Saha, 2018). They have identified the social, economic and political resources, the individual and collective strategies as well as the institutional measures that allow some women to survive in these extremely competitive and uncertain environments, and even to reach high levels of artistic reputation and economic remuneration (Buscatto, 2018; Karttunen, 2009; Provansal, 2023; Steedman, 2024).

Some scholars studying gender inequality in arts and culture have noticed, in their fieldwork, that female art students, artists and cultural intermediaries experience sexist practices and sexual violence. But, until now, very few scholars conducted fieldwork that explicitly focuses on gender-based violence in certain artistic and cultural sectors and connected their findings to the rich, yet 'fragmented' literature (Walby, 2013) on gender-based violence. Before presenting the state of the art related to this topic, let us discuss the key concepts of 'gender-based violence' and 'the *continuum* of sexual violence' developed in gender studies literature.

A Legacy of Feminist Thinking and Feminist Movements

Second-wave feminist movements and feminist thinking have helped to render visible the silenced experiences of sexual violence and to understand their social meaning. Challenging biological determinism and individualised approaches to violence against women, feminist thinkers reframed the issue, emphasising its systemic character and its inscription in gendered relations of power.

In the late seventies, British sociologist Jalna Hanmer (1977) stated that violence against women, and the fear of violence, is a form of social control by men over women and a way to maintain women's subordination. Violence, and the threat of violence, contribute to exclude women from certain social areas (investing certain occupations, for example), to restrict their fields of possibility (limiting their geographic mobility or artistic freedom), and to force them to behave in a certain way ('shut down the seduction' when interacting with cultural intermediaries (Buscatto, 2021)). Furthermore, Hanmer argued that 'not only should a definition of violence be based on the perspective of the victim, but that women's definitions covered a wide spectrum of abuses' (Hanmer & Maynard, 1987, p. 6).

Exploring the 'Continuum of Sexual Violence' as Conceptualised by Kelly

Pressure, abuse and coercion are also central to Liz Kelly's definition of 'the *continuum* of sexual violence' (Kelly, 1987). The concept makes it possible to describe the extent of women's experiences of sexual violence, from the everyday and routine intimate violations to criminalised and lethal forms of violence, affecting women across a lifetime, and to articulate them with the perpetuation of women's oppression. Kelly emphasises as well that a study of violence should be based on women's subjective experience and definition of violence rather than on the use of discrete categories organised along their degree of gravity.

Scholars have thus examined how the definition and the identification of sexual violence may change over time and vary according to social, cultural, political and legal contexts. For example, in a study conducted with editorial workers from two types of magazines—a feminist magazine and a heterosexual male pornographic magazine—Kirsten Dellinger and Christine Williams (2002) explore how the identification and the labelling of experiences of unwanted sexual behaviours as sexual harassment depend on the organisational culture and workplace norms. Comparing the social, cultural, legal and political contexts of the definition of sexual harassment in the United States and France, Abigail Saguy (2000) underlines that it is defined as a discrimination based on sex in American law while considered as a form of sexual violence in France, and that the consequences of such behaviours are very different for their perpetrator in these two national contexts. Kimberlé Crenshaw (1991) has also argued that women's experiences of violence and the way they are handled, or not, by political discourses and practices, depend on women's location at the intersection of several systems of inequality related to gender, class and race.

Feminist activists and researchers have identified and studied a large range of categories of violence (sexism, sexual harassment, rape, domestic violence, incest, cyber-harassment, femicide, etc.) exerted in diverse social contexts and locations (family, public space, higher education, work, social media, etc.) and perpetrated in a great majority by men against women. The development of research on gender and violence and the implementation of public policies to prevent and fight violence went along with the multiplication of categories to name it and the spread of 'umbrella terms' (Boyle, 2018) in the academic, activist, media and political spheres.

Gender and Violence: Naming the Issue

'Violence against women', 'men's violence against women', 'male violence against women', 'patriarchal violence against women', 'sexist and sexual violence', 'gender-based violence': the choice of a category comes with advantages and limitations. The first three expressions place the focus on the identity of the victims and/or of the perpetrators of violence. Unlike 'violence against women', which implies women's vulnerability, talking about 'men's violence against women' emphasises men's responsibility (Boyle, 2018), violence against women being predominantly committed by men. But it may convey an essentialist explanation of violence, men being the aggressors and women the victims 'by nature'. In 1993, the United Nations Declaration on the Elimination of Violence against Women defined 'violence against women' as 'any act of gender-based violence that results in, or is likely to result in physical, sexual, or psychological harm or suffering to women, including threats of such acts, coercion or arbitrary deprivation of liberty, whether occurring in public or private life'.[5] Prevalence research has shown the pervasiveness of violence in women's lives (Brown et al., 2020). However, there have been recent debates about extending the theoretical frameworks of gender-based violence to analyse violence against children (Whittier, 2016), gender and sexual minorities (Brown et al., 2020) and minoritised groups of men (Peretz & Vidmar, 2021). 'Patriarchal violence against women' tends to be used by scholars working on violence occurring in the family, such as domestic violence and incest, to 'point at the social system that underpins them'[6] and in which women's work and bodies are exploited by men (Giacinti et al., 2024, p. 4). The distinction between sexist violence and sexual violence in the fourth expression hides the *continuum* of the different forms of violence experienced by women.

---

5   See https://docs.un.org/en/A/RES/48/104
6   Our translation.

These limitations compelled us to use the notion of 'gender-based violence' to emphasise that gender, as a social relationship and a system of power relations, is the organising principle of violence and to consider a diversity of victims targeted because of their sex, their gender identity or gender performance, and their sexual orientation. Gender-based violence refers to all forms of violence, whether verbal, physical, sexual, psychological or economical, interpersonal or institutional, committed in both public and private spheres against people due to their claimed or assigned gender identity, sexual orientation, or location in the hierarchy of masculinities.[7] All contributing chapters in *Gender-Based Violence in Arts and Culture: Perspectives on Education and Work* articulate an analysis of violence through the lens of gender inequalities and gendered power relations at play within artistic and cultural work and educational contexts.

Gender-Based Violence in Artistic and Cultural Work and Education: State of the Art

Despite the richness of the literature on gender-based violence, very few studies have documented and addressed the forms, meanings and consequences of violence perpetrated against women and gender and sexual minorities in the artistic and cultural worlds. And as mentioned above, despite the growing visibility of the topic, few researchers specialised in these fields have explored the experiences of women and gender and sexual minorities with gender-based violence. And when they did, they primarily focused on the various forms of physical, verbal and non-verbal sexual harassment in artistic and cultural work, and to a lesser extent, in educational settings within the arts and culture sectors. A number of common findings emerge from these limited studies.

First, researchers have described the prevalence of sexual harassment in artistic and cultural workplaces (Crowley, 2021; Hennekam & Bennett, 2017; Idås et al., 2020). They have underlined that female workers in these environments are much more affected by sexual harassment than

---

7   Masculinities are organised along a hierarchy depending on their distance to 'hegemonic masculinity' and their intersections with other systems of domination (Connell, 2005).

their male colleagues, and employees from other sectors (Kleppe & Røyseng, 2016; North, 2016).

Second, they have reported how sexual harassment produces and is the product of gender inequality and gender relations in artistic and creative occupations (Buscatto et al., 2021; Crowley, 2021; Giuffre & Harris, 2019; Hennekam & Bennett, 2017; North, 2016). And they have identified, in the organisational culture, the organisation of work and the structures of employment, some factors and mechanisms sustaining sexual harassment in the artistic and creative industries. Sexualised workplaces, working processes and the content of artistic work blur the lines between what is considered a normal part of the job and what constitutes sexual harassment, making it more difficult to identify and report sexual harassment (Dellinger & Williams, 2002; Giuffre & Harris, 2019; Hennekam & Bennett, 2017). For example, in the theatre world, the line between work expectations and abusive behaviours is not easy to draw because the work of both male and female actors relies on attraction, intimacy and eroticism (Kleppe & Røyseng, 2016). 'Ambiguous industry demands', the valorisation of 'edginess' and the emphasis on artistic requirements contribute to obscuring reprehensible behaviours in the modelling industry as well (Crowley, 2021). Additionally, the celebration of talent, genius and charismatic authority perpetuates a tolerance of sexual harassment in artistic and cultural work and education. This tolerance is shared by victims, co-workers and superiors, enabling it to remain an essential aspect of the occupational culture of classical music (Trachman, 2018), the media industry (North, 2016) and the creative industries (Hennekam & Bennett, 2017). Patti Giuffre and Deborah Harris (2019) have described how, in the culinary industry, abusive behaviour by male 'creative genius' chefs is tolerated, or even excused, due to their professional success and creative abilities; restaurateur and author Jen Agg coined the term 'genius asshole' to explain how this trope helps to trivialise such behaviour. Finally, the individualisation of careers, intense competition for work, precarious employment situations and recruitment practices via informal professional networks put female workers in a vulnerable situation and make them dependent on men in positions of power able to make and break careers (Crowley, 2021; Hennekam & Bennett, 2017; Kleppe & Røyseng, 2016; Trachman, 2018).

A third key finding, linked to these structural work and employment factors, is the low proportion of women denouncing cases of sexual harassment because of the fear of retaliation and the potential negative outcomes on their career, and because of the lack of structures and procedures for reporting it (Dellinger & Williams, 2002; Giuffre & Harris, 2019; Idås et al., 2020; Kleppe & Røyseng, 2016; North, 2016; Trachman, 2018). As a result, some women feel compelled to leave their cultural and artistic careers, reflecting the broader structural barriers that prevent them from fully participating in these fields.

Assessing and Explaining Gender-Based Violence in Artistic and Cultural Work and Education

Despite their meaningful contributions, these works have some limitations, which prompted us to develop this collective book to thoroughly assess and explain gender-based violence in those environments. Most studies focus mainly on the experiences of gender-based violence of women already working in the arts and we know very little about the effects of gender-based violence in artistic education on the perpetuation of gender inequality in artistic careers. While several structural factors enabling and sustaining gender-based violence have been identified, their consequences for the access to artistic and cultural work, artistic careers and for creativity remain under-investigated. Most researchers also adopt an extensive definition of the creative industries or the artistic sectors, making it more difficult to describe precisely how these mechanisms operate within particular cultural and artistic work contexts. Furthermore, the analyses tend to focus solely on sexual harassment rather than investigating 'the *continuum* of sexual violence' as suggested by Kelly (1987), and do not always distinguish between gender-based violence, gender inequality and discrimination. Some studies also focus not on women's own experiences but rather on their views about sexual harassment in their occupational environment. Finally, we know very little about how gender-based violence is experienced by ethno-racial, gender and sexual minorities, and challenged in these fields.

Based on seven case studies conducted in several artistic and cultural worlds—opera, visual arts, popular music, screen industries, photography and theatre—and a wide range of countries—Finland, France, Japan, the United Kingdom and the United States—this book thus aims to deal with these limitations by offering a comprehensive sociological, cultural and feminist analysis of gender-based violence in artistic and cultural education and work. To do so, the authors address several issues. First, they open the analysis of gender-based violence not only to criminal offences such as rape, sexual violence, harassment or assault, but also to everyday sexism as part of a *continuum* of sexual violence. Secondly, they document the contexts, structures, power relations and routine practices that enable and sustain gender-based violence in artistic and cultural sectors. Analysing its historical foundations and social logics, the authors emphasise its structural character against commonly held psychologising and individualising explanations. Third, they study how gender-based violence is being silenced and normalised. Fourth, they reveal the social conditions, practices, measures and strategies used to challenge, denounce, address and stop gender-based violence. Last but not least, they offer and discuss multiple, original methodologies for studying gender-based violence. In the remaining sections of this introduction, we will briefly address how the key insights were systematically uncovered through these case studies.

Investigating Gender-Based Violence beyond Statistics

The research presented in this book is not based on one-off projects but rather on entire academic careers dedicated to studying artistic labour markets and gender issues. And this deep and long-term knowledge enriches the authors' study of gender-based violence in several ways.

Historically, quantification has been a way to objectify and to document the extent of gender-based violence. This is not the case when it comes to arts and cultural sectors, where very few quantitative studies, if any, have been conducted by researchers, governmental institutions, artistic institutions and activists, in those sectors, mostly due to high costs and lack of human resources. To frame the case studies within their specific contexts, the authors necessarily draw on industry statistics, underscoring their significance in the pursuit of equality. However, while acknowledging the importance of 'feminist counting', they all seek to delve deeper beyond just statistics of equality. Achieving a simple male-female balance may not fully capture the complexities of gender dynamics, power structures and intersectional inequalities that shape women's and gender and sexual minorities' experiences and opportunities in the arts. Indeed, the focus of the seven chapters oscillates between everyday practices and their structural foundations while the methodologies they use could be described as feminist, and share a politically activist orientation. Consequently, calls for research participation were often spread, in part, with assistance from feminist associations or groups in the arts. As opposed to general studies conducted in creative industries, this epistemological approach allows for 'thick' descriptions of gender-based violence as well as for a deep understanding of its causes and its consequences.

Moreover, most authors in the book acknowledge that their samples are not fully representative, often comprising a relatively low number of respondents and exhibiting a bias toward individuals interested in gender issues and with personal experience. And this choice, based on a strong knowledge of the artistic or cultural worlds being investigated, is key in their ability to identify gender-based violence in its complexity. The researchers have then used various measures to include not just those who identify as female and victims, but to embed the research within a comprehensive understanding of the underlying structures and the workings of gender-based violence. Not all authors aim for generalisability; instead, they focus on providing nuanced, contextual analyses that describe 'some of the ways in which content and workplace culture interact and explore[s] new directions for thinking about the questions raised', as Anna Bull states in her chapter (Chapter 6). Interestingly, many of these apparently non-generalisable observations and findings recur in other art fields and countries throughout the book.

Thanks to their deep and long-term knowledge of the art sector, the researchers are thus able to give a rich and detailed view of what is at stake in these fields, enhancing our knowledge about contexts and structural processes enabling violence as well as about the meaning of such experiences for victims. It allows the authors to contextualise their findings by drawing on their extensive experience in researching the artistic sectors and their operational logics and could thus exceed the limits of quantification. The following four sections outline the four main findings this book brings to the study of gender-based violence in artistic and cultural work and education.

Grasping the Inclination of Art Worlds toward Gender-Based Violence through the Identification of Its Various Forms

First of all, this book brings to light the many ways gender-based violence occurs in artistic and cultural worlds. By doing so, it reveals how these spaces are conducive to gender-based violence through many ordinary, and sometimes invisible, practices. The case studies demonstrate that while those practices may seem innocuous, and are sometimes even invisible to people who experience or witness them, they participate in creating an educational or professional world laden with gender-based violence. Thanks to a thorough description of gender-based violence in its various forms, along Kelly's '*continuum* of gender-based violence', the case studies also describe in detail a wide range of sexist and sexual behaviours which constitute the daily, ordinary experience of many female students and professionals in artistic and cultural sectors.

For instance, using a detailed questionnaire describing many different potential sexist and sexual acts in their study of gender-based violence in the French opera world (Chapter 2), Marie Buscatto, Soline Helbert and Ionela Roharik reveal that not only do many practices participate in creating a gender-based violent art world (more than three-quarters of respondents reported having experienced an act of gender-based violence as victims), but also that the range of acts is very numerous, from sexist remarks, insistent flirting, sexist jokes or obscene, saucy and embarrassing comments to unwanted touching of sexual or erogenous areas, or sexual assault. Interviews conducted with female and male singers confirmed that sexist practices were not only part of the daily life of opera workers, but that even those of them who initially claimed not to be victims and witnesses of such sexist acts were, in fact, experiencing them in their daily lives without recognising them as such. Thanks to an extensive collection of many gender-based violence acts, most of them being considered sexist, this case study shows how strongly the French opera world fosters gender-based violence.

Another instance here is the qualitative study carried out in the

Japanese popular music industry by Chiharu Chujo: 'when asked in the context of a more nuanced understanding of "sexual harassment"—including manifestations such as sexist remarks, persistent flirtation and derogatory jokes about sexuality or appearance—respondents clearly confirmed recurrent encounters with such incidents' (Chapter 3). While those interviewees did not consider those practices as sexual harassment at first (and thus worth denouncing or even mentioning to an interviewer conducting a study on sexual harassment), they did describe such situations freely when specifically asked about them. And the ways they described those sexist practices clearly indicated that those practices were mostly tolerated by women on a daily basis, not because they were harmless or insignificant, but because of power relations (such as hierarchy and client/customer relationships) that constrained them to accept the practices. They developed tactical ways to try to protect themselves from being harmed—from escaping those situations to accepting them as inevitable. But overall, only a few of them reacted actively to fight them, and this happened only when they could use their professional legitimacy gained over time or benefit from the support of strong networks. Through a study designed to elicit testimonies extending the definition of gender-based violence to daily sexist practices, Chujo was able to not only describe how conducive to gender-based violence the Japanese music industry is (including the experience of sexual violence as such), but also how difficult it is for women to escape such a gender-based violent world. The same can be said of all the artistic and cultural worlds explored in this book, from the Helsinki School, a Finnish photography training and branding initiative (Chapter 5), to the French contemporary art education scene (Chapter 4) and the New York theatre world (Chapter 7).

It should be noted here that the strong involvement of the researchers in gender issues made this empirical approach possible. Indeed, even if in the aftermath of #MeToo, research participants are supposedly more inclined to discuss their experiences of gender-based violence, they are still at risk of losing work opportunities if their identities are revealed, because of the gendered power dynamics prevalent in most art worlds. And this is even more important in artistic and cultural worlds where reputations are at stake, and precarity and instability are key elements in the development of one's career. The instances of violence may have been traumatic for the interviewees, demanding special sensitivity from the interviewer, as clearly exemplified in Bull's strategy of acknowledging potential trauma in her interviewing techniques while studying gender-based violence in screen industries fields (Chapter 6). Extra measures have been used to ensure the confidentiality and anonymity of the research participants, unless those participants had already expressed their points of view in the media, as was the case in Leena-Maija Rossi and Sari Karttunen's study of sexual harassment in the Helsinki School (Chapter 5).

The Production of Gender-Based Violence as the Result of Cumulative Social Processes

A second contribution of the case studies presented in this book is expanding our understanding of the social processes which produce such an omnipresence of gender-based violence in artistic and cultural education and work. While the authors are genuinely interested in the experiences of workers and students, they aim to go further and uncover the underlying structures which enable those experiences to happen and to be tolerated even when harmful to the victims. They seek 'to report on the social conditions which allow the production of gender-based violence and grasp its various sociological dimensions', as described by Buscatto, Helbert and Roharik (Chapter 2). The political aim, whether explicitly declared or not, is to expose and dismantle the mechanisms and structures maintaining the gendered order in the arts. Gender-based violence is not treated as a marginal, interpersonal or private issue, but as a form of social control that contributes to the subordination of women and gender and sexual minorities in the arts.

For instance, Mathilde Provansal shows how varied cumulative social processes participate in producing various forms of gender-based violence in the French elite art school she investigated (Chapter 4): 'A first social process providing a "conducive context" (Kelly, 2016) for gender-based violence is the sexualisation of female students in a context of "hierarchised gender diversity" (Cardi et al., 2005). The last expression refers to the unequal distribution of power and authority between men and women within art schools'. While women tend to be a majority as students, men tend to act as teachers, but more to the point, sexualisation of female students tends to be a norm which affects all their encounters and educational resources, from recruitment to training to job opportunities. And the same phenomenon is observed in all the artistic and cultural worlds studied in this book, whatever the level of feminisation—music, theatre, visual arts, photography or screen industries.

Moreover, Provansal observes a strong dependency of students on their instructors to launch their careers: as is also the case in all art sectors, men in power are key in opening doors and assuring the artist's future, whatever the stage of her career. Another social process which participates in producing such gender-based violent art worlds is the blurred boundaries between the private, educational and professional spheres. Not only are many events which could be considered as private—cocktails, dinners, holidays, love relationships—an integral part of artistic lives, but the production of artworks is based on the mobilisation of intimate experiences and bodies whether they consist in visual or photographic artworks, musical or theatrical performances.

Last but not least, very few public policies and procedures enable victims or witnesses to denounce gender-based violence in open, safe and transparent contexts. We should note once more that the strong involvement of Provansal in this art school as a researcher in the long run enabled her to identify the social processes that contribute towards the production and perpetuation of a violent gender-based art world. Indeed, the data collection spanned from 2014 to 2022: over this long period of time, she conducted interviews with art school graduates and personnel, an ethnography of entrance exam, and analysed documents produced by feminist art student and teacher collectives.

Gender-Based Violence Affects Women's Creativity and Careers in Many Ways

The case studies presented in this book explore the many ways gender-based violence affects women's careers. One obvious consequence is that some women, confronted with sexist practices or subjected to sexual violence, withdraw from such art worlds to avoid further exposure to these practices, as clearly identified in the case study of photography students affiliated with the Helsinki School by Rossi and

Karttunen (Chapter 5). Some of them are traumatised and may go through psychological counselling, while others reject such practices and refuse to be part of such sexist and abusive environments. Another consequence is that even those who survive such experiences (as victims or as witnesses) tend to find their professional reputation and the quality of their artworks diminished due to demeaning practices that reduce women to their bodies and sexual appeal, as observed by Provansal in the French elite visual art school she studied (Chapter 4). Some of those women may also refuse to go along with sexist practices and risk losing professional opportunities, labelled as boring, lacking appeal or too loud, as identified by Buscatto, Helbert and Roharik in the context of French opera (Chapter 2).

Another direct and little explored consequence of the inclination of artistic and cultural worlds to gender-based violence is its influence on creative content. In their study of the pervasiveness of sexual harassment in the Finnish photography export and training initiative, the Helsinki School, Rossi and Karttunen show how female photographers were compelled to produce images in which the 'female bodily capital also emerges as a resource to be used in photographs. For instance, the branding effort has to some extent utilised the bodily capital and aesthetic labour of its female members' (Chapter 5). In some images, women appeared as powerless victims; in other cases, they were pushed to photograph their nude bodies or to draw on their personal trauma as part of their creative practice. Looking through Helsinki School photo books, and combining visual and textual materials in their analysis, Rossi and Karttunen reached the assessment that 'several female artists associated with the Helsinki School appear to have been strategically used both for crafting the collective image of the School and enhancing the market success of the branding effort, implying an economic form of gender-based violence'.

Drawing on a study of eighteen workers in the UK screen industries who had been subjected to sexual harassment or violence at work since 2017, Bull focuses 'on a subset of these accounts in which interviewees described producing content relating to sexuality, gender-based violence or harassment—across journalism, factual entertainment and drama/comedy—at the same time as negotiating sexual harassment or violence within the workplace in which this material was being produced' (Chapter 6). In some cases, producing such content makes the workplace even more conducive to gender-based violence. In other cases, it becomes a resource for those victims to talk about their traumatic experience and label it as gender-based violence. But overall, the study that this chapter drew on found that few employers of the UK screen industries took an actively anti-sexist approach to workplace culture (Bull, 2023).

These case studies suggest that cultural production under conditions of gendered dependency relations and gender-based violence may shape both the content and form of artistic works, constraining the creative agency of women artists and influencing the narratives and representations they produce. While activist women aim to provide artistic representations that contribute to recognising and denouncing gendered abuse, there are others whose work continues to reaffirm the patriarchal symbolic order (see, for example, Canlı & Mandolini, 2022; Mandolini & Williamson Sinalo, 2023). In sectors such as photographic art (Chapter 5) and the screen industry (Chapter 6), women may be expected, even compelled, to use their bodies, sexual experiences and personal traumas as commodities in their artwork to advance their careers. Moreover, many women engage in producing representations of violence against women within contexts marked by workplace harassment or violence. Further research is necessary to fully understand the impact of these circumstances on women's creative practices and the representation of gender-based violence in cultural works.

Gender-Based Violence Tends to Be Silenced

While most of the time women acknowledge that the consequences of gender-based violence are harsh, both psychologically and professionally, they tend not to speak up. And this is the case even when confronted with blatant cases of sexual misconduct which could lead to legal action—sexual harassment, sexual assault or rape. All case studies show that the social processes which make those artistic and cultural worlds conducive to gender-based violence are also silencing the victims. Fear seems to be the common denominator in the production of silence: fear of losing one's job (or of not being recruited for the next one), fear of being expelled from the artistic and cultural world, fear of being disparaged publicly as too seductive or sexy, fear of being considered as a lousy colleague, fear of being attacked personally, fear of not being believed due to the strong legitimacy of the predator (as, for example, a talented and renowned artist).

In her study of sexual harassment of New York theatre professionals, Bleuwenn Lechaux shows that this constant fear is key in explaining why so few criminal cases are brought to justice despite the development of measures to enable such denunciations (Chapter 7). Her research, conducted through a field survey totalling several weeks spread over the years 2015 and 2017, supplemented by twenty-eight interviews in 2020, builds upon her prior work on theatre professionals in New York and Paris, which involved 126 semi-structured interviews conducted between 2007 and 2010. Through her long-term involvement in this sector, she is able to show that, while the #MeToo movement made the issue of sexual harassment visible and openly legitimated any action against sexual predators, denunciations nonetheless remain infrequent and challenging to engage in for the victims, due to the heavy psychological and professional costs of speaking out. If the exposure of criminal offences has pushed the issue of sexual harassment to the top of the public agenda and procedures for fighting sexual harassment have been formalised (e.g., the Callisto project and tool, intimacy direction through choreographic techniques, *pro bono* mediation), 'legal measures nevertheless seem to be of little help in worlds where hiring practices remain governed by the uncertainty and arbitrariness of subjective artistic choices'.

This assessment goes one step further in highlighting the necessity of studying the *continuum* of violence to better elucidate how criminal sexual offences are integrated into the structural and systemic functioning of artistic and cultural worlds. Moreover, addressing this issue entails combating sexism, as it is through sexist practices that the groundwork for sexual offences is established. This leads us to discuss a further revelation from our case studies: the conditions which sometimes allow employees to speak up and to reduce sexist and sexual violence in artistic and cultural worlds.

From Silencing to Speaking Up: A Long Road to Go

As discussed in the preceding sections, women tend not to speak up, even when victims or witnesses of legally reprehensible sexual offences. However, our case studies also show that this tendency not to denounce gender-based violence may be partly questioned thanks to at least three types of actions.

Lechaux (Chapter 7) as well as Alice Laurent-Camena (Chapter 8) identify how informal groups, through the exchange of experience and information, may help women to label their experience and sometimes even to act upon it. For instance, in her ethnographic work on the French electronic music world, Laurent-Camena shows how passing on rumours between women about some male predators not only gives an increased legitimacy to the denunciation, but sometimes enables those women to protect themselves from such predators by excluding them from their projects. It does not affect the predator's reputation or ability to perform music, but it does create a safer work environment for those women who decide to act on the shared rumour. So-called intimacy coordinators may also be called for on theatre, opera or cinema stages. 'By offering a guarantee of preserving emotional safety through learning what we might call "stage consent"', they help prevent directors from using their position to abuse women (Chapter 7). Public denunciations of sexual abuse, through social media and press releases, are quite effective, as they often lead to the end of the predator's career or profoundly shake it (as seen in the case of the Helsinki School, Chapter 5). They are however very rare, as observed by Laurent-Camena, not only because they require a large amount of proof and need to be defined as criminal acts to reach such a public level of denunciation, but also because members of the electronic music world prefer to handle denunciations internally and to avoid such public accusations, whenever possible.

In her conclusion, Laurent-Camena considers how '"exemplary" public accusations can paradoxically deter victims from speaking out, in addition to the other obstacles they encounter along the denunciation process. The egalitarian ethos, at least concerning the stance against gender-based violence, does not fundamentally disturb the gendered organisation of this art world.'

Conclusion

This book builds toward a comprehensive understanding of gender-based violence in artistic and cultural education and work, exploring its causes as well as its consequences, from silencing the victims to enabling them to speak up—even if in rare cases. However, while it makes significant contributions to this topic, much remains to be examined regarding gender and sexual minorities and men as victims. Despite a strong intention to address gender-based violence affecting gender and sexual minorities—queer, non-binary, transgender and non-heterosexual individuals—as well as men, the authors were unable to do so due to the very limited number of cases encountered during their studies.

Gender-based violence in artistic and cultural worlds does primarily affect women and is mostly implemented by powerful men. However, specific case studies focusing on minoritised victims need to be developed to better understand those phenomena and articulate them with gender-based violence affecting women. We strongly advocate for the development of such case studies in the future, as this book has aimed to expand our understanding of gender-based violence affecting women workers and students in artistic and cultural worlds. For the same reason, while researchers focused on unveiling the ways gender-based violence is produced, legitimised and perpetuated over time, they were unable to implement an intersectional approach (Buscatto et al., 2020)—another development that is called for in future research. And we hope that researchers from all around the world will develop case studies addressing gender-based violence in Latin American, African and Asian countries, since it was beyond the scope of our research to do so.

The book is divided into three parts to provide a comprehensive examination of gender-based violence in artistic and cultural education and work. Part I explores the systemic factors that underpin gender inequalities and gender-based violence, focusing on power dynamics, normalised practices and institutional structures that perpetuate these practices. Part II shifts the focus to the creation of representations of gender-based violence in cultural and artistic works, examining the intersection of creation, representation and the lived experiences of those affected. Part III investigates efforts to challenge and confront gender-based violence within artistic and cultural environments, highlighting the strategies and actions used to address and disrupt these harmful practices.

References

Alcalde, C. M., & Villa, P.-I. (2022). *#MeToo and beyond. Perspectives on a global movement.* University Press of Kentucky. https://doi.org/10.2307/j.ctv2mm210k

Banks, M., & Milestone, K. (2011). Individualization, gender and cultural work. *Gender, Work and organization,* 18(1), 73–89. https://doi.org/10.1111/j.1468-0432.2010.00535.x

Becker, H. S. (1982). *Art worlds.* University of California Press.

Bielby, D. (2009). Gender inequality in culture industries: Women and men writers in film and television. *Sociologie du travail,* 51(2), 237–252. https://doi.org/10.4000/sdt.16462

Boyle, K. (2018). What's in a name? Theorising the inter-relationships of gender and violence. *Feminist Theory,* 20(1), 19–36. https://doi.org/10.1177/1464700118754957

Brook, O., O'Brien, D., & Taylor, M. (2020). *Culture is bad for you. Inequality in the cultural and creative industries.* Manchester University Press. https://doi.org/10.7765/9781526152152

Brown, E., Debauche, A., Hamel, C., & Mazuy, M. (Eds) (2020). *Violences et rapports de genre. Enquête sur les violences de genre en France.* Ined Éditions. https://doi.org/10.4000/books.ined.14719

Bull, A. (2019). *Class, control, and classical music.* Oxford University Press. https://doi.org/10.1093/oso/9780190844356.001.0001

Bull, A. (2023). *Safe to speak up? Sexual harassment in the UK film and television industry since #MeToo.* Screen Industries Growth Network, University of York. https://screen-network.org.uk/wp-content/uploads/2023/10/Safe-to-Speak-Up-full-report.pdf

Bull, A., & Scharff, C. (2023). *Voices for change in the classical music profession.* Oxford University Press. https://doi.org/10.1093/oso/9780197601211.001.0001

Buscatto, M. (2018). Feminisations of artistic work: Legal measures and female artists' resources do matter. *Revista Todas as Artes,* 1(1), 21–38. https://doi.org/10.21747/21843805/tav1n1a2

Buscatto, M. (2021). *Women in jazz. Musicality, femininity, marginalization.* Routledge. (Original work published in 2007). https://doi.org/10.4324/9781003177555

Buscatto, M., Helbert, S., Roharik, I. (2021). L'opéra, un monde professionnel hanté par les violences de genre. *Les Cahiers de la SQRM,* 22(1), https://doi.org/10.7202/1097857ar

Buscatto, M., Cordier, M., & Laillier, J. (Eds) (2020). *Sous le talent: la classe, le genre, la race. Agone,* Special issue, 65.

Canlı, E., & Mandolini, N. (2022). Aesthetics in distress: Gender-based violence and visual culture. Introductory note. *Vista*, 10. https://doi.org/10.21814/vista.4071

Cardi, C., Naudier, D., & Pruvost, G. (2005). Les rapports sociaux de sexe à l'université: au cœur d'une triple dénégation. *L'Homme & La Société*, 4(158), 49–73. https://doi.org/10.3917/lhs.158.0049

Connell, R. W. (2005 [1995]). *Masculinities* (2nd ed.). Routledge. https://doi.org/10.4324/9781003116479

Crenshaw, K. (1991). Mapping the margins: Intersectionality, identity politics, and violence against women of color. *Stanford Law Review*, 43(6), 1241–1299. https://doi.org/10.2307/1229039

Crowley, J. E. (2021). Sexual harassment in display work: The case of the modeling industry. *Gender & Society*, 35(5), 719–745. https://doi.org/10.1177/08912432211036890

Dellinger, K., & Williams, C. (2002). The locker room and the dorm room: Workplace norms and the boundaries of sexual harassment in magazine editing. *Social Problems*, 49(2), 242–257. https://doi.org/10.1525/sp.2002.49.2.242

Farrow, R. (2017, October 10). From aggressive overtures to sexual assault: Harvey Weinstein's accusers tell their stories. *The New Yorker*. https://www.newyorker.com/news/news-desk/from-aggressive-overtures-to-sexual-assault-harvey-weinsteins-accusers-tell-their-stories

Flinn, M. C. (2024). *Drawing (in) the feminine: Bande dessinée and women*. The Ohio State University Press. https://doi.org/10.26818/9780814215142

Giacinti, M., Hamel, C., Roca i Escoda, M., Bayer, V., & Couchot-Schiex, S. (2024). Politiques publiques face aux violences patriarcales: l'État de nos désillusions et de nos avancées. *Nouvelles Questions Féministes*, 43(2), 4–13. https://doi.org/10.3917/nqf.432.0004

Gill, R. (2011). Sexism reloaded, or, it's time to get angry again! *Feminist Media Studies*, 11(1), 61–71. https://doi.org/10.1080/14680777.2011.537029

Gill, R. (2014). Unspeakable inequalities: Post feminism, entrepreneurial subjectivity, and the repudiation of sexism among cultural workers. *Social Politics*, 21(4), 509–528. https://doi.org/10.1093/sp/jxu016

Giuffre, P., & Harris, D. A. (2019). *Taking the heat: Women chefs and gender inequality in the professional kitchen*. Rutgers University Press. https://doi.org/10.36019/9780813571270

Hanmer, J. (1977). Violence et contrôle social des femmes. *Questions Féministes*, 1, 68–88.

Hanmer, J., & Maynard, M. (Eds). (1987). *Women, violence and social control*. Palgrave Macmillan. https://doi.org/10.1007/978-1-349-18592-4

Hatzipetrou-Andronikou, R. (2018). *Joueuses d'instruments traditionnels: Apprentissage, socialisation professionnelle et genre dans les musiques traditionnelles en Grèce* (Doctoral dissertation, École des Hautes Études en Sciences Sociales). HAL Archives Ouvertes. https://theses.hal.science/tel-01979092v1/file/Hatzipetrou-Andronikou_Th%C3%A8se.pdf

Haymann, S., & Brzezowska-Dudek, L. (Eds) (2022). *#MeTooThéâtre*. Libertalia.

Hennekam, S., & Bennett, D. (2017). Sexual harassment in the creative industries: Tolerance, culture and the need for change. *Gender, Work and Organization,* 24(4), 417–434. https://doi.org/10.1111/gwao.12176

Hesmondhalgh, D., & Baker, S. (2015). Sex, gender and work segregation in the cultural industries. *The Sociological Review*, 63(S1), 23–36. https://doi.org/10.1111/1467-954X.12238

Idås, T., Orgeret, K., & Backholm, K. (2020). #MeToo, sexual harassment and coping strategies in Norwegian newsrooms. *Media and Communication*, 8(1), 57–67. https://doi.org/10.17645/mac.v8i1.2529

Jones, D., & Pringle, J. K. (2015). Unmanageable inequalities: Sexism in the film industry. *The Sociological Review*, 63(S1), 37–49. https://doi.org/10.1111/1467-954X.12239

Kantor, J., & Twohey, M. (2017, October 5). Harvey Weinstein paid off sexual harassment accusers for decades. *The New York Times*. https://www.nytimes.com/2017/10/05/us/harvey-weinstein-harassment-allegations.html

Karttunen, S. (2009). *"Kun lumipallo lähtee pyörimään": Nuorten kuvataiteilijoiden kansainvälistyminen 2000-luvun alussa* ["It's kind of like a snowball starts rolling": The internationalisation of young visual artists in Finland]. Taiteen keskustoimikunta.

Kelly, L. (1987). The continuum of sexual violence. In J. Hanmer & M. Maynard (Eds), *Women, violence and social control* (pp. 46–60). Palgrave Macmillan. https://doi.org/10.1007/978-1-349-18592-4_4

Kelly, L. (2016, March 1). The conducive context of violence against women and girls. *Discover Society*. https://archive.discoversociety.org/2016/03/01/theorising-violence-against-women-and-girls/

Kleppe, B., & Røyseng, S. (2016). Sexual harassment in the Norwegian theatre world. *Journal of Arts Management, Law & Society*, 46(5), 282–296. https://doi.org/10.1080/10632921.2016.1231645

Le Monde. (2018, January 9). Nous défendons une liberté d'importuner, indispensable à la liberté sexuelle [Editorial]. *Le Monde*. https://www.lemonde.fr/idees/article/2018/01/09/nous-defendons-une-liberte-d-importuner-indispensable-a-la-liberte-sexuelle_5239134_3232.html

Mandolini, N., & Williamson Sinalo, C. (2023). Introduction. In C. Williamson Sinalo & N. Mandolini (Eds), *Representing gender-based violence* (pp. 1–21.). Palgrave Macmillan. https://doi.org/10.1007/978-3-031-13451-7_1

Miller, D. L. (2016). Gender and the artist archetype: Understanding gender inequality in artistic careers. *Sociology Compass*, 10(2), 119–131. https://doi.org/10.1111/soc4.12350

North, L. (2016). Damaging and daunting: Female journalists' experiences of sexual harassment in the newsroom. *Feminist Media Studies*, 16(3), 495–510. https://doi.org/10.1080/14680777.2015.1105275

Peretz, T., & Vidmar, C. M. (2021). Men, masculinities, and gender-based violence: The broadening scope of recent research. *Sociology Compass*, 15(3), 1–18. https://doi.org/10.1111/soc4.12861

Provansal, M. (2020). Comment 'faire la différence'? La fabrique des inégalités de sexe, de classe et de race à l'entrée des beaux-arts. *Agone*, 65, 105–127.

Provansal, M. (2023). *Artistes mais femmes: Une enquête sociologique dans l'art contemporain*. ENS Éditions.

Provansal, M. (2024). Precarious professional identities: Women artists and gender inequality within contemporary art. *L'Année Sociologique*, 74(1), 85–116. https://doi.org/10.3917/anso.241.0085

Ramstedt, A. (2024). *Classical music, misconduct, and gender. A feminist study on social imaginaries and women musicians' experiences of gender inequality in Finland* (Doctoral dissertation, University of Helsinki).

Ravet, H. (2011). *Musiciennes: Enquête sur les femmes et la musique*. Autrement.

Saguy, A. C. (2000). Employment discrimination or sexual violence? Defining sexual harassment in American and French law. *Law & Society Review*, 34(4), 1091–1128. https://doi.org/10.2307/3115132

Saha, A. (2018). *Race and the cultural industries*. Polity Press.

Steedman, R. (2024). *Creative hustling: Women making and distributing films from Nairobi*. MIT Press. https://doi.org/10.7551/mitpress/14127.001.0001

Stokes, A. (2015). The glass runway: How gender and sexuality shape the spotlight in fashion design. *Gender and Society*, 29(2), 219–243. https://doi.org/10.1177/0891243214563327

Trachman, M. (2018). L'ordinaire de la violence: Un cas d'atteinte sexuelle sur mineure en milieu artistique. *Travail, genre et sociétés*, 40(2), 131–150. https://doi.org/10.3917/tgs.040.0131

Walby, S. (2013). Violence and society: Introduction to an emerging field of sociology. *Current Sociology*, 61(2), 95–111. https://doi.org/10.1177/0011392112456478

Whittier, N. (2016). Where are the children? Theorizing the missing piece in gendered sexual violence. *Gender & Society*, 30(1), 95–108. https://doi.org/10.1177/0891243215612412

Wreyford, N. (2018). *Gender inequality in screenwriting work*. Palgrave Macmillan. https://doi.org/10.1007/978-3-319-95732-6

PART I
GENDER-BASED VIOLENCE, POWER RELATIONS AND THE REPRODUCTION OF GENDER INEQUALITIES

Introduction

The three chapters constituting the first part of this book draw attention to the gender hierarchies and power dynamics, and to the professional practices and representations, that produce and perpetuate gender-based violence in artistic and cultural worlds.

In Chapter 2, Marie Buscatto, Soline Helbert and Ionela Roharik use a quantitative survey to reveal the pervasiveness of sexist and sexual violence mainly committed by powerful men against women in the French opera world. Despite their omnipresence and their harmful psychological and professional effects, the authors find that victims and witnesses rarely report these acts to the relevant authorities. To understand this paradox, the authors draw on interviews with female and male opera singers and show how gender-based violence is entangled in the professional habits and representations of this occupational environment.

Chiharu Chujo's Chapter 3 focuses on sexual harassment in the Japanese music industry. While female workers tended to minimise and even deny their experiences of sexual harassment during the interviews she conducted with them, they also recounted the various strategies implemented to address these situations. To make sense of this discrepancy, Chujo explores the social and economic conditions which perpetuate and normalise sexual harassment in this hierarchical and precarious artistic work environment. The lack of engagement for gender equality in the music industry, stigma avoidance and the emotional investment required by their artistic activity are possible explanations of the artists' positionalities towards sexual harassment.

In Chapter 4, Mathilde Provansal focuses on French artistic higher education as one institutional space of gender-based violence in the contemporary art world. Writing on a largely feminised artistic educational context, she emphasises the gender asymmetry in the distribution of power in schools of visual arts, students being predominantly women and men being a majority among instructors. She argues that unequal power relations and age relations have an effect on the type of gender-based violence that are identified and denounced by students. Provansal then turns to the social processes that constitute the scaffolding of gender-based violence in art schools and explores how the latter limits women's creative abilities, professional networks and work opportunities.

Overall, these chapters reveal that the processes producing the *continuum* of sexual violence in artistic work and education are cumulative and embedded in routine professional practices, making it more difficult for victims and witnesses to challenge them.

2. French Opera: A Professional World Haunted by Gender-Based Violence[1]

Marie Buscatto, Soline Helbert and Ionela Roharik

Introduction

In the years following the 2017 #MeToo movement, the French classical music world has experienced a huge social media increase of testimonies and informal discussions related to gender-based violence. In August 2020, a storm broke over the professional world of opera: French soprano Chloé Briot announced in *La Lettre du Musicien* that she had lodged a complaint against a fellow singer, whom she accused of sexually assaulting her on stage during an opera performance of *The Flood*,[2] declaring that she wanted to 'put an end to the law of silence' (Banes Gardonne, 2020). The information was immediately relayed and discussed in various media, as evidenced by Clément Buzalka's lengthy column on the *France Musique* radio website dated August 21, 2020 (Buzalka, 2020). At the time, no other victim had publicly denounced any wrongdoing, but in private conversations, it was a hot topic.

Although the complaint was dismissed on September 19, 2022, it

---

1   The content of this chapter was originally published as an article in issue 22(1) of the journal *Les Cahiers de la Société québécoise de recherche en musique* (SQRM) (Buscatto et al., 2021). I would like to thank the editorial committee, consisting of Vanessa Blais-Tremblay, Jean Boivin, Vicky Tremblay and Jordan Meunier, for their permission to publish this work in this book in a reduced English version.
2   *L'inondation* [*The Flood*], by Francesco Filidei and Joël Pommerat, produced in 2019 at the Opéra Comique (Paris, France).

did raise a number of questions. Are sexual assaults commonplace in the opera world? Are they symptomatic of a wider sexist pattern in this professional world? Can we really speak of a 'law of silence'? If so, what are the risks for those who report sexual violence and/or sexist acts? Is the opera world conducive to gender-based violence against female opera workers? Those questions were at the basis of a study conducted in France in 2020 among professional opera singers (who make up half of the respondents) and other professionals involved in the production of an opera performance, such as, for example, orchestral musicians, technical staff, conductors, chorus members and administrative staff.

In this chapter, we report on the social conditions which enable gender-based violence and explore its various sociological dimensions.[3] To best answer the above questions, we defined gender-based violence broadly, encompassing all forms of violence—whether verbal, physical or psychological, interpersonal or institutional—committed based on gender-related assumptions about one's gender or sexuality. We are certainly addressing the topic of legally characterised sexual violence such as rape, harassment, touching or sexual assault. But we also seek to study gender-based violence in its wide variety of 'ordinariness' (Trachman, 2018) within the work environment: from disparaging sexist remarks to sexual jokes, insistent flirting, or derogatory jokes about sexuality or looks. Gender-based violence is thus considered along a *continuum* in the sense articulated by Liz Kelly (1987).

After having presented opera as a collective and hierarchical work environment supervised by men, we describe the omnipresence of sexist and sexual misconducts, mostly carried out by men of power and suffered by female singers. We then identify the low level of denunciation of these acts, despite their heavy psychological consequences on both the

---

3   Having adopted an intersectional analysis (Buscatto, 2016), our study informs the issue of gender-based violence by sex, age, occupation, employment status and type of employer structure. The literature also mentions other social determinants that can affect the propensity to suffer and/or to report such acts, in particular racialisation (Appert & Lawrence, 2020; Buscatto et al., 2020). However, this study did not allow us to add items related to racialisation for various practical and statistical reasons. First, addressing this topic in a rigorous manner would have made the questionnaire very cumbersome and difficult to circulate. In addition, dealing with the issue of racialisation would have required access to a sufficient number of racialised people on which to base the analysis. However, this was not feasible through the Internet, as this demographic is still very rare in French opera.

victims and the witnesses, due to the many fears raised by denunciation. Finally, we focus on the structural foundations of the omnipresence of this gender-based violence and its low level of denunciation in connection with a professional environment that is conducive to gender-based violence.

Methods

The quantitative data for this survey conducted in France were obtained by means of an anonymous questionnaire drawn up in 2020. The questionnaire was distributed on the webquest.fr platform, then made available on the website of the *ComposHer* association, dedicated to the promotion of female classical composers, and more broadly to the place of women in the classical music world.

All opera professionals (singers, orchestral musicians, technical and administrative staff, conductors and choirmasters, stage directors, artistic agents) were asked to respond to the questionnaire. Distribution began on May 31, 2020, mainly via social networks and e-mail. On Facebook, a large number of different groups of arts professionals were approached to distribute the link. The link was also widely relayed within WhatsApp support groups created during the first wave of show cancellations linked to the COVID-19 pandemic. We successively re-sent the questionnaire to members of these networks in July, September and November 2020, more explicitly inviting responses from men as well as people who did not consider themselves victims. Instagram and Twitter were also used as outreach tools. At the same time, delegates from choirs and—to a lesser extent—professional orchestras were contacted, some of whom agreed to circulate the link to their colleagues. Lastly, in November and December 2020, the Paris Opera's health, safety and working conditions committee (CHSCT) e-mailed the link to all the company's artistic, technical and administrative staff.

Comprising some fifty questions, the form covers a wide range of themes linked to sexism in the world of opera: sexist behaviour, the impact of age and physical appearance on careers, stage attire, the impact of menstruation and menopause on instrumental and vocal skills, and professional problems linked to pregnancy and maternity. Men were also invited to respond to the first three themes. In this chapter, we analyse the responses to the first part of this questionnaire, devoted solely to sexist and sexual behaviours, in relation to the eighteen interviews we conducted with opera singers.

These semi-structured interviews, lasting between one and two hours, were conducted by telephone (fifteen) and face-to-face (three) from May, 2020. Three men and fifteen women were interviewed, eight of whom had completed the online questionnaire. Varying in age, professional level and career conditions (temporary and salaried chorus artists, soloists at the beginning of their careers, confirmed or internationally renowned singers, artists retired from the stage, etc.), the singers interviewed shared their experiences of gender-based violence in the workplace.

Given the conditions under which the survey was carried out and the response rate (336 questionnaires received), the scope of the questionnaire may appear limited. The literature abounds in references dealing with the limitations of online surveys, and these agree on their main disadvantage: the non-probabilistic nature of samples, due to the impossibility of controlling who responds to the questionnaire in relation to all those called upon to answer (Dussaix, 2009; Ganassali, 2008; Lindhjem & Navrud, 2011; Stephenson & Crête, 2011). The sample we are working on is no exception to this possible shortcoming. Moreover, these studies have also shown that Internet surveys generally yield lower response rates compared to other distribution methods, typically capturing around 11% of the estimated target population (Lozar Manfreda et al., 2008). Our sample corresponds to around 10% of the estimated reference population and is therefore within the usual limits for this type of survey. Although this bias is closely linked to the lack of statistical representativeness of the samples, it nevertheless plays a favourable role in the reliability of the results, as the respondents are often more interested in the subject than the general population.[4]

More 'concerned' by sexist behaviour and sexual violence, women were far more likely to respond to our survey, and their diligence is more assertive: within fifteen days of it going online, 115 of the 252 women (46%) had already completed the form, and more than half were singers (38 soloists and 30 chorus singers). While fewer men responded

---

4   According to several sources consulted in 2017, there were around 12,000 salaried employees in the opera world; the level of feminisation is close to that of the theatrical world (49%).

promptly (30 out of a total of 83 men who completed the questionnaire: 36%), singers once again predominated, accounting for almost three-quarters of this group of prompt respondents (15 soloists and 7 choir singers). It thus appears that, by primarily gathering the words of victims and witnesses of gender-based violence, this survey makes it possible to grasp the *continuum* of violence as some people experience and/or observe it. Although we cannot speak of statistical representativeness, in the articulation between questionnaires and interviews, we can on the other hand recognise the survey's sociological significance. Even more so since, as Didier Frippiat and Nicolas Marquis put it, responding via the Internet makes individuals less sensitive to the intrusive nature of the questions than when they respond by other means, and 'it enables them to report more non-standard or socially undesirable behaviour' (Frippiat & Marquis, 2010, p. 63).[5]

The responses to the questionnaires, and then to the interviews, proved to be very revealing on a subject that most often arouses silence, fear and embarrassment, as also attested by the analysis we were able to draw from them.

Please note that, even if the questionnaires allowed for people who did not identify as men or women to answer, only one person answered 'other'. Moreover, most sexist and sexual acts which were observed or experienced concerned persons who identified as women. A new survey is necessary to address people who identify as non-binary or gender-queer.

Opera as a Collective and Hierarchised Work Organisation Supervised by Men

Opera is an artistic genre that allows the simultaneous encounter of several art forms and requires the collaboration of a large number of artists, technicians and administrative staff. In the pit and on stage, in some works and in certain opera houses, there may be as many as 180 artists; backstage, in the workshops and offices, between several dozen and several hundred other collaborators may be involved in the creation of an artwork. For example, the Opéra national de Paris employs 1,500

---

5   Our translation.

people, all categories combined (Ndiaye & Rivière, 2021).

The work in an opera house is by nature collective and responds to a strongly hierarchical organisation. Large budgets are placed in the hands of powerful directors. The production of a show is entrusted to a conductor, a director and a technical director, each supported by one or more assistants and stage managers.

Hierarchies also exist within the different groups of artists. In the pit, the positions of soloists, first instruments and tuttis structure the orchestra, as do seniority and status (permanent or temporary employees), factors that also determine positions within the choirs. As for the hierarchies among the soloists, they are established according to notoriety, career levels, age and the importance of the roles interpreted in the work performed. Finally, it appears that management positions are largely occupied by men.[6]

Having described the working environment in which opera singers evolve their careers, let us now turn to the specific identification of sexist and sexual conducts in this profession.

The Omnipresence of Sexist and Sexual Acts: Women as Victims,[7] Men of Power as Aggressors

Sexist and sexual acts are numerous and recurrent. They are also varied, mainly affect women and are often perpetrated by men of power.

A High Prevalence of Sexist and Sexual Acts

Three-quarters of the people who agreed to fill out the questionnaire did so as victims of sexist and sexual acts (252 out of 336 people), while 13% of them did so as witnesses (44 out of 336) and 12% avoided the question (40 out of 336)—10% of women and 17% of men did not answer the question. While the witnesses (68%) and the alleged aggressors (74%) are mostly men, the victims are mostly women (84.5%).

---

6   For an example, see the program of the Opéra national de Paris, 2019/2020 season.
7   The term 'victim' was preferred to survivor for two main reasons. On the one hand, in our questionnaires and interviews, victim was the way we described this experience. On the other, even when asked to speak about their experiences freely, people would describe themselves as victims and not as survivors.

Moreover, these sexist and sexual acts are recurrent: only 20.5% of the witnesses and 27% of the victims consider that the reported sexist or sexual act is of an exceptional nature. Recurrence was noted by more than three-quarters of the witnesses (77%) and almost as many of the victims (72%). Near-permanence is observed by just under a third of witnesses and a quarter of victims. If we look only at singers, soloists or members of a choir, which represents half of the respondents (172 out of 336), the percentages are very close.

A Wide Variety of Sexist and Sexual Acts, Some Recurrent Practices

In the general population (252 victims out of 336 people who answered the questionnaire), we note a wide variety of sexist and sexual acts, from 'sexist remarks or jokes' (for 84% of women and 56% of men) to 'unwanted sexual acts' (5 women and 2 men), as well as 'incivilities, unpleasant or rude behaviours because of sex' (57.5% of women and 23% of men) or 'obscene, filthy or embarrassing comments or jokes' (57.5% of women and 44% of men).

If sexist and sexual acts are very frequent, unwanted physical sexual acts or acts with a sexual connotation are also denounced by significant proportions of the sample. When we focus on male and female singers only, these proportions are even higher, especially for female singers. First, female singers are the most frequent victims (115) of such acts, compared to male singers (24). It then appears that remarks, sexist jokes, insistent flirting, or obscene, saucy and embarrassing comments and jokes are experienced as 'background noise' by all men and women, even more so if they are singers. At least half of male singer-victims and 80% of female singer-victims have been subjected to such behaviours. The omnipresence of 'dirty jokes' during rehearsals and social moments mentioned by the female singers we interviewed is a striking fact.

Certain behaviours seem to be even more 'addressed' to women, whether they are singers or not: at least half of the female respondents were subjected to them, in much higher proportions than men. Such behaviours include 'differential treatment by the chief director', 'incivility, unpleasant or rude behaviour because of your gender', 'embarrassing remarks about your appearance or your dress' and/or 'obscene, saucy and embarrassing comments and jokes'. In our study, women were more subjected to remarks about their appearance and/or to vulgar humour, which demeans them either by sexualising them or by harassing them with uncivil, rude, unpleasant acts of a sexual nature.

Other acts are more relevant to men, whether singers or not, such as 'derogatory comments about your possible homosexuality', 'derogatory comments about your possible heterosexuality', 'unwanted touching of a sexual or erogenous area' or 'other inappropriate/unwanted physical contact'. The 24 male singers who were victims were primarily subjected to degrading remarks about their supposed sexuality (homosexual or heterosexual) and unwanted sexual contact, most often by another man.

Men of Power as Main Aggressors

The overwhelming majority of the offenders are men. For all the acts mentioned (319 people) by men or women, 74% of the perpetrators are men (248 cases); 19% of the respondents name both men and women as perpetrators (63 cases); women are only a minority of the perpetrators (4 cases).

In the case of the female singers who were victims (115), the person who perpetrated the sexist or the sexual behaviour was most often a man who had direct power over them: a conductor (47 cases: 41%), a choir director (15 cases: 13%), a stage director (39 cases: 34%), a singing teacher (29 cases: 25%), an agent (9 cases: 8%) or the director of an opera institution (25 cases: 22%). This finding is consistent with another result of the questionnaire. When asked whether in their experience conductors, choirmasters or stage directors apply gender-specific working methods, 52% of female singers (69 out of 132 singers, whether victims or witnesses) answered yes. A much smaller proportion of chorus singers (36%, or 22 out of 61) responded yes compared to soloists (66%, or 47 out of 71).

However, sexist or sexual behaviours can also be perpetrated by a male colleague, such as a singer or an instrumentalist (80 cases out of 115: 69.5%), or by a member of the technical staff (25 cases out of 115: 22%) or the administrative staff (9 cases out of 115: 8%). There were no major differences between the female singers according to whether they were soloists or members of a choir.

On the other hand, female temporary singers, as well as the youngest and oldest women, seem to be subjected to sexist or sexual behaviours even more often than other singers. Male singers, even though fewer in number identify themselves victims (24 cases out of the 83 men who answered: 29%), are also more often targeted by men in positions of power.

A Very Low Level of Reporting despite the Heavy Psychological and Professional Costs

The questionnaire confirms the low level of reporting of these sexist and sexual acts, especially to supervisors and external authorities. However, these incidents are often widely known among those involved and have serious psychological and professional consequences for the affected individuals.

A Low Level of Reporting to the Hierarchy or to an External Authority

Our analysis includes 295 people among the 336 respondents in the sample: 251 victims and 44 witnesses. Forty people were neither victims nor witnesses, while one person, who identified their sex as 'other', had to be removed from the analysis for statistical reasons.[8]

The responses to the questionnaire highlight a general observation: when sexist or sexual misconduct occurs, whether as victims or as witnesses, people are often able to discuss it with those around them and may take action in the moment. However, very few formally report it through the hierarchy or to an external authority.

Some trends seem to emerge:

a) Men are more likely to react on the spot (49% against 37% for women); among singers these proportions are even more

---

8   The expression 'removed from the analysis' here refers only to counting operations. This choice is purely technical. Indeed, this case being 'too singular', it could not be treated in a rigorous manner in the context of our study and thus allow for generalisable conclusions.

marked: 58% of male singer victims against 38% of female singer victims.

b) Women, on the other hand, mainly talk to someone close to them (58% of women against 46% of men; 61% of female singers against 44% of male singers). Sometimes they decide not to react at all: 48% of women, victims or witnesses, against 39% of men.

c) The answers concerning the denunciations to a hierarchical superior or to an external authority are in much lower proportions: 18% of the respondents sometimes report to a hierarchical superior and only 6% to an external authority. These proportions remain relatively similar, whatever the different populations: men/women/singers/non-singers, etc.

d) When we cross-checked the responses, only 43 people reported having no reaction when they experienced or witnessed these sexist or sexual acts. We deal with this group and the reasoning behind its formation in the next paragraphs.

Heavy and Known Psychological Consequences for the People Concerned

One might have imagined that the low level of reporting to management or to an outside party, as well as the high incidence of non-reaction at the time, were due to the low psychological impact of sexist and sexual acts on the individuals concerned. However, the opposite is true, as can be seen from the analysis of reported feelings about these acts.

Sexist and sexual acts weigh on women... and on men. Whether one is a victim or a witness, the impact of these acts is important, even if we observe a certain degree of relativisation among men. They are less angry (54% of men versus 68% of women say they felt angry) and more often say they did not feel particularly uncomfortable (16% of men versus 5% of women). Female singers, and especially soloists, are the most affected by the psychological consequences of the attacks (for example, 68% of soloists who were victims of sexist and sexual attacks claim to have lost confidence in themselves after the attacks and 42% felt ashamed and humiliated by the attacks).

Finally, it should be noted that the small group of those who do not speak out and who do not denounce such behaviours (the group of 43 people) presents a particular profile in the sense that it is composed of people more affected than the others by the loss of self-confidence (52%) and by shame (56%). Non-reporting, which is certainly a minority action, cannot be associated with a relativisation of these acts, but rather with possible guilt-tripping of the victims or witnesses.

At the Heart of a Low Level of Denunciation

What fears could explain the low level of denunciation to the hierarchy or to an external authority? Here we must look at the fears that seem to hinder whistleblowing. Once again, the interviews corroborate the answers given in the questionnaire. Fear is the feeling involved in 3 of the 4 causes of non-reporting selected by more than 30% of the respondents (general population, victims or witnesses): 'fear for the future of your career' (32%), 'fear of being seen as a pain in the ass' (34%) or 'in order not to attract attention, not to make waves' (40%), which implicitly implies a fear of being exposed. These proportions are higher among women, with respectively 34%, 39% and 45%.

When we ask those who have denounced the facts, such fears seem to be well-founded: even if most of them have been taken seriously, 35.5% have not been believed, while for 63% of them no action in their favour has been taken. Moreover, these respondents were not believed, even though the perpetrators' actions were often known, repeated and common (for a large majority of the people (60%) who denounced such acts, the misconduct was known and repeated).

If we now look at the people who believe they missed out on professional opportunities after rejecting a sexual advance—83 people (33%) out of the 251 victims (men and women)—we find the following results.

First, the proportions are similar for men and women: roughly $1/3$, $1/3$, $1/3$. For men, out of 39 victims, 13 believed they missed out on opportunities, 12 say they did not and 12 have never faced such a situation. For women (212 victims), 70 say yes, 67 say no, 71 have never been in this situation, and 4 did not respond.

Secondly, it is among singers that the phenomenon seems to be the most frequent: 39% of singers say they have missed opportunities, while only 26% of non-singers experienced this situation. Out of 139 male and female singer victims, 54 said yes (39%), 37 no (27%), 46 never in the situation (33%), 2 non-responses (1%), while for the non-singers, there are 113 victims: 29 yes (26%), 42 no (37%), 40 never in the situation (35%), 2 non-responses (2%).

Finally, among male and female singers, it is men more than women who say they have missed opportunities: 11 men out of 24, i.e. almost half, against 43 women out of 115 (37%). For male singers: out of 24 singers, 11 said yes, 6 said no, 7 said they had never been confronted with this type of situation. For female singers: out of 115 victims, 43 said yes, 31 no, 39 never faced the situation, 2 non-responses.

Anger as the Main Driving Force behind the Rare Denunciations

What, then, are the main reasons for denunciation, even by a small minority, 'despite' an unfavourable context? The analysis of the responses to the questionnaire provides a first clue, even if it does not allow us to explain its social foundations, for lack of the necessary data. Indeed, anger appears to be by far the main motivation for denunciation: 81% of the singers who denounced these acts gave anger as their main motivation, while the other motivations (such as loss of confidence, demotivation, shame or intimidation) were always less than 40%. And whistleblowing seems to go hand in hand with a worsening work atmosphere. However, the factors that encourage a person to take the risk of whistleblowing because of his or her high level of anger are not known and merit a specific investigation, focused on these people and the social conditions that produce whistleblowing inside or outside the opera world.

A Professional Environment Conducive to Unreported Sexist and Sexual Acts

How can we explain both the prevalence of sexist and sexual acts and the low level of reporting to management or to an outside authority, despite the negative psychological and professional consequences of not reporting?

In line with the approach of Elizabeth Armstrong et al. (2006) on rape at US student campuses, Kirsten Dellinger and Christine Williams (2002) on sexual harassment in two magazines and Mathilde Provansal on gender-based violence in visual art schools (Chapter 4 in this book), we analysed the work environment and shared professional norms.

The Hypersexualisation of Women Singers: Uncontrolled 'Drifts'

As observed in former studies, physical seduction is often central to the profession of the opera (Stephenson, 2012), and more broadly that of classical musicians (Ravet, 2011). This phenomenon thus affects various elements of the professional lives of opera artists, both on and off stage. Strong emphasis on physical seduction frequently leads to the hypersexualisation of women in the field. This environment can make it especially challenging for some individuals —particularly those in positions of power—to construct 'clear' boundaries between expected professional behaviors tied to artistic expression or performance and harmful, sexist or sexual acts that constitute gender-based violence, which can deeply affect women's physical and mental well-being and professional opportunities.

As for the female characters embodied by the opera singers, there is a strong presence in the artworks of seductive and amorous women. The plots proposed in most of the operas often revolve around the love of a man and a woman, a feeling thwarted by the presence of other men. The female characters, who are less numerous than the male characters, are usually involved exclusively in love issues, are the object of love or desire of several male characters at the same time, and are frequently victims of violence. Some works, such as *Don Giovanni*, *Susannah* or *L'Arianna*, even feature explicit rape scenes, prompting feminist musicologists to consider different ways in which these artworks can (or cannot) be taught and staged without promoting a 'rape culture' (Curtis, 2000; Cusick & Hershberger, 2018). This near-systematic connection of female characters' participation in the love plot in the artworks thus tends to carry over into the working atmosphere surrounding the singers.

When asked, 'When you play a cross-dressing character, does it change the way others look at you during the production?', one singer responded:

> Yes, absolutely. Because the fact of not being in a seductive relationship
> on stage changes the relationship with those who are in the rehearsal
> room. There is a form of confusion between what happens on stage and
> off stage. People can be seduced by what you give off on stage, by your
> character. And during the rehearsal [period], this seduction can continue
> off stage, over a coffee, a drink. That's what can sometimes create trouble.
> [...] So it happens less when you play men. (Amanda, opera singer, 30–
> 40 years old)

The staging still tends to sexualise these female characters and to set
up explicit love scenes. The search for modernity by stage directors
who want to 'dust off' opera still involves the exploitation of the sexual
imagination, with sensual characters and explicit references to sexuality.
Such stagings seem to potentially open the door to sexist and sexual
acts, direct or indirect, outside of any social control, because of the
lack of clear limits between the actual requirements of the role, the
interpretations given by male directors or singers, and the physical and
psychological integrity of women singers on and off stage. Indeed, as
one respondent states:

> Sex scenes in the theatre are choreographed, as are sword scenes, for
> which a specialist is usually called in. For sex scenes, we don't call anyone
> and we do it behind closed doors, so as not to disturb. [...] In the cinema,
> there are people who are called on the sets to manage the sex scenes,
> to protect the bodies, to make everything professional. And there, [in
> opera,] if I am embarrassed by certain words or gestures, I look like a bad
> artist. (Céline, opera singer, 30–40 years old)

During the interviews, the singers regularly mention outfits that overly
sexualise their bodies: plunging necklines, very short shorts, transparent
or slit miniskirts, which are often not at all necessary for the roles they play.

Some stage directors, singers or production managers seem to
pursue these women assiduously at any time of the day or night, 'steal'
kisses from them outside of working hours, touch intimate parts of their
bodies during rehearsals and outside of any artistic necessity, or make
degrading remarks about their physique. Also mentioned are rehearsals
of scenes, especially love scenes, where male singers or directors touch
their breasts or private parts, without any connection with the needs of
the production. One singer indicates that she wears sweaters tucked into

her pants in order to avoid wandering hands, while another explains: 'on several occasions, I've found myself thinking about what to wear before going to the rehearsal'.

As this last example indicates, women opera singers thus learn to 'shut down the seduction' (Buscatto, 2021) to avoid sexual violence—harassment, insistent flirting, attempted rape or rape, touching—and verbal or physical sexist acts. Unless the role imposes it, some of them choose not to wear suggestive clothes and behave in a distant way: they avoid answering text messages, refrain from drinking with these men, tuck their sweaters into their pants during rehearsals, steer clear of uncomfortable gestures, emphasise a stable relationship with a male musician or producer, or highlight their maternity or role as a mother...

The presence of sexist and sexual acts does not stop there. Indeed, the appeal of women singers is constantly mobilised to promote the works in which they perform, as well as to advance their careers, weakening in return their ability to protect their physical and mental integrity. Female singers are required to participate in promotional events and encouraged to charm and engage critics, financiers, programmers or their public, potentially exposing them to the risk of unwanted sexual behaviour:

> If there are a few pretty girls on the set, the director of protocol will insist heavily that they come to the dinner or cocktail party after the show [...] we wait for these singers in front of their dressing rooms. (Mylène, opera singer, 30–40 years old)

A final point shows the double-bind nature of sexism at work in this professional world, due to this hypersexualised image of women singers. When women decide to denounce sexual violence, they are subjected to a paradox. Having been transformed into sexual objects, they are often blamed for the violence they experience, unless they can prove otherwise. They are expected to justify their behaviour as exemplary, and the slightest deviation or misstep is interpreted as the cause of the abuser's reprehensible actions. One woman who was sexually abused—forcibly kissed several times and harassed via messages and in front of witnesses by her director—decided not to report him after observing the denigrating remarks and the difficulties suffered by a colleague who had previously reported a sexual assault.

To our prompt 'You indicated that you didn't talk about the things you had been through for fear of being blamed,' this young singer replies:

> It's for women in general. X filed a complaint, and I know how it goes. People analyse your actions to see if you didn't provoke the situation. It's always the same... off-beat messages from managers, sometimes at one in the morning. At the beginning, you are very young, you wonder what will happen if you don't answer, if they will cancel your contract. So, you answer. And then they tell you "if you answer at midnight, don't be surprised if afterwards...". Because of this, I never wanted to be under the spotlight of this kind of investigation! (Coline, opera singer, 20–30 years old)

A Highly Competitive, Uncertain and Anxious World

Theatre, music and dance are saturated, competitive and precarious art worlds (Menger, 2005). The number of people who aspire to be artists far outnumbers the number of artists that those professional worlds can accommodate. And, as in the creative industries studied by Sophie Hennekam and Dawn Bennett in the Netherlands (2017) or in the New York theatre world (Lechaux, Chapter 7 in this book), this seems to work against women on several levels.

First, for young singers, whether soloists or choir members, there is a great risk of not being hired again if they report harassment or denounce abusers, which in turn favours predatory behaviours. Each production they participate in may be their last. If they do come forward, these women risk being categorised as 'bitchy', as 'mood breakers', as conflict creators. This fear is at the heart of the difficulty of denunciation, as has already been shown by the analysis of the answers to the questionnaires. This concerns not only the female soloists, but also the young female choristers. Indeed, if the women choristers who hold a permanent position, often aged over thirty, can benefit from relative protection from the choir's management, the younger women choristers, hired as 'extras'—and therefore in a more precarious position—seem to be more often subjected to gender-based violence:

> In fact, in a choir, you are always with the same colleagues, there are some heavyweights, but there is a form of protection that is established. In the group, if a man is really too heavy, he could be put aside, like in a pack. But what can happen is that these heavyweights will attack the

'extras' because their position is more fragile. This happened to me when I was a student. At that point, the 'pack' no longer plays its protective role. (Cécile, singer, 40–50 years old)

In the same vein, those women already present in this art world and rather well established in their position, while less likely not to be recruited in future productions, often seek to improve their artistic lot, at least until they reach the age of thirty-five or forty: gaining access to 'interesting' positions and roles allows them precisely to make the career they desire and not to lock themselves into a 'modest' artist position (Buscatto, 2019). Young choristers, even stable ones, may aspire to become soloists, while soloists seek to get access to roles that are more suited to their tastes (and voices). In these circumstances, one can avoid denouncing gender-based violence in order not to be 'blacklisted'. Furthermore, if solidarity between women or between colleagues is very weak, sexist or sexual behaviours which are observed or experienced may not be denounced to avoid risking one's reputation and career, as was also observed by Chiharu Chujo in the Japanese music industry (see Chapter 3 in this book):

When we work on the same production, of course, we get along well and there is mutual support. But given that the business is very competitive, it makes it difficult to be truly united. Everyone does what they can to pursue their careers. (Alice, opera singer, 30–40 years old)

Artistic Success and Talent as an Excuse for Reprehensible Behaviours

Some victims or witnesses justify their failure to denounce gender-based violence by referring to the 'talent' of the aggressor, his creative abilities, his artistic greatness. It is as if those who have power are also those whose artistic talent is recognised. Such great artistic talent would justify accepting behavioural 'deviations' when they exist, and in particular sexist and sexual behaviours even when they are judged as misplaced or reprehensible by these same people (see in this book the same process as observed by Rossi and Karttunen in the Finnish photography world (Chapter 5) or Lechaux in the New York theatre world (Chapter 7)):

There is a very strong omerta in this milieu. These conductors are very talented, and can be charming and healthy in their work, which also protects them, and makes us look past their unhealthy behaviours. (Mylène, opera singer, 30–40 years old)

Speaking of a very legitimate conductor in the world of music, a male instrumentalist interviewed mentioned numerous reprehensible behaviours—including an alleged rape for which a legal complaint has been filed—known to all and never denounced, neither in the world of opera nor in a court of law.

One opera singer commented:

Oh yes, X—a renowned director—, it was 'Minitel rose' [an 'erotic Minitel', Minitel being a French videotex service of the time], he skipped the administrator. At the time, it's not that you weren't free to say no, I did, but you had the associated hassle. That's what I said about the [Plácido] Domingo case [...] everybody knew that his first prize in his contest was the girl he managed to fuck. Everybody defended him saying: 'but such an attractive man, he didn't need that'. Of course, he did, it was his way of doing things. X and Domingo, it's the same, they are guys who piss around their bed at night, who mark their territory.

To our question, 'You mean they totally confused sexual seduction with hiring people?', the same singer replies:

But yes, and nobody ever told them. For example, I have corrected people in dinner parties who said, 'Well, attacking such a great artist, who has done nothing...'. No. You don't know what he did. In fact, I know, but let's say that we don't know! (Amélie, opera singer, 50–60 years old)

Another element that is specific to the world of opera is the fact that, although gender-based violence deeply troubles the majority of those affected on an individual level, it is often considered 'normal'. As a result, it is seen as a set of 'deviations' that are impossible to limit, given the inherently creative nature of the profession:

I think that in our profession there is a part of seduction, whether with the public or among colleagues, which can generate ambiguity, but there are drifts. [...] We are in a very liberated world, and liberation can go as far as unwanted behaviour. (Coline, opera singer, 20–30 years old)

Finally, these same people who have power over others are people who are adulated by the public, by the media, by colleagues; in some cases, this 'success goes to their heads' and would lead them to think that 'anything goes' because of their talent. The low levels of reporting may convince them of this possibility:

> There is also a thin line between playing and 'not playing'. It's silly to say, but there are colleagues, success goes to their heads and because you have a voice, anything goes. In the beginning, I have worked in major opera houses and played smaller roles with superstars, and there are some who think they can do anything. I was totally asexual in the way I dressed, in a turtleneck, too big, there was even a tenor who managed to pull the collar of my sweater to see my breasts instead of saying hello. (Jade, opera singer, 40–50 years old)

Conclusion

The opera world is conducive to gender-based violence, committed mainly by powerful men towards women, even more so when they are singers. It still favours a low level of denunciation to the hierarchy or to an external authority, both by the latter and by the colleagues who witness it. There are many structural elements that contribute to the production and legitimisation of recurrent gender-based violence: dirty jokes, disparaging remarks about physical appearance, insistent flirting, physical or sexual touching and assault, and even rape. These include the hypersexualisation of female characters on the opera stage, the emphasis on the physical seductiveness of female singers in order to be recruited, the high degree of uncertainty affecting the employment and careers of these female artists, and the tolerance by opera staff of the 'excesses' and sexist and sexual behaviours of the big names of opera by virtue of their 'genius' and artistic freedom.

Gender-based violence can then be thought of as a *continuum* as defined by Kelly (1987), ranging from the most everyday gender-based acts to legally punishable sexual violence. These sexist and sexual acts cause heavy psychological costs for a significant number of the victims. But fear for one's career, reputation and future dominates when it comes to reporting these acts to a hierarchical or external authority, even when these acts are legally reprehensible, thus feeding a feeling of impunity.

Although the vast majority of the victims who responded to the questionnaire are cisgender women, we must not forget the gender-based violence perpetrated on men by other men or on gender minorities. Even if few men and only one person who neither identified as a man nor a woman responded to the questionnaire, making it impossible to process their answers rigorously, at least two elements indicate this potential reality. On the one hand, the men who responded are often victims themselves, and their experiences of victimisation are frequently perpetrated by other men. On the other hand, based on the few interviews we conducted with men, the violence they encounter often appears to be perpetrated by men in positions of power, particularly those who identify as homosexual. A specific investigation is needed to enrich these initial findings and assess how far binary and heteronormative norms affect the creation and legitimation of gender-based violence in the world of French opera.

By its very nature, gender-based violence harms the careers of women who are subjected to it because it generates a lack of confidence, and feelings of shame or anger: it can result in exclusion if they denounce these acts, or self-exclusion, if they are personally affected. But it also has a potentially negative influence on their careers, insofar as these women are forced to develop strategies that hinder their professional integration in order to protect themselves. This includes efforts to 'shut-off the seduction' (Buscatto, 2021), and thus, incidentally, to limit interactions with the men of power who nevertheless control the resources necessary for securing work and gaining recognition. Gender-based violence consequently also affects the slow feminisation of artistic work (Buscatto, 2018).

Through the specific case of the French opera milieu, we have thus demonstrated the prevalence of gender-based violence in this professional environment, and the reasons for its production and its denial. The aim was also to contribute to a wider reflection on gender-based violence in the art worlds in the twenty-first century: the structural foundations of the production and non-reporting of gender-based violence, as revealed by the #MeToo movement, are indeed deeply embedded in the very functioning of the artistic universe—characterised by precarious careers, hyper-competition, an ideology of talent, and the hypersexualisation of women. These foundations must be identified and explained in terms of their specific modes of operation if we are to better understand the different ways in which they negatively affect the professional trajectories of women artists.

References

Appert, C. M., & Lawrence, S. (2020). Ethnomusicology beyond #MeToo: Listening for the violences of the field. *Ethnomusicology*, 64(2), 225–253. https://doi.org/10.5406/ethnomusicology.64.2.0225

Armstrong, E. A., Hamilton, L., & Sweeney, B. (2006). Sexual assault on campus: A multilevel, integrative approach to party rape. *Social Problems*, 53(4), 483–499. https://doi.org/10.1525/sp.2006.53.4.483

Banes Gardonne, J. (2020, August 19). La chanteuse Chloé Briot porte plainte pour agression sexuelle. *La Lettre du Musicien*. https://lalettredumusicien.fr/article/la-chanteuse-chloe-briot-porte-plainte-pour-agression-sexuelle-6648

Brown, E., Debauche, A., Hamel, C., & Mazuy, M. (Eds) (2020). *Violences et rapports de genre: Enquête sur les violences de genre en France*. INED. https://doi.org/10.4000/books.ined.14719

Buscatto, M. (2016). 'Intersectionnalité': À propos des usages épistémologiques d'un concept (très) à la mode. *Recherches sociologiques et anthropologiques*, 47(2), 103–118. https://doi.org/10.4000/rsa.1744

Buscatto, M. (2018). Feminisations of artistic work: Legal measures and female artists' resources do matter. *Revista Todas as Artes*, 1(1), 21–38. https://doi.org/10.21747/21843805/tav1n1a2

Buscatto, M. (2019). 'Modest' artists standing the test of time: Artistic 'vocation', yes... but not that alone! *Recherches sociologiques et anthropologiques*, 50(2), 9–26. https://doi.org/10.4000/rsa.3416

Buscatto, M. (2021). *Women in jazz: Musicality, femininity, marginalization*. Routledge. https://doi.org/10.4324/9781003177555 (Original work published 2007)

Buscatto, M., Helbert, S., & Roharik, I. (2021). L'opéra, un monde professionnel hanté par les violences de genre. *Les Cahiers de la Société québécoise de recherche en musique*, 22(1–2), 49–67. https://doi.org/10.7202/1097857ar

Buscatto, M., Cordier, M., & Laillier, J. (Eds) (2020). *Sous le talent: Le genre, la classe, la 'race'. Agone*, Special issue, 65.

Buzalka, C. (2020, August 21). La soprano Chloé Briot accuse un chanteur d'agression sexuelle. *France Musique*. https://www.francemusique.fr/actualite-musicale/la-soprano-chloe-briot-accuse-un-chanteur-d-agression-sexuelle-86916

Curtis, L. (2000). The sexual politics of teaching Mozart's *Don Giovanni*. *NWSA Journal*, 12(1), 119–142. https://doi.org/10.1353/nwsa.2000.0003

Cusick, S. G., Hershberger, M. A., Will, R., Baranello, M., Gordon, B., & Hisama, E. M. (2018). Sexual violence in opera: Scholarship, pedagogy, and production as resistance. *Journal of the American Musicological Society*, 71(1), 213–253. https//doi.org/10.1525/jams.2018.71.1.213

Dellinger, K., & Williams, C. L. (2002). The locker room and the dorm room: Workplace norms and the boundaries of sexual harassment in magazine editing. *Social Problems*, 49(2), 242–257. https://doi.org/10.1525/sp.2002.49.2.242

Dussaix, A.-M. (2009). La qualité dans les enquêtes. *Modulad*, 39, 137–171.

Frippiat, D., & Marquis, N. (2010). Les enquêtes par Internet en sciences sociales: Un état des lieux. *Population*, 65(2), 309–338. https://doi.org/10.3917/popu.1002.0309

Ganassali, S. (2008). The influence of the design of web survey questionnaires on the quality of responses. *Survey Research Methods*, 2 (1), 21–32. https://doi.org/10.18148/srm/2008.v2i1.598

Hennekam, S., & Bennett, D. (2017). Sexual harassment in the creative industries: Tolerance, culture and the need for change. *Gender, Work and Organization*, 24(4), 417–434. https://doi.org/10.1111/gwao.12176

Kelly, L. (1987). The continuum of sexual violence. In J. Hanmer & M. Maynard (Eds), *Women, violence and social control. Explorations in sociology* (pp. 46–60). Palgrave Macmillan. https://doi.org/10.1007/978-1-349-18592-4_4

Lindhjem, H., & Navrud, S. (2011). Using internet in stated preference surveys: A review and comparison of survey modes. *International Review of Environmental and Resource Economics*, 5(4), 309–351. https://doi.org/10.1561/101.00000045

Menger, P.-M. (2005). *Les intermittents du spectacle: Sociologie d'une exception*. Éditions de l'EHESS. https://doi.org/10.4000/books.editionsehess.1581

Ndiaye, P., & Rivière, C. (2021). *Rapport sur la diversité à l'Opéra national de Paris*. https://www.caribopera.fr/wp-content/uploads/2021/03/RapportsurladiversiteONP21.pdf

Opéra National de Paris. https://www.operadeparis.fr

Ravet, H. (2011). *Musiciennes: Enquête sur les femmes et la musique*. Éditions Autrement.

Shaver-Gleason, L. (2018, January 26). *The morality of musical men: From Victorian propriety to the era of #MeToo* [Unpublished talk]. Utah State University.

Stephenson, E. L. (2012). *If there's no 'fat lady,' when is the opera over? An exploration of changing physical image standards in present-day opera* (Master's thesis, University of Denver). https://digitalcommons.du.edu/cgi/viewcontent.cgi?article=1626&context=etd

Stephenson, L. B., & Crête, J. (2011). Studying political behavior: A comparison of internet and telephone surveys. *International Journal of Public Opinion Research*, 23(1), 24–55. https://doi.org/10.1093/ijpor/edq025

Trachman, M. (2018). L'ordinaire de la violence: Un cas d'atteinte sexuelle sur mineure en milieu artistique. *Travail, genre et sociétés*, 40, 131–150. https://doi.org/10.3917/tgs.040.0131

3. Navigating the Boundary between Subjection and Agency: Gender-Based Violence in the Japanese Popular Music Industry

Chiharu Chujo

Introduction

In March 2023, a BBC documentary exposed the critical issues of power imbalances and gender inequities within the Japanese music industry (Mobeen, 2023). The high-profile sexual abuse scandal involving Johnny Kitagawa, a prominent figure in the Japanese music industry, brought to the forefront systemic issues that demand meticulous examination.[1] Six years after the #MeToo movement,[2] the Japanese popular music industry appears to be finally addressing the pervasive gender-based

---

1   The scandal surrounding Johnny Kitagawa, founder of Johnny & Associates, revealed decades-long sexual abuse allegations involving underage male trainees in Japan's music industry. The case highlights systemic issues, including power imbalances, media complicity and inadequate legal protections, while challenging cultural norms that perpetuate silence around abuse. This has sparked calls for reform within the entertainment industry and broader societal accountability.

2   The limited impact of the #MeToo movement in Japan can be attributed to the deeply entrenched patriarchal values and societal norms that discourage open discussions about sexual harassment and gender-based violence (GBV). Hasunuma and Shin (2019) highlight that, unlike in other countries, the #MeToo movement in Japan has progressed more slowly, with fewer women coming forward publicly and those who do often choosing to remain anonymous. This phenomenon is further entrenched by the legislative landscape—which has historically failed to recognise sexual harassment as a criminal offence, perpetuating a culture of impunity (Hasunuma & Shin, 2019).

   https://doi.org/10.11647/OBP.0436.03

violence (GBV) entrenched in the sector. Nevertheless, as a vibrant and culturally significant realm, it has long harboured complex gender power dynamics that deserve scholarly examination.

The Japanese music industry is characterised by its diversity and dynamism and offers a wide range of genres to cater to the preferences of the public, such as J-pop, J-rock, J-hip-hop, enka, anime and idol. Each genre in Japan has its own dedicated group of fans, distinctive characteristics and cultural significance. Against the backdrop of this vibrant yet complex industry, it is imperative to consider the broader gender dynamics at play in Japan. The nation ranks 118th out of 146 countries in the 2024 Global Gender Gap Report (Kusum et al., 2024), underscoring the staggering gender disparities that prevail within the fabric of society. Moreover, gender discrimination remains pervasive in the music industry. The business has traditionally been dominated by male musicians and male-focused themes, posing challenges for female artists to achieve success. The disparity in gender representation is particularly pronounced in the rock and hip-hop genres, where male artists dominate.[3] The idol system is another example of significant gender inequality in Japanese music. Idol groups, consisting mainly of young female performers, dominate the music scene in Japan, with their strict beauty criteria, limited artistic independence and the commodification of female artists[4] (Chujo & Wartelle-Sakamoto, 2021; Naitō, 2021). In production, management and leadership positions, men also have more power and influence than women.[5] The existing disparity in leadership roles perpetuates gender inequality and limits the availability of music industry opportunities for women.

---

3   Based on my personal research, the Fuji Rock Festival 2022 featured a total of 163 artists and groups, out of which only 26 were female. In *Musicman*, a database of the popular music industry that has been widely utilised as a crucial business resource in the sector, the category of 'musicians' (background musicians, songwriters and lyricists) also has a low representation of women (42 out of 302), and only 1% of sound engineers are women (2 out of 140).

4   The commodification and gendered image shaping observed in the Helsinki School, as discussed in Chapter 5 by Leena-Maija Rossi and Sari Karttunen, finds resonance in the Japanese idol culture, where hypergendered norms dictate the visual and professional personas of female artists.

5   According to my research on the websites of prominent record labels, such as Avex Japan, Nippon Columbia, Pony Canyon, the Sony Music Group, Universal Music Japan, Victor Entertainment, Warner Music and Yamaha Music Communications, only Pony Canyon has a board composition with more than 10% women, specifically 11.8% (2 out of 17 members).

Over the past few years, a few studies have highlighted such gendered norms within the popular music world. Hypergendered expectations for women in prominent musical roles and the constrained contexts encompassing their professional and private lives have been documented (Chujo & Wartelle-Sakamoto, 2021; Naitō, 2021; Hyôgen no Genba Chôsa Dan, 2021; Takeda, 2017). Nevertheless, the examination of gender discrimination and, more specifically, GBV within the Japanese popular music industry and the social structure that has maintained these issues remains a notably underexplored domain within the academic sphere in Japan. The reasons for this require further investigation.

This chapter seeks to address this research gap, delving into the GBV inherent in the Japanese popular music scene and providing a nuanced analysis of the societal and structural factors that perpetuate it. Through an in-depth examination, this research aims to contribute valuable insights to the broader discourse surrounding gender dynamics within the Japanese popular music industry.

Academic Silence: A Lack of Research on Gender-Based Violence in the Japanese Music Industry

As defined by the European Commission (n.d.), GBV refers to 'violence directed against a person because of that person's gender or violence that affects persons of a particular gender disproportionately'. If this violence can take 'many forms' (Council of Europe, 2019, p. 18), GBV refers to situations in which individuals are treated unequally and unfavourably because of their gender. In reference to Liz Kelly's (1987) definition of violence, which suggests the notion of a *continuum*, violence against women occurs on a spectrum rather than in isolated incidents. This emphasises the interconnectedness and normalisation of different forms of violence, ranging from subtle behaviours and objectification to more overt forms. Violence, therefore, can be embodied in 'disparaging sexist remarks [...] sexual jokes, insistent flirting, or derogatory jokes about sexuality or looks' (Chapter 2 in this book). These are the most common practices—so embedded in everyday life that the victims themselves would hardly be aware of their nature and psychological, economic or institutional effects. It is noteworthy that gender roles and expectations, male privilege, sexual objectification and inequalities in power and status have served to legitimise, invisibilise, sexualise and perpetuate certain forms of violence against women (Russo et al., 2006). In considering this definition and the potential elements which perpetuate GBV, I will examine the situation of women in the Japanese popular music industry.[6]

The issue of GBV in the music world has remained largely overlooked in Japan in 2024, persisting even in the wake of the #MeToo movement. Within academia, a mere forty-three articles emerge in Japanese when searching the term 'gender-based violence', and a similarly limited 205 articles appear with the same keyword in English on CiNii, a search engine for Japanese academic references.[7] In the realm of art, there exists a scarcity of academic works on GBV to date—with minimal exploration of the subject, particularly within the field of music. Notably, academic attention has primarily focused on the representation of violence, primarily in the realm of painting (Ikeda et al., 2010), with even fewer studies addressing the same theme in the domain of music.[8] Despite the release of several government reports[9] on GBV since 2000, particularly on issues such as domestic violence, stalking, trafficking and sexual harassment, there is an absence of government statistics specifically identifying these problems within the arts.

Several grassroots associations have taken action despite this academic and institutional silence. In 2021, the voluntary organisation *Hyôgen no Genba Chôsa Dan* (Research Group for Artist's Voice) published its research report on sexual harassment in various artistic fields. This organisation investigates harassment in the arts and includes artists, writers, researchers, filmmakers and professionals from various fields. The survey, which included 1,449

---

6   This chapter defines the music industry based on research involving music producers and distributors (Hesmondhalgh, 2018; Hirsch, 1972; Yagi, 2010). The scope of the music industry encompasses four main areas: 1) music creation, which involves individuals such as directors, sound engineers and artists; 2) live performance, which includes professionals such as public address (PA) operators, lighting technicians, event promoters and organisers; 3) music distribution, which involves activities such as promotions, sales and retailing; and 4) music industry copyright work.

7   Author's research, April 2024.

8   As of the current date in 2024, the only study that has addressed sexual harassment issues in the Japanese music world is Ōtera's (2021) research on music colleges in Japan.

9   See the Gender Equality Bureau Cabinet Office's website: https://www.gender. go.jp/policy/no_violence/e-vaw/chousa/h11_top.html

people of all genders, is categorised by artistic field, workplace injury and working conditions. Of the 1,161 respondents (of all genders), most reported verbal sexual harassment related to their appearance or age, but almost half also reported physical harassment.

The survey, which provides a comprehensive overview of sexual harassment in the arts, does not fully cover the music sector. Only 204 (9.2%) of the respondents belonged to the music field, and the music section has only twelve short comments, significantly fewer than other sections (Hyôgen no Genba Chôsa Dan, 2021). Moreover, according to James Paul Gee's (2014) metaphor of communication as an 'iceberg', respondents with explicit insights into violence may not fully capture the nuances of the latent violence of the unspoken society. Indeed, interviews may not cover all aspects of social violence. However, interviews can be combined with other research methods, such as cultural artefact analysis, to better understand violence and its many forms in a particular context.

In this chapter, I thus seek to complement the aforementioned study by conducting a more in-depth analysis of GBV affecting individuals working in the music industry. Specifically, it will focus on the experiences of those employed behind the scenes in technical and industry roles, as well as on the challenges faced by the artists themselves. While the mentor-disciple relationships in opera (see Chapter 2 in this book) and the emotional labour in visual arts education (see Chapter 4 in this book) illustrate structural challenges in European contexts, similar issues arise in Japan's music industry. These dynamics resonate with the precarious conditions of freelance workers in New York theatre (see Chapter 7 in this book). Nevertheless, I aim to identify the specific features of cases within the Japanese music industry. After outlining my methodology, this chapter will proceed with the presentation of key observations, which will then be analysed to provide insightful interpretations. To conclude, I will discuss future perspectives stemming from this analysis.

Methodology

Commencing in 2019, my research endeavours have centred on qualitative investigation, employing semi-structured interviews and observational methods, within the context of the music industry, encompassing both female and male participants. Snowball sampling methodology was chosen for participant recruitment. Similar to the British and American film industries (Patriotta & Hirsch, 2016; Wreyford, 2015), the French jazz scene (Buscatto, 2021) or the creative industries (Hesmondhalgh & Baker, 2010), Japanese popular music is a closed society composed of informal networks. Given the nature of this milieu and my geographical base in France, the establishment of relationships within these professional circles initially demanded strategic efforts. Regrettably, the onset of the global pandemic necessitated a two-year hiatus in my research activities—impeding the continuation of fieldwork, particularly observational components.

The initial selection of interviewees relied on personal networks, with individuals often identified through associations with friends or colleagues with whom preexisting professional or personal relationships were established. Subsequently, during a six-month research stay in Japan in 2023, I conducted additional fieldwork and broadened my network in this domain. Social networking sites, notably X (formerly Twitter), were utilised as platforms to solicit interview participants, yielding responses from eight volunteers. So far, a total of seventeen individuals have been interviewed, encompassing a wide range of professional backgrounds and age groups. Most of the participants are female musicians from different genres.[10]

The demographic breakdown is as follows:

- Female musicians: 9.
- Other female music professionals (music magazine writer, idol make-up artist and radio director): 3.
- Male musicians and sound engineer: 5, with 1 self-identifying as queer.

The semi-structured interviews, characterised by flexibility and depth, varied in duration, ranging from one to three hours. After a general conversation about the course of their lives and careers, I used six main questions to gain a deeper understanding of their perspectives.

---

10   The present study primarily focuses on GBV as experienced by cisgender women in the Japanese music industry, reflecting the composition of the sample and the sociocultural context under examination. It is acknowledged, however, that this approach does not fully encompass the experiences of LGBTQIA+ individuals or account for the complexities of non-binary and intersectional identities. Consequently, it is essential for future research to extend the scope of inquiry to encompass diverse gender identities and sexual orientations, thereby addressing the intricate intersections between GBV and these identities.

Although the questions were listed, they were not always asked in the same sequence; at times the sequence changed, depending on the topic and the situation. The questions covered whether they have experienced:

1. unconscious gender bias,
2. a lack of confidence in their own work,
3. ridicule/criticism,
4. overt gender discrimination (*akiraka na seisabetsu*),
5. sexual harassment (*sekuhara*), and
6. difficulty in accessing information and funding in the industry as a woman.

Questions 1, 4 and 6 pertain to gender discrimination, whereas 3 and 5 more directly relate to GBV. Number 3 is also acknowledged as a characteristic of gender-based discrimination. Number 2, addressing an outcome of both gender discrimination and violence, was included based on insights from the *Be the Change: Women in Music 2022* survey report (Kahlert et al., 2022). The report notes that a significant number of women participants grapple with self-esteem issues. In fact, the interviews revealed a deliberate choice not to directly use the terms 'gender-based violence' (*jendâ ni motozuku bôryoku*) or 'sexual violence' (*seibôryoku*). Instead, the term 'sexual harassment' (*sekuhara*) is utilised, as it encapsulates one facet of GBV. According to the National Personnel Authority (NPA),[11] a Japanese public administrative agency, sexual harassment is defined as:

a. sexual behavior in the workplace that makes others uncomfortable, especially the fact that:
   - an employee offends other employees;
   - an employee offends a person other than the employee with whom the employee comes into contact in the performance of his or her duties;
   - a non-employee offending an employee, or;
b. sexual behavior by an employee outside the workplace that is offensive to other employees.

---

11   See https://www.jinji.go.jp/seisaku/kinmu/harassment/10-10.html

Here, 'sexual behaviours' include (i) behaviours based on sexual interest or desire, (ii) behaviours based on a sense that roles should be assigned according to gender and (iii) behaviours based on prejudice regarding gender orientation or gender identity.

Considering the NPA's definition, this term may align closely with the definition of GBV previously outlined. In the Japanese context, however, *seibôryoku* and *sekuhara* carry distinct connotations for many individuals. *Sekuhara*, for many, is perceived as something more ingrained in everyday life, appearing more relevant and at times less severe than violence. On the other hand, *seibôryoku* is generally considered something more overtly violent by most people, although there is a growing understanding in journalism that *sekuhara* is also a form of GBV.[12] Finally, for the sixth inquiry, I also conducted a parallel investigation by posing identical interrogatives to individuals identifying with the contrasting gender, thereby eliciting a comparative analysis of their perceptions and sentiments regarding the subject matter.

Due to the small number of male informants, this article places a particular focus on the issues of sexual harassment (*sekuhara*) as attested by female informants. Considering this sociolinguistic nuance, I subsequently undertake an in-depth analysis of the informants' discourses. Initially seeming to deny the existence of violence, I will explore these discourses, acknowledging the intricate sociolinguistic landscape that shapes their narratives.

Ambivalent Discourses: No Sexual Harassment, Even If...

Violence is deeply ingrained in the everyday interactions in the Japanese music industry to such an extent that those who encounter it are often unaware of its presence, as highlighted in Mathieu Trachman's (2018) study on what he refers to as 'ordinary violence'. During my research, most of the informants denied the presence of physical sexual assault

---

12　Yukiko Itoh (2022) notes that the term 'sexual violence' (*seibôryoku*) was first used in the early 2010s in Nippon Hōsō Kyōkai (NHK)'s narrative on sexual violence. She examines the actual damage caused by sexual violence and the structural problems that society only became aware of in 2015. Through interviews with victims and actor-narrators, she identifies their hidden realities.

or physical violence (i.e. any direct use of physical force, such as hitting or kicking) in their professional field—except for Aki, a singer who suffered constant sexual harassment from her agency's president:

> The president of the office I was working in at the time was an old man, and he was very powerful in the industry. I was constantly being sexually harassed, and I was about seventeen, so mentally, I didn't really know how to escape. [...] I thought that if I went on like that I would break down, so I decided to stop. When I told them that I wanted to quit, they told me that I was the record company's 40th anniversary newcomer, so if I quit for that reason, it would make their position in the industry worse. So they asked me to stop. They said, 'We just want you to continue. It would be a problem if you quit'. (Aki,[13] July 19, 2019)

Despite facing tangible and legally sanctionable harassment, Aki was unable to pursue any legal or media-related recourse but chose to pursue an avenue of escape, as elucidated further in this chapter. This decision was influenced by power dynamics inherent in her relationship with her president and considerations related to her professional career. Nevertheless, when analysing what was said by my respondents, one can identify 'commonplace gender-based violence'.

Rumours

Most of the informants have some form of musical education from their youth, from junior or senior high school. Some of them have higher education, such as attending universities specialised in music or at least performing musical activities at their university. In such surroundings, all female informants testified that they faced gender discrimination in their artistic recognition but denied having experienced physical sexual harassment. However, many of them confirmed that their friends and colleagues had experienced sexual harassment by their mentor during lessons:

> I myself am quite secure, but in reality I feel it's a mess [at the university]. We have trainings in quite a small room [...] that you couldn't see inside from the front [...] But during my time at university, all these [doors with small] windows were taken out [...]. They said it was because

---

13   Most informants expressed a preference for anonymity; hence, all names attributed to informants in this chapter are pseudonyms.

someone had done something really terrible to someone else during a class. I remember that. (Nao, July 25, 2023)

'Minor' Harassment in Unofficial Settings: Gender-Based Violence Not Being Considered as Such

When asked in the context of a more nuanced understanding of 'sexual harassment'—including manifestations such as sexist remarks, persistent flirtation and derogatory jokes about sexuality or appearance—respondents clearly confirmed recurrent encounters with such incidents. One of the most relevant cases is after-work drinks with colleagues, which is a relevant custom in the music industry, as Sophie Hennekam and Dawn Bennett (2017) highlight in their work on sexual harassment in Dutch creative industries. In these moments, which 'often go with a loosening of professional etiquette and potentially high level[s] of drinking' (Boni-Le Goff, 2022, p. 55), sexual behaviours are often considered insignificant or negligible by the perpetrator and even their close peers, such as colleagues, because they do not appear harmful from the outside.

> Much of the people I talk to at the sales fairs are men, so when I am asked to have a meeting with them, sometimes I wonder if it's a work meeting or just a dinner. In the end, we end up talking almost entirely without talking about work [...]. I want to be careful about that. But if I'm told that it's a meeting, I have to go, don't I? (Aki, July 19, 2019)

It is worth noting that these respondents seem confused rather than embarrassed or angry about such flirtatious behaviour from their male colleagues. In fact, these respondents were unsure whether such behaviour could be considered sexual harassment. They seem to be in a constrained situation where they have no choice but to accept it for the sake of their professional position, even though there are no tangible promises or assurances for their professional careers.

Lookism and Ageism

In a similar way to American popular culture (Leschner, 2019), the female body is vocally objectified in everyday contexts in the Japanese popular music industry. Although most informants denied having experienced direct physical sexual harassment, they talked extensively about sexist (or hypergendered) notions of appearance evoked by their peers. Most of them testified about the restrictive expectations of how women should look and how old they should be: 'I think the kind of people who are considered singers are a bit like they're being told what to do. They're like the guy in the band telling them to dress up like a country cowgirl or something' (Saki, August 3, 2022).

Sometimes, such lookism privileges women, but it is to enhance the atmosphere or merely to decorate the environment. Eminent pianist Eri (July 19, 2023) testified that she had seen many hotel restaurants offer a job exclusively to female pianists because 'the place would look better if a woman in a dress played the piano'. In such a case, according to her, her agent 'gets angry' with her if she wears her glasses.

However, in such circumstances imposing gendered norms on their appearance, as is the case of flirting in informal settings, the informants seem to be reluctant to consider such practices as sexual harassment.

> I myself don't get [sexually harassed] ... I don't, but I still feel like there's quite a lot in costumes and that sort of thing. I think that a certain amount of exposure is expected. Also, I'm speaking in terms of compliments, but I often see situations where I'm praised for being unusually sexy. I think there are a lot of outfit problems [...]. When I wear something like that [i.e. the dress, people say] it's glamorous or something like that. Male musicians are supposed to wear tails and so on. But women are told that it's nice to wear something like that, and I found it a bit disgusting the way they said it. And if you have a job that requires you to wear something like that, or if it's a visual performance, you must wear a dress or something. It might not go as far as sexual harassment but ... (Nao, July 25, 2023)

Strategies to Escape or Resolve Challenging Situations

In such instances—ranging from inappropriate remarks and lookism to more subtle forms of coercion in professional interactions—the informants appeared to adopt a posture wherein they refrain from categorising themselves as recipients of harassment. There is an evident lack of certainty or consideration regarding the seriousness with which their experiences might be acknowledged as instances of violence. The process of raising critical consciousness regarding these perceived acts of violence appears elusive or intangible. Nevertheless, and quite surprisingly, they also articulated strategies indicative of their proclivity to either evade or resolve the challenging situations they encounter.

Escaping from the Situation

Regarding the potential solution of escaping from the situation, one course of action involves departing from restrictive and detrimental environments, as exemplified by Aki. However, as articulated in her testimony, she initially encountered challenges in taking this step due to resistance not only from her immediate superior but also from the agency itself. The agency dissuaded her from severing ties with the agent to prevent potential damage to its reputation.

Acting against the Situation

Certain individuals face challenges and make efforts, both passively and actively, to overcome difficult circumstances. Marie Buscatto (2021) states that French female jazz musicians intentionally diminish their sexual allure to prevent harassment. Similarly, one of the respondents in my study elucidated her method of establishing an atmosphere that dissuades flirtatious propositions, effectively conveying her unequivocal rejection of such advances. Another approach involves utilising a structural framework to establish a prominent musical standing in order to discourage harassment. Active resistance primarily entails the act of publicly condemning or criticising something. Only a single interviewee revealed instances of violence that occurred in the 1980s. The artist expressed strong opposition to GBV in her music, which was considered notably radical and transgressive (Chujo & Aizawa, 2021). Most informants who encountered such challenges responded in a passive manner.

Letting It Be

Several informants attested to their inability to evade or rebuff certain behaviours exhibited by the audience, particularly persistent advances. One of them—Yuki, who plays as a DJ in many venues in Tokyo— recounted seeking advice from a female and more experienced colleague regarding flirtatious behaviours of male audience. In response, the colleague advised her to endure and tolerate such occurrences.

> I remember a senior member of the club staff saying that it was a water trade [*mizushôbai*] ... When she said it was a water business, I was shocked [...] and at the same time, I thought that was right. So I thought that if my activities were supposed to be a water business, then it would be simpler to just let it be. (Yuki, 26 July 2023)

Mizushôbai, colloquially known as 'water business', serves as a slang term denoting an eating and drinking establishment with an uncertain income. In common parlance in Japan, however, it typically connotes sex work. Rather than contesting or opposing this characterisation in the context of her musical activities, the informant acknowledged and accepted this association. It is noteworthy that Yuki sought to align herself with the discourse articulated by her senior colleague—notwithstanding harbouring reservations, owing to the considerable esteem she held for the latter.

Recourse to Professional and Familial Networks

Certain informants provided testimony indicating that they were able to avert offensive behaviour or verbal abuse through the support of their social networks. Many of them have familial connections—often with their fathers or male peers occupying elevated hierarchical positions, affording them a form of protective buffer:

> My father is a man who has done a lot in my milieu, and he is respected for his contribution. So I think that because I'm his daughter, I've got a certain freedom to do what I want. [...] There's nothing more to it than that, so it's a daughter category. So there's no depth to it, nothing special. I am not an 'individual'. (Saki, August 3, 2022)

Saki, whose father is a distinguished musician and owns a concert hall, acknowledged the power dynamics within her milieu. Her father occupies an esteemed position, consequently framing her identity primarily as the 'daughter of this person'.

Another informant—Miki, who has engaged in several intimate relationships with her male peers—explicitly refuted any suggestion that these relationships have influenced her musical activities. She asserted that she 'does not want to relate it' to her own professional pursuits.

Simultaneously, however, she acknowledged that these relationships afford her a sense of equality with her male peers:

> I think that being in a romantic relationship may have made it possible for us to speak as equals. I mean, with the band members. Until then, I kind of thought that I might not have had much to say about the arrangements or the performance side of things [...] because I have a complex. [...] But now that having gone through a romantic relationship, I know that it's okay to talk about anything I think. [...] Without that [i.e. the romantic relationship], maybe I would have been a complexed person. (Miki, September 11, 2023)

For this young musician, establishing an intimate relationship with a member of their (male-dominated) group served as a means of overcoming her musical 'complex' towards her male peers. Similar to Saki, who benefits from her father's recognition, acknowledgement from her male partner is deemed essential for her to establish professional legitimacy in relation to other male peers. It is noteworthy, however, that, in contrast to Saki, she does not perceive the relationship with a male peer as problematic when its impact is perceived positively. Furthermore, age and professional stage, which are tied to one another, are societal factors that influence women's positions. Some interviewees, all above the age of forty, stated that they do not require this form of action since they have advanced enough in their careers and have a particular reputation.

Socialised Coercion Preventing Recognition of Violence

These testimonials divulge a discourse marked by ambivalence among the informants. While, on the one hand, the informants either denied or expressed uncertainty about encountering sexual harassment and consistently refrained from explicitly mentioning GBV, on the other hand, their narratives inadvertently affirm, even unconsciously, the manifestation of certain effects associated with aspects of GBV, in line with the concept of a *continuum*: subtle sexist behaviours, rooted in underlying attitudes, beliefs and social structures, are normalised and perpetuated in their professional activities.

The emergence of a paradox is evident—where, despite denying instances of harassment, informants consistently adopt strategies aimed at proactively 'avoiding' such situations. This prompts an investigation into the discrepancy: why, if they claim not to have experienced sexual harassment, do they use language and actions that reflect deliberate avoidance? In the following section, an examination of the social and economic milieu in which the informants work will help to grasp the paradoxical position adopted by the informants.

One could posit a hypothesis suggesting that sexual harassment, encompassed within the broader framework of gender violence, is not cognizantly acknowledged by the informants. Drawing from Nakane Tae's[14] (2023) ethnographic exploration of (weak) mobilisations within the music world, it is elucidated that participants in this milieu often dissociate their identity as artists, performers or music professionals from that of traditional workers (*rōdōsha*). According to Bård Kleppe and Sigrid Røyseng (2016, p. 293), Norwegian theatre is a representation of what Max Weber (2013/1922) refers to as 'charismatic communities', where members must recognise the authenticity of the charismatic leader and conform accordingly. This principle defines relationships between members as 'strictly personal' (Kleppe & Røyseng, 2016, p. 293) and based on their own standards. Ensuring professional and career security therefore requires prioritising relationships with powerful individuals over other rational factors. In line with Kleppe and Røyseng's analysis, Nakane suggests that the concept of 'labour rights' or 'labour mobilisation' might not resonate with these professionals in the music industry, as they do not perceive themselves as conventional workers. Nakane's analysis provides grounds to hypothesise that in addition to the awareness of workers' rights being limited, the awareness of women's rights or GBV may also be low among female practitioners in the music world. Indeed, all interviewees explicitly mentioned that, prior to their engagement in the interviews, they had scarcely contemplated the position of women in the realm of employment. Despite their expressed interest in the subject, their reflections on the place of women in the workforce were minimal. The limited discussion of women in the labour market in the specified situation may indicate larger issues in sectors such as the Japanese music industry—including insufficient attention to gender equality, as my previous research revealed (Chujo, 2023); a lower number of female artists; unequal opportunities and recognition;

---

14   This chapter follows Japanese naming conventions, where the family name precedes the given name (e.g., Nakane Tae). This format is used consistently throughout.

and insufficient measures to combat gender-based discrimination and violence. Furthermore, the absence of active involvement indicates that the policies of gender equality in the arts, particularly in music, may be insufficient or nonexistent in terms of promoting equal treatment and preventing GBV. While generalising from these testimonies would be premature, the prevailing discourse on mobilisation against GBV may find limited resonance within such an environment.

An additional hypothesis posits that the informants deliberately (albeit unconsciously) refrain from acknowledging the presence of violence in their lives. As Gunilla Carstensen (2016) observed, determining whether an act qualifies as sexual harassment can often be ambiguous due to factors such as the specific circumstances, context and a lack of clarity, as the definition of sexual harassment is imprecise. Furthermore, drawing on insights from Henry Greenspan's (2019) discourse analysis of Holocaust survivors[15] and Blandine Veith's (2010) life history research on migrant women, deliberate positionalities may be assumed during interviews, with informants choosing to omit certain experiences that are challenging to articulate.

The paradoxical discourse observed in our informants could potentially result from such intentional positionalities. Their hesitancy in addressing uncomfortable situations may be explained by an ambivalent standpoint. As per the analysis of Japanese sociologist and feminist Ueno Chizuko (2010), women inadvertently contribute to feelings of self-hatred (*jiko-ken'o*) and the process of perceiving others as different or alien (*tasha-ka*). First, women internalise feelings of resentment towards society, and second, they deliberately create distance between themselves and others who experience discrimination or violence in order to avoid being stigmatised. What information can be uncovered when informants employ the strategy of othering to prevent feelings of self-hatred within their limitations? Here are three potential factors that

---

15 Greenspan (2019) characterises silence in his discourse analysis of Holocaust survivors as unsaid, incommunicable, unbearable, and irretrievable. A survivor may choose not to talk about the unspoken, while the things that cannot be communicated are difficult to put into words. Unbearable refers to the intense emotional suffering that survivors may choose not to discuss, while irretrievable describes the loss of loved ones, communities, and a feeling of belonging. Greenspan asserts that his Holocaust survivor research holds great significance, emphasising that it is equally relevant to all of us.

can affect the positioning of the informants.

Hierarchical Relationships with Seniors

Initially, the interviewees found themselves constrained within three restrictive relationships that impede their ability to denounce GBV in their surroundings: commercial relationships with audiences and fans, professional relationships with peers and hierarchical relationships with elders. In the context of the latter, reference is made to Inagaki Kyōko's (2017) work, which posits that Japanese art worlds embody a distinct concept of master–disciple relationships or ingratitude. The Japanese art world is highly hierarchical—as in the case of orchestra (Ravet, 2015) or opera (Buscatto et al., in this book) in France and, based on the principle of networking, the creative cultural sphere in the UK (Hesmondhalgh & Baker, 2010).

However, studies by Inagaki (2017) and Ōtera Masako (2021) on harassment in Japanese music colleges emphasise that in the Japanese social context, the master supports the disciple, and the disciple in turn repays the debt owed to the master over a long period. Many of the informants in my research appear to uphold such hierarchical relationships with their older peers, expressing sentiments such as 'that person has always been good to/taken care of me, so I don't want to betray them'. Although not explicitly acknowledging the constraints arising from these hierarchical relationships, it appears that they are hesitant to confront instances of GBV, particularly if their senior colleagues fail to acknowledge their grievances seriously. Yuki observed the hierarchical connection within her DJ community and its gendered component. She posited that male DJs place a higher importance on hierarchical relationships compared to their female counterparts. Therefore, women, who are already facing disadvantages, should exercise caution in selecting their male partners in order to uphold their social standing. She witnessed that her romantic involvement with her ex-boyfriend, who was seven years her senior, influenced her male coworker, who was four years older than her, and regards her boyfriend as a mentor, to grant her approval:

> Women must be extremely cautious about who they date, or they will
> be hurt later on. [...] Because the man you choose directly affects your

future activities. [...] It's like a pretty traditional male-female connection, like the old-fashioned couple feeling. This is 'my girl' stuff. It's difficult to change the old ways (Yuki, July 26, 2023).

Here, the manifestation of societal norms and standards with respect to interpersonal connections becomes evident. Yuki's discourse implies that women are subject to close examination and judgement depending on their selection of a spouse, which then impacts their social status and engagements. Although Yuki admitted that there are archaic standards, she also suggested that it is hard to question or overthrow them. The notion of conforming to predetermined roles, such as 'my girl' or 'his girlfriend', highlights the lasting impact of gendered power dynamics paradigms. This leads to the second aspect: the emotional investment.

Emotional Labour and Emotional Blackmail

Second, all the informants exert substantial effort to interact amiably with their audience and colleagues in their professional spheres. The emotional investment involved in this effort can be framed as 'emotional labour', a concept elucidated by Arlie Hochschild (1979) in the context of certain service industries. Japanese sociologist Takeda Keiko (2017) has highlighted the emotional labour inherent in the idol business, particularly concerning the relationships with fans. The informants who tolerate the sexist behaviours of their customers appear to be grappling with a similar dynamic. They are expected to maintain a pleasant demeanour towards their customers and refrain from expressing anger, even if confronted with provocative behaviour. It is noteworthy that this expectation for emotional labour is accentuated within the context of seniority relationships, as discussed earlier. Consequently, shaping relationships with colleagues, especially those in more senior positions, becomes a norm.

Precarious Status as Freelance

Third, it is noteworthy that all the informants operate independently, particularly in their musical pursuits, without the backing of an agency. Moreover, within the realm of art worlds, an inherent ambiguity exists in demarcating boundaries between work and nonwork, potentially elucidating the comparatively low level of mobilisation among workers (Takahashi, 2023). Sociologist Takahashi Kaori highlights the awareness within art professions, which often materialises at the intersection of the notions of 'work' and 'inciting things' (*yaritaikoto*); 'work' pertains to artistic practices adapting to external demands for remuneration, while 'inciting things' refers to artistic practice stemming from intrinsic motivation and undertaken for its own sake. Within the domain of artistic occupations, the notion of 'work' encompasses meeting external criteria in return for monetary remuneration. This encompasses various assignments, initiatives or duties performed to fulfil the requirements of clients, employers, colleagues or the public. Conversely, 'inciting things' refers to artistic pursuits driven by personal enthusiasm and motivation. These are (or are supposed to be) artistic endeavours pursued solely for the pleasure of producing—without the primary objective of financial profit or outward acclaim, as Angela McRobbie (2016) argues in her research on the circumstances of creative labour in Britain. This differentiation emphasises the dual nature that artists frequently encounter: managing the requirement to support themselves financially through their job while fostering their own creative instincts and manifestations. Actors and actresses in these spheres often rely on the latter to safeguard their artistic identity. Consequently, when faced with workplace injustices and possessing limited discretion, they may find themselves in situations where they cannot adapt or manage decisions as they typically would. This phenomenon is not unique to the informants' experiences but has been demonstrated in other studies encompassing members of musical groups (Nomura, 2023) and amateur idols (Kamioka, 2021, 2023). These performing professions frequently lack fixed contracts and provide few assurances of stable economic situations for the artists involved. In such a precarious environment, the informants may find themselves desensitised to annoying conduct.

Socialised coercion occurs when professional norms and expectations are internalised, making GBV prevention difficult. Drawing on Ueno Chizuko's theoretical framework (2010), the informants' ambivalence reflects a complex dynamic between self-loathing and stigma avoidance. These elements reveal the complex social structures that perpetuate GBV in the music industry. In essence, the informants' deliberate positionalities are deeply entwined with societal expectations, making socioeconomic and cultural contexts crucial to addressing GBV in the music industry.

Conclusion

This research illuminates the pervasive yet overlooked issue of daily harassment faced by the informants in their professional pursuits. The prevalent trivialisation of such experiences, often overlooked or not consciously acknowledged, highlights a significant gap in the recognition of GBV within the Japanese music industry. Persistent advances and seemingly innocuous remarks are inadequately categorised, perpetuating an environment where the concept of violence remains elusive. This lack of recognition is compounded by the presence of restrictive hierarchical relationships, the imposition of emotional labour and an overarching environment that demonstrates limited awareness of women's rights.

These findings exhibit similarities with patterns observed in other artistic and cultural domains—such as cinema, theatre, opera or other creative works in Western countries, where incidents of harassment and discrimination may also be minimised or disregarded. Within this particular context, it is evident that the Japanese music industry exhibits a distinct characteristic: the hierarchical arrangement of connections within Japanese society, primarily centred around age and mentor–disciple relationships, strengthens the power dynamic between not only men and women, but also men and men, and women and women. This subsequently impacts the professional trajectories of individuals.

The existence of rigid hierarchical structures, along with the enforcement of emotional labour, intensifies the situation, resulting in an environment that displays a lack of understanding regarding women's rights. The failure to acknowledge GBV is a recurring theme in different fields, which mirrors the wider societal beliefs and systems that enable the continuation of such conduct.

Despite these insights, it is crucial to acknowledge the study's limitations. The underrepresentation of men in the sample underscores the need for a more diverse participant pool to capture a comprehensive spectrum of experiences. Furthermore, additional research is required to tackle the absence of viewpoints from male actors in the industry. Homosociability contributes to the structure that can perpetuate GBV, as in Patricia Yancey Martin and David L. Collinson's (1999) or Michele Rene Gregory's (2009) observations of male homosociability in the workplace. Such studies should encompass a wider spectrum of voices and narratives. Understanding the complex dynamics of relationships between male actors in Japanese social interactions is crucial for comprehending its significant impact on professional experiences and outcomes. In moving forward, addressing these limitations and continuing to investigate the nuanced dynamics within this professional milieu will contribute to a more comprehensive understanding of the challenges faced by individuals, paving the way for informed interventions and policy changes that foster a safer and more equitable working environment.

References

Boni-Le Goff, I. (2022). Sexual violence as an invisible process in white-collar work. In D. Grisard, A. Erismann & J. Dahinden (Eds), *Violent times, rising resistance: An interdisciplinary gender perspective* (pp. 51–64). Seismo Press. https://doi.org/10.33058/seismo.30758

Buscatto, M. (2018). Feminisation of artistic work: legal measures and female artists' resources do matter. *Todas as Artes. Revista Luso-brasileira de Artes e Cultura*, 1(1), 21–38. https://doi.org/10.21747/21843805/tav1n1a2

Buscatto, M. (2021). *Women in jazz: Musicality, femininity, marginalization.* Routledge. https://doi.org/10.4324/9781003177555 (Original work published 2007)

Buscatto, M., Helbert, S., & Roharik, I. (2021). L'opéra, un monde professionnel hanté par les violences de genre. *Les Cahiers de la Société québécoise de recherche en musique*, 22(1–2), 49–67. https://doi.org/10.7202/1097857ar

Carstensen, G. (2016). Sexual harassment reconsidered: The forgotten grey zone. NORA—*Nordic Journal of Feminist and Gender Research*, 24(4), 267–280. https://doi.org/10.1080/08038740.2017.1292314

Chujo, C., & Aizawa, N. (2020). Women's movements in 1970s Japan. In E. Boris, S. T. Dawson & B. Molony (Eds), *Engendering transnational transgressions* (pp. 133–146). Routledge. https://doi.org/10.4324/9781003050384-10

Chūjō, C., & Wartelle-Sakamoto, C. (2021). L'hyperféminisation des chanteuses japonaises : shōjo kashu et aidoru. *Transposition*, 9. https://doi.org/10.4000/transposition.5910

European Commission. (n.d.). What is gender-based violence? *European Commission.* https://commission.europa.eu/strategy-and-policy/policies/

justice-and-fundamental-rights/gender-equality/gender-based-violence/
what-gender-based-violence_en

Gee, J. P. (2014). *How to do discourse analysis*. Routledge. https://doi.
org/10.4324/9781315819662

Greenspan, H. (2014). The unsaid, the incommunicable, the unbearable, and
the irretrievable. *The Oral History Review*, 41(2), 229–243. https://doi.
org/10.1093/ohr/ohu033

Gregory, M. R. (2009). Inside the locker room: Male homosociability in the
advertising industry. *Gender, Work and Organization*, 16(3), 323–347. https://
doi.org/10.1111/j.1468-0432.2009.00447.x

Hasunuma, L., & Shin, K. (2019). #MeToo in Japan and South Korea: Activism,
backlash and solidarity. *Journal of Women, Politics & Policy*, 40(4), 499–523.
https://doi.org/10.1080/1554477x.2019.1563416

Hennekam, S., & Bennett, D. (2017). Sexual harassment in the creative industries:
Tolerance, culture, and the need for change. *Gender, Work & Organization*,
24(4), 417–434. https://doi.org/10.1111/gwao.12176

Hesmondhalgh, D. (2018). *The cultural industries*. SAGE. https ://uk.sagepub.
com/en-gb/eur/the-cultural-industries/book250830

Hesmondhalgh, D., & Baker, S. (2010). *Creative labour: Media work in three cultural
industries*. Routledge. https://doi.org/10.4324/9780203855881

Hirsch, P. (1972). Processing fads and fashions: An organization-set analysis
of cultural industry systems. *American Journal of Sociology*, 77(4), 639–659.
https://doi.org/10.1086/225192

Hochschild, A. R. (1979). Emotion work, feeling rules, and social structure.
American Journal of Sociology, 85(3), 551–575.

Hyôgen no Genba Chôsa Dan. (2021).'*Hyôgen no genba' harasumento hakusho*
2021. https://www.hyogen-genba.com

Hyôgen no Genba Chôsa Dan. (2022). *Hyôgen no genba jendâ baransu hakusho*.
https://www.hyogen-genba.com

Ikeda, S., & Kobayashi, M. (Eds). (2010). *Shikakuhyōshō to ongaku*. Akashishoten.
https://doi.org/10.20591/ongakugaku.58.1_51

Inagaki, K. (2017). *Kyōiku bunka no shakai-gaku*. Hōsōdaigaku Kyōikushinkōkai.

Itoh, Y. (2022, Dec.). Les violences sexuelles à travers les médias depuis 2000.
L'Atelier doctoral des études japonaises de la SFEJ, Société française des études
japonaises, Paris, France. https://hal.science/hal-04109147v1

Kahlert, J., Das, A., & Cirisano, N. (2022). *BE THE CHANGE—Women in Music*
2022. TuneCore. https://www.believe.com/sites/believe/files/2022-05/Be-
The-Change-x-2022-Women-in-Music.pdf

Kamioka, M. (2021). Aidoru bunka ni okeru 'cheki': Satsuei ni yoru kankeisei no kyōka to kashika. *Tetsugaku*, 147, 135–159. https://doi.org/10.14992/00020093

Kamioka, M.. (2023). Geinō to iu rōdō: 'Aidoru wārudo' ni oite kyōyū sareru jōnetsu no kachi. In S. Matsunaga, T. Nagata & K. Nakamura (Eds), *Shōhi to rōdō no bunka shakaigaku* (pp. 141–158). Nakanishiya Shuppan.

Kelly, L. (1987). The continuum of sexual violence. In J. Hanmer & M. Maynard (Eds), *Women, violence and social control* (pp. 46–60). Palgrave Macmillan. https://doi.org/10.1007/978-1-349-18592-4

Lechner, E. (2019). The popfeminist politics of body positivity: Creating spaces for 'disgusting' female bodies in US popular culture. *Revue française d'études américaines*, 158(1), 71–94. https://doi.org/10.3917/rfea.158.0071

Martin, P. Y., & Collinson, D. (1999). Gender and sexuality in organizations. In M. Ferree, J. Lorber & B. Hess (Eds), *Revisioning gender* (pp. 285–310). Sage.

McRobbie, A. (2016). *Be creative: Making a living in the new culture industries.* Polity Press.

Naitō, C. (2021). *Aidoru no kuni no seibōryoku.* Shinyōsha. https://doi.org/10.19018/nihonkindaibungaku.106.0_239

Mobeen, A. (2023, March 6). Japan's J-pop predator: Exposed for abuse but still revered. *BBC News.* https://www.bbc.com/news/world-asia-64837855

Nakane, T. (2023). 'Rōdō' kategorī ni aragau ongakuka tachi ni yoru rentai e no mosaku: Geijutsusei to rōdōsei no aida ni aru 'rōdō-tekina mono' no jirenma o megutte. In S. Matsunaga, T. Nagata & K. Nakamura (Eds), *Shōhi to rōdō no bunka shakaigaku* (pp. 223–240). Nakanishiya Shuppan.

Nomura, H. (2023). Yume o ou tame ni seishain ni naru: Bunka geijutsu katsudōsha no rōdō o tou. In S. Matsunaga, T. Nagata & K. Nakamura (Eds), *Shōhi to rōdō no bunka shakaigaku* (pp. 121–140). Nakanishiya Shuppan.

Ōtera, M. (2021). Issues of harassment related to teacher-student relationships in music colleges. *The Bulletin of Art Institute, College of Art, Nihon University*, 1(0), 16–27. https://doi.org/10.57544/nichigei.1.0_16

Pal, K. K., Piaget, K., & Zahidi, S. (2024, June 11). *Global gender gap report* 2024. World Economic Forum. https://www.weforum.org/publications/global-gender-gap-report-2024/

Pandea, A. R., Grzemny, D., & Keen, E. (2020). *Gender matters* (2nd ed.). Council of Europe. https://doi.org/10.3917/coe.pande.2019.01

Patriotta, G., & Hirsch, P. M. (2016). Mainstreaming innovation in art worlds: Cooperative links, conventions and amphibious artists. *Organization Studies*, 37(6), 867–887. https://doi.org/10.1177/0170840615622062

Ravet, H. (2015). *L'orchestre au travail: Interprétations, négociations, coopérations.* Vrin. https://doi.org/10.4000/sdt.877

Russo, N. F., & Pirlott, A. (2006). Gender-based violence: Concepts, methods, and findings. *Annals of the New York Academy of Sciences*, 1087(1), 178–205. https://doi.org/10.1196/annals.1385.024

Takahashi, K. (2023). 'Yaritai koto' to 'shigoto' no bunri, kinsetsu, kanri: Bijutsusakka to ongakuka no jissen o jirei to shite. In S. Matsunaga, T. Nagata & K. Nakamura (Eds), *Shōhi to rōdō no bunka shakaigaku* (pp. 103–120). Nakanishiya Shuppan.

Takeda, K. (2017). Raibu aidoru, kyōdōtai, fan bunka: Aidoru no rōdō to fan komyunitī. In T. Tanaka, A. Yamamoto & T. Andō (Eds), *Dekigoto kara manabu karuchuraru sutadīzu* (pp. 117–134). Nakanishiya Shuppan.

Ueno, C. (2010). *Onnagirai: Nippon no misojinī*. Kinokuniya Shoten.

Veith, B. (2011). Lorsque les silences parlent dans les récits de vie : Comment analyser la complexité du social ? *L'Homme et la Société*, 176–177(2), 151–169. https://doi.org/10.3917/lhs.176.0151

Wreyford, N. (2015). Birds of a feather: Informal recruitment practices and gendered outcomes for screenwriting work in the UK film industry. *The Sociological Review*, 63(S1), 84–96. https://doi.org/10.1111/1467-954X.12242

Yagi, R. (2010). Uncertainty absorption mechanism of organizations in the music industry: A theoretical discussion of the existing papers by Hirsch. *Yokohama Kokusai Shakai Kagaku Gakkai*, 15(3), 161–177.

4. Gender-Based Violence in French Art Schools and the Reproduction of Gender Inequality in Contemporary Art

Mathilde Provansal

Introduction

In September 2020, the association 'Balancetonecoledart' ('expose your art school')—created by current and former students of the Institut Supérieur des Beaux-Arts de Besançon (the School of Visual Arts of Besançon, a provincial French town)—published several testimonials on social media. The name of the association and the illustration accompanying the posts, a pink pig roasting on a spit on a black background, echo the #BalanceTonPorc movement ('expose your pig'), a hashtag created in 2017 by a New York-based French journalist to raise awareness about the prevalence of sexual misconduct at work and inviting women to disclose the names of harassers. The Instagram and Facebook accounts of 'Balancetonecoledart' published a dozen written testimonials of sexual harassment, sexual assaults and rape. Each testimonial was accompanied by a trigger warning and the legal definition of the offence. Shortly after, the Chief Prosecutor of Besançon launched a call for testimony and students at other art schools created their own pages on social media to share experiences of violence. More recently, the testimonies that accompanied the publication of a manifesto 'for a #Metoo of the art world' called attention to the fact that art schools are one of the sites of gender-based violence in the contemporary art (Manifesto XXI, 2024).[1]

---

1   These testimonies are published daily on the Instagram account 'metoo.art

    https://doi.org/10.11647/OBP.0436.04

Contrary to gender-based violence in university and elite academic institutions (Ahmed, 2021; Armstrong et al., 2006; Bereni et al., 2003; Briquet, 2019; Brown et al., 2020; Cardi et al., 2005; CLASCHES, 2014; Hirsch & Khan, 2020; Schüz et al., 2022), gender-based violence in art schools remains largely under-documented. Research about gender inequality in artistic education is quite recent because for years the myth of the self-educated artist prevailed and artistic training was not considered a key step in artistic careers, except for classical music and ballet (Buscatto et al., 2020). Yet, investigating this topic may enrich our understanding of gender-based violence in higher education, and more broadly of the gender order in contemporary art. Women have constituted an increasingly large majority of visual arts students in France over the past thirty years (DEPS, 2023; Galodé, 1994). In the last two decades, more than 60% of art school students were women (DEPS, 2023). However, in 2019, only 41% of visual artists were women (DEPS, 2023), and they continue to be less visible on the contemporary art market and in institutions (Provansal, 2023). Such discrepancy between women's presence in schools of visual arts and their professional outcomes in contemporary art is not specific to France and can be found in other countries such as Australia (The Countess, 2019), Finland (see Chapter 5 in this book), Germany (Schulz et al., 2016), Poland (Gromada et al., 2016), the United Kingdom (Robinson, 2021) and the United States (Frenette et al., 2020).

Based on the case of French schools of visual arts, this chapter explores the role that gender-based violence in artistic education plays in perpetuating gender inequality in contemporary art. Gender-based violence refers to 'all forms of violence, whether verbal, physical or psychological, interpersonal or institutional, committed by men as men against women as women, in both public and private spheres' (Simonetti, 2016, p. 681). Liz Kelly's notion of the *continuum* of women's experiences of sexual violence (Kelly, 1987) makes it possible to articulate various forms of violence, both verbal and physical, encompassing everything from the everyday intimate intrusions to criminalised offences. Gender-based violence is also understood as a form of social control which acts to maintain women's subordination and limits women's field of possibilities (Hanmer & Maynard, 1987). The notion underlines the inscription of these various forms of violence in gender relations and their role in the reproduction of gender hierarchies (Delage et al., 2019). Although violence against women is the predominant form (Brown et al., 2020), Ilaria Simonetti adds that gender-based violence also refers to the experiences of men whose masculinity does not fit the norm of 'hegemonic masculinity' (Connell, 2005). This chapter focuses on women's experiences of violence, as I do not have sufficient data to study violence experienced by men and LGBTQ+ individuals. Also, I underline the articulation of gender violence with other systems of inequality when there is sufficient data to do so (Crenshaw, 1991). In this chapter, I study the forms of gender-based violence experienced by female students in public French art schools, the social processes that produce and sustain them, and their consequences for women's integration in the contemporary art world. Overall, this chapter aims at emphasising how gender-based violence in artistic education contributes to maintaining gender segregation and thus to perpetuating gender inequality (Hattery, 2022) in the art world.

Box 1. The French Fine Arts Higher Education System and the 'École des Arts Plastiques'

In France, the Fine Arts Higher Education Network comprises forty-four institutions that welcome more than 11,000 students, a majority of whom are women (69% in 2021) (DEPS, 2023). Students are admitted to art schools via a competitive entrance exam after the baccalaureate. These schools give access to Bachelor and Master degrees in art, design and communication (DGCA, 2018).

The 'École des Arts Plastiques' (EAP) is one of these forty-four art schools.[2] Between 1995 and 2013, the school welcomed around 550 students per year, the majority of whom were women (59%) and students from privileged social and economic background (60% of students have at least one parent who belongs the socio-professional category 'Top executive/liberal professions'). The school belongs to the 'elitist segment' of artistic formation (Galodé & Michaut,

---

2   Art schools are distinct from departments of visual arts at universities.

2003) and aims for artistic excellence, both in terms of recruitment and training. Its five-year curriculum is entirely devoted to artistic practice and is not aimed at alternative careers in design or graphic design. I consider that studying in this prestigious, selective and art-oriented school is a sign of interest in an artistic career. The 'pedagogy of creation' (Moulin, 2009) of the EAP stands out by the fact that students have to find a studio, and are placed under the leadership of a 'studio head' (a 'chef d'atelier'), at the beginning of their studies. Students from various cohorts work on their personal work in this collective work space.

Unfortunately, there is no quantitative survey on the prevalence of gender-based violence in art schools. However, the topic is not new and there are several institutional and feminist initiatives documenting it. In a report on women's place in art and culture (Gonthier-Maurin, 2013) presented to the French Senate in 2013, the issue of sexual harassment in art schools was brought up by Reine Prat, a high-ranking civil servant and author of two famous reports on gender inequalities in live performance arts (Prat, 2006, 2009), and Giovanna Zapperi, a professor of contemporary art history at the art school of Bourges at the time. Both emphasised that in art schools, 'generations of "Lolitas" work under the aegis of mentors who are most often men, most often of a certain age' (Gonthier-Maurin, 2013, p. 18).[3] More recently, art schools were included in the survey on student living conditions conducted in 2020 by the French Observatory of Student Life (Belghith et al., 2021). However, the sample of respondents is too small to analyse the prevalence of sexual violence in art schools. In February 2020, a survey on 'sexist and sexual violence and harassment' in the artistic and cultural higher education system was conducted for the Ministry of Culture by Egae, a consulting company specialised in discrimination, gender equality and sexual violence. Each institution received its own results, but no synthesis has been published by the Ministry of Culture. Finally, between March 2020 and July 2022, *Les Mots de Trop* ('the last straw'),[4] a collective created by three female students in 2019, launched a call for

---

3   My translation.
4   See https://lesmotsdetrop.fr/index.html

testimonies of discrimination in art schools. Their platform has collected more than four hundred anonymous testimonies of various forms of gender-based violence and discrimination in art, design and architecture places of education in France, Belgium and Switzerland (Les Mots de Trop, 2022).

Data and Methods

The data used for this study was collected during two different fieldworks. The first period of fieldwork is from my PhD thesis on gender inequality in contemporary art (Provansal, 2023). In particular, I conducted interviews with twenty-seven women and twenty men who graduated from a prestigious French art school, which I call 'École des Arts Plastiques' (EAP), between 1992 and 2014. Four artists who did not graduate from the EAP were interviewed as well. During these interviews, I asked questions about their trajectory before, during and after art school. I also interviewed six professors of the EAP. The great majority of these interviews were conducted before the #MeToo movement, from 2014 to 2018.

Gender-based violence was not a core topic of the interviews. But it was sometimes addressed by interviewees when answering questions about the atmosphere of the studio they were working in at the EAP, about their relations with their instructors and classmates, and about their experiences of instructors' misconduct. I sometimes asked explicitly whether they had experienced or witnessed sexual harassment during their studies. However, as gender-based violence was not the core of my research, I decided not to ask for many details in order to have time to talk about their careers. It's also worth noting that some interviewees shared their experiences and views on this topic as former students and as professors in schools of visual arts. This material, however, has some limitations. First, it was not collected to study gender-based violence in art schools. Second, I interviewed graduates who studied for at least five years in this school. Therefore, my sample does not capture individuals who may have left the school because of gender-based violence.

During this first period of fieldwork, I also did an ethnography of the first-year entrance exam of the EAP for one year out of the past ten years.[5] I observed the interviews of eighty-seven candidates and the deliberations of the jury on these applications. I conducted a quantitative analysis of a database I built with the 740 applications for this exam.

The second period of fieldwork was conducted in 2021–2022. I interviewed seven female instructors working in different art schools, two members of the Ministry of Culture in charge of this question (one current, one retired), three current or former art school students involved in feminist collectives (two women, one non-binary person), and one member of CLASCHES (an anti-sexist collective fighting sexual harassment in higher education). The interviews with instructors cover various topics such as their own professional trajectory, their teaching experience in art schools, their relations with students, faculties and members of the administration, the existing measures to prevent and fight against gender-based violence and to support victims, their role in the implementation of this policy and the consequences that public disclosure of gender-based violence in their school have had on their working conditions. In addition, I analysed documents written by *Les Mots de Trop* and a guide on 'sexist and sexual violence' produced by a collective of feminist art school instructors (La collective d'enseignantes & H·Alix Sanyas, 2023).

In the first section of this chapter, I describe the different forms of gender-based violence experienced by women during their studies in art schools. In the second section, I explore the social processes and relations that enable gender-based violence in the arts and that contribute to obscuring it. The third section addresses the consequences of gender-based violence on women's professionalisation in art schools.

The Various Forms of Gender-Based Violence Experienced by Women in Art School

Reported Gender-Based Violence Is Mainly Exerted by Male Instructors

The majority of gender-based violence reported in interviews by graduates of the EAP and in the testimonies collected by *Les Mots de Trop* was exerted by male instructors against female students.

---

5   I do not give the exact year to ensure anonymity of the individuals I observed.

A large number of female and male respondents reported various forms of everyday sexism and misogyny:

> Sexist remarks, jokes you hear all the time. Basically, you have to, especially in sculpture because it's physical and it's a real commitment of the body, so you hear that you can't hold on very long or that such and such an artist is very ballsy, yeah, you get lots of remarks like that, you still get lots of representations like that.[6] (Interview with a twenty-eight-year-old woman)

Sexist remarks and jokes are made about female students' work on intimacy, body, femininity, sexuality or when using techniques and media socially constructed as 'feminine'. Several female students were also told by professors that women would stop their artistic practice shortly after graduation because they would get married or have children. During the evaluation of her artistic work to validate her diploma, a predominantly masculine jury made comments about a pregnant student. She did not receive her diploma and wondered afterwards whether the jury had taken her work less seriously because she was pregnant. One female professor also reported a case where sexism was articulated with ableism. Some male professors refused a deaf student the equal treatment she was asking for and made sexist comments about her:

> Well, I did hear that it was basically a kid having a tantrum and that it wasn't, they didn't say she was completely hysterical, but it was close, you know. (Interview with a female instructor of the EAP)

Experiences of sexism represent a great majority of testimonies collected by *Les Mots de Trop*. Around 40% of the testimonies detail experiences of misogyny and sexism, and male instructors are involved in half of these cases (Les Mots de Trop, 2021).

Several female graduates of the EAP reported various forms of unwanted sexual attention as well. It mainly consisted of male instructors staring or leering at female students. For example, the twenty-eight-year-old woman quoted above said: 'oh well, looking at your breasts, yes, that happens very often during interviews'. Another thirty-three-year-old woman criticised 'the male gaze at the female model':

---

6   All interview excerpts have been translated by the author.

It's a question of a man of a certain age, who's in a position of power, who's going to look at a young girl who's, we're not even talking about physical attraction because attraction isn't the word, there's really no point in saying it, but who's reduced to her body of a twenty-year-old woman.

Unwanted sexual attention can take the form of unwanted physical contact to establish a sexualised relationship with a student. For example, a thirty-year-old-woman said that her studio head put his hands on her hips while she was working. She did not understand what was happening and felt very uncomfortable. Some male instructors commented on women's appearance or clothes as well. Some instructors' behaviours were also reported by female students as ambiguous and 'insidious', and they did not know whether to qualify it as a form of sexual attention or not. For example, a professor asked a former female student to see her work in her very tiny apartment. She did not understand why he would not look at her work at school and felt very uncomfortable. She tried to keep physical distance and to appear very cold during this meeting. According to her, it would have been easy to have sex with him but she did not want to. Sometimes, these forms of unwanted sexual attention are hidden behind artistic matters as, for example, when a male professor suggests a female student to be naked for a performance or a photography project.

None of the graduates labelled these experiences as sexual harassment or abuse. However, one former female graduate and several female instructors mentioned cases of 'abuse', 'sexual harassment' and 'rape' at the EAP. One thirty-seven-year-old woman reported that a professor tried 'to abuse' a foreign student within the school. Interviews with female professors revealed that two students filed a sexual harassment complaint against a professor. They both had to withdraw the complaint under pressure from the school.[7] According to one instructor, one student was raped by a male instructor who had sexual relations with many students.[8] Female instructors working in other art schools reported various forms of everyday sexism as well as cases of sexual harassment and rape mainly committed by male instructors with female students (see also Chapter 5 in this book).

---

7   This happened before 2010.
8   Women from all generations talked about these sexual relations, which they had mainly heard about and that one experienced personally. The rape happened within the past ten years.

Gender-Based Violence among Students Is More Difficult to Identify

The interviews I conducted with the graduates of the EAP also contain accounts of gender-based violence exerted by male students against female students. However, it seems easier for students and graduates to identify and disclose gender-based violence when it is committed in a relation characterised by hierarchy, an asymmetrical distribution of power and age difference. For example, gender-based violence disclosed on the Facebook and Instagram accounts of 'Balancetonecoledart' Besançon and Marseille do not contain testimonials of gender-based violence among students.[9] Likewise, among the 432 testimonies received by *Les Mots de Trop*, 225 involved male instructors and only 13 involved students (Les Mots de Trop, 2022, p. 29). A former female student I interviewed during the second period of fieldwork talked easily about her experiences of sexual harassment and sexual aggression committed by male instructors, but she did not want to answer any questions about physical violence committed by her boyfriend who was a student as well. The interviews with the female and male graduates of the EAP contain more examples of the various forms of gender-based violence exerted by male instructors toward women than examples of gender-based violence committed between students. The great majority are also described by female graduates. They reported sexist remarks and sexist jokes made by some of their classmates, negative comments and remarks about their work, experiences of unwanted physical contact and unwanted sexual attention. These forms of violence were usually mentioned when I asked questions about how the graduates found a studio or about its organisation and atmosphere:

---

9   According to its Facebook page, 'Balancetonecoledart' Besançon aims at 'promoting and developing aid and assistance for victims of sexual violence of any kind committed in art schools'. However, in a Facebook post published on September 24, 2020, the association described the aims of the movement in a statement, writing that it aims 'to publish any testimony relating to violence of any kind—sexist, lgbtqphobic, racist, validist, classist, psychophobic, bitchphobic—having been committed by one or more members of the teaching and/or management teams (or by other people holding any authority, occasional or regular, within the school) over students'.

It was a very, very, rather macho studio, with only boys. It was, I called it the studio of the great apes, you see it was Ohoh (*she shouts loudly in a deep voice*) I pee the farthest, I yell the loudest, I smoke the most joints, I'm the strongest, I do the biggest paintings, well you see that was the atmosphere. (Interview with a forty-three-year-old woman)

The guys were quite aggressive. [...] They were macho and everything, unbearable. And then, there was one in particular who ruined our day because he talked all day. He was drunk. You had to bear it. (Interview with a twenty-eight-year-old woman)

No woman reported any case of sexual abuse or rape, but one woman experienced physical, verbal and psychological violence committed by her partner, who was a student in the school as well. One possible explanation of the fact that instances of gender-based violence exerted by male students on female students are more difficult to identify and to condemn by the victims and their classmates than the ones exerted by male instructors towards students is that the latter take place in unequal power relations clearly identified by students. On the contrary, the seemingly shared experience of being an art school student might obscure the structural character of gender-based violence among students (Brook et al., 2020) and its inscription in unequal gender relations.[10]

Before exploring the consequences of this *continuum* of gender-based violence on women's professionalisation, the next section identifies some social processes and relations that constitute the scaffolding of gender-based violence in art schools.

Social Processes and Relations Sustaining Gender-Based Violence in Art Schools

Several mechanisms produce gendered power structures that enable and sustain gender-based violence in art schools, and that might contribute to silencing victims.

---

10   The authors explain how the shared experience may be an obstacle to identifying and rendering visible social and gender inequalities in the creative industries.

The Sexualisation of Female Students

A first social process providing a 'conducive context' (Kelly, 2016) for gender-based violence is the sexualisation of female students in a context of 'hierarchised gender diversity' (Cardi et al., 2005). The last expression refers to the unequal distribution of power and authority between men and women within art schools, and in particular at the École des Arts Plastiques. While women now comprise two thirds of art school students, faculty—especially in artistic practices—have long been overwhelmingly male (Vandenbunder, 2014). For example, in 2015, women represented less than a third of the instructors of the EAP, and, in particular, three quarters of studio heads were men. The sexualisation of female students contributes to the trivialisation of sexual interactions between male professors and female students and obscures the relations of power and authority between them.

First, instructors and gatekeepers may use women's physical appearance to evaluate and select female artists at different stages of their career (Provansal, 2024; see also Buscatto et al.; Chujo; Lechaux, in this book). As I have shown elsewhere (Provansal, 2023, 2024), the sexualisation of female candidates happens right from the beginning of artistic education, as mentioned by a male graduate of the EAP:

> The girls who enter the school are very, very pretty. I mean, there really are a lot of them. And it's not something you can count scientifically, but if you're honest with yourself, it's there, you know. I've already heard teachers in the corridors after first-year juries saying that this year we've gone a bit too far, that we've taken too many girls for their looks. Well no, maybe it didn't mean that, but maybe they found their work interesting, maybe it didn't mean that. But what it did mean was that at the end of the day, uh, on the first-year class photo, it's going to look weird, and they said so themselves, so there's something odd about it. Do you see what I mean?
> Interviewer: We've got …
> … we went a bit overboard this year, I mean every year it's like that. And so, I don't know how to take it, because there's a kind of game that's very strange. (Interview with a twenty-eight-year-old man)

The 'hierarchised gender diversity' of the jury (twenty men versus four women the year I conducted my observation) and the high uncertainty of the artistic quality of the candidates open the door to the sexualisation of female candidates. In other art worlds where women are a majority, such as theatre (Moeschler & Rolle, 2014) or dance (Sorignet, 2010), women's academic degrees and artistic experience matter in their selection. But for women, these resources are less important for entering the EAP than their 'personality'. More than a third of the observed female candidates got selected for their 'personality' while it was the case for only one out of the nineteen admitted observed male candidates. In particular, the physical appearance of female candidates was often brought up during the deliberation even though it is not a professional resource in the visual arts. For some female candidates, their look and appearance were the only elements discussed during the deliberation.

Once admitted to the EAP, seduction is considered to be part of the game and former students of the EAP compare, for example, the search for a studio to speed dating. However, the process does not entail male students' sexualisation. According to female and male interviewees, women's physical appearance is used by some studio professors to select female students. A thirty-two-year-old woman said about her studio head:

> You know, he used to do interviews with first-years and all that, and he used to make jokes like 'oh yeah, I took little [female] first-years like that' (*she makes a kissing noise*), you know.

Likewise, former graduates of the EAP I interviewed often referred to 'pretty girl quotas' to explain why women are a majority in the school, and to justify their presence in studios run by men:

> There's obviously a cast like that, because all the chicks who were in my studio were very pretty, and even today, if you go to the EAP, it's, well, it's visible. (Interview with a forty-five-year old woman)

Interviews with female instructors working in other art schools reveal that using physical appearance to evaluate and select female artists is not restricted to the EAP. A female instructor, for example, mentioned that faculties used to 'rate [female] students' asses in exams from one to ten'.

Second, according to the interviewees, romantic and sexual relationships between instructors and students at the EAP were not uncommon during their studies. They are trivialised by some respondents who consider them to be common at university. The EAP would thus be like any other higher education institution. These relations are all the more tolerated as they are attributed to the openness and transgressive character of artistic circles. Some respondents emphasise that female students are no longer minors and are thus old enough to consent or not.[11] According to many interviewees, the issue of gender-based violence in art schools is a complex one because there can be 'true love stories', too:

> But afterwards, you hear stories but you have to take a step back because it's complex, these stories of, it's really complicated. There are also love stories, there are also attractions, that's what you can't do, it's difficult to do, there's no question of judging, but these stories are complicated. I mean, on principle, it's not great that teachers sleep with their students. (Interview with a forty-one-year old woman)

Several women underline that they became aware of the relations of power and authority behind these sexualised interactions once they became instructors in art schools themselves.

Third, in art schools, relations between instructors and students are strongly personalised and individualised, which works to reinforce and to normalise the sexualisation of female students and to obscure the dimensions of power in these relations. It also has the effect of blurring the boundary between the private and educational spheres (see below).

Finally, the naturalisation of men's flirting behaviours and men's sexual urges serves to obscure the hierarchical dimension of the relation and the structural character of gender-based violence. These behaviours are attributed to the 'temperament' of male professors and to the 'personality' of female students, in particular to their lack of 'character' and weakness. This form of victim blaming puts female students in charge of setting limits and saying no to sexual interactions with their professor. For example, in the following excerpt, a thirty-seven-year-old woman witnessed what she calls the 'abuse' of a female student. Her essentialist explanation of sexual violence is enhanced by harmful stereotypes and racialised gendered myths about Asian women:

---

11   Likewise, it seems that the cases of sexual violence in French cinema that are considered outrageous are the ones involving very young girls, not the ones involving women above the age of eighteen. For example, see *À l'air libre* (2024).

This girl, she was Japanese or Chinese, I mean Asian. So already she was lacking in language skills. Often, in fact, these women artists [...] they have a completely different culture of attitude, a little self-effacing, a bit submissive in the face of men, in the face of authority, in the face of the prestige of this school, too. In their attitude one often feels a rather strong weakness of presence [...] So they are perfect victims. [...] I say that some personalities are more fragile than others and that in fact when there are structures like that, which are very sexist, very macho, well these women (*she whistles*), it's complicated.

Students' Dependency on Their Instructors to Launch Their Career

A second mechanism perpetuating gender-based violence is linked to the organisation of the artistic work of art school students. In art schools as well as in the contemporary art world, there is an oversupply of would-be artists and thus strong competition for access to professional networks and visibility. Like models in the fashion industry (Crowley, 2021), students are placed in a situation of 'asymmetric information' and rely on their instructors to learn the 'rules of art' (Provansal, 2023). They are taught in an informal way, for example via studio heads' personal anecdotes shared with a limited number of students. This works to place students in a dependent position and to make it more difficult for them to denounce experiences of gender-based violence (see also Chapter 5 in this book). This dependent position is even more precarious and vulnerable for female students when they are expected to play the seduction card to obtain the support of a mentor:

He [a studio head] had a weird relationship with young girls, you know. He'd been going out with one of his former students for a very long time, his favorite of the studio was a girl who posed naked on her sculptures [...] who did things with honey, a mattress, and very sensual stuff, and he'd suggest 'ah well it would be nice if you did that, that performance but naked, it would be more interesting' [...] So I ran away. [...] He had his favorites, who were always the pretty girls, and he helped them out a lot when they left school. There was a very clear seduction relationship. (Interview with a twenty-eight-year-old woman)

The Blurred Boundaries between the Private, Educational and Professional Spheres

The blurred boundaries between the private, educational and professional spheres is a third mechanism producing a conducive context for gender-based violence in schools of visual arts (see also Chapter 5 in this book), and in other cultural and artistic fields such as the screen industries (Chapter 6, this book) and the theatre (Chapter 7, this book). Several students interpret the professional expectation to develop a personal artistic vision as an injunction to expose themselves. For example, some students work with their own intimate experience in their artworks, especially in their first years of artistic education. However, it can put them in a vulnerable position when they share their intimacy with their professors. For example, *Les Mots de Trop* (2021) writes:

> At least in France, art schools are perceived as places where you have to focus work on personal feelings, stories, experiences—thereby being exposed to a certain kind of vulnerability.

Some female instructors and students explained how this expectation can be manipulated by male instructors to sexualise female students, suggesting that they be nude in their work and likening it to a way of exposing oneself or transgressing boundaries. Similarly, Bleuwenn Lechaux (Chapter 7) depicts how emotions and intimacy permeate professional theatre practices and make it more difficult to denounce sexual harassment.

Students might also share friendly and intimate moments with their professors during school trips, artist residencies, student parties and other moments of sociability within or outside the school. A French female instructor described her shock when she took her first teaching position in a French art school after spending the first part of her career abroad:

> And then (*laughs*), it's (*laughs*), it's the great, the great revelation of art schools in France, that I don't know of course, uh because in my first year if you want I arrive and uh I'm confronted with something that completely stuns me that is uh teachers who throw parties to celebrate students' diplomas by inviting strippers.

The sexual harassment and rapes described in the testimonies of female instructors or collected by 'Balancetonecoledart' and involving students and male instructors or members of the administration took place in contexts like parties or school trips where the boundaries between the private, educational and professional spheres were blurred (see also Chapter 5). As mentioned before, this helps to obscure the relation of power between male professors and female students.

The Flawed Implementation of Policies against Gender-Based Violence in Artistic Higher Education

For many years, there was a lack of human resources, infrastructures and measures to prevent and to fight gender-based violence in art schools but also to support victims socially, psychologically and legally. This worked to silence and to sustain gender-based violence. The lack of legal or professional sanctions, the fact that some schools put pressure on students to drop complaints and the lack of support by the administration and other instructors for students and professors who reported cases of violence do not encourage women to disclose gender-based violence and to file a complaint.

Since 2017, some measures to regulate sexist and sexual violence have been implemented in art schools: charters for equality and diversity, mandatory training on sexist and sexual violence, committees for equality and diversity, the possibility to contact 'Allosexism', a listening unit opened by the Ministry of Culture to report and find support for gender-based violence in the arts. However, access to and the implementation of these measures vary depending on the status of the school (national versus local), some measures remain unknown, such as 'Allosexism', and some have limitations due to a lack of clear procedures. For example, students are sometimes part of equality committees and might find it difficult to hear testimonials about sexual violence, some instructors have leaked what they have heard to protect colleagues, members of these committees are not necessarily trained to handle issues about sexist and sexual violence, and there are no clear procedures on how to handle cases of reported violence. One female instructor, for example, regretted the lack of guidance, training and human resources needed to define and implement such measures:

But above all, to act quickly, let's say relatively quickly, decisions had to be made. And these decisions had to be taken in a concerted and considered manner. We had to know what type of structure we wanted to have. Was it to be an external structure? If so, which one? Or do we want an internal structure? So, we write it, we build it, we make it. Is it a paid job? There's no budget. So, it's people from the institution. Who are they, volunteers? If so, how many? What's their status? You see. And all that has to be thought through, thought out and discussed with professionals. I'm not a professional, I wasn't a professional. In fact, I didn't have an answer and I said so. I said I didn't have any answers, I only had questions to ask, in other words, we now need to have a clear path. Nothing exists! We have to do everything. How do you do it? You can't do it in a week.

According to the interviewed female instructors in charge of defining and implementing measures to regulate sexist and sexual violence, the lack of a 'clear path' limits the effect of these new policies. Furthermore, the absence of support and the sometimes strong resistance from some of their colleagues or members of the administration hindered the implementation of gender-based violence policies.

In reaction to the lack of information and measures to prevent and fight gender-based violence in art schools, feminist collectives formed by students or instructors created their own tools (booklets, websites, etc.) such as the self-defense guide for art students by *Les Mots de Trop* (2022) or the guide to fighting against sexist and sexual violence in art schools written by female instructors (La collective d'enseignantes & H·Alix Sanyas, 2023).

The range of verbal and physical violence experienced by female students in art schools is not without consequences on their professionalisation. In particular, it constrains women's field of possibilities in terms of artistic practice, professional networks and work opportunities.

The Consequences of Gender-Based Violence on Women's Professionalisation

Women's Workspace Instability

A first consequence of this range of verbal and physical violence exerted by both professors and students is the instability of a place to work for female students. At the EAP, several women decided to change studios, sometimes several times during their studies, because of the control exerted by male students on the workspace, or to escape a sexist, macho and misogynistic atmosphere, or because they did not feel comfortable with the inappropriate relationships between their studio head and female students, or because they wanted to work with a professor who would support their work. A thirty-three-year-old woman, for example, explained how 'a group of extremely confident guys, five or six of them' controlled women's access to studios of artistic practice:

> Little macho guys who were insufferable, unbearable, and leering, too. And I know that a lot of girls didn't go to those studios because they were afraid of those guys. Like the studio downstairs, there was a kind of an old painter who had a crew like that of guys who were there like zombies, who'd been there for years at the EAP, you even got the feeling they were part of the walls, who laid down the law a bit, who took the biggest wall.

The instability of the workspace constrains women's professionalisation. It hinders women's access to professional networks, as well as to the professional norms and representations that organise artistic work (Provansal, 2023). For example, a woman described herself as an 'artist without a fixed studio', and she regretted that she 'never managed to find a kind of mentor' to support her, who could transmit to her 'the rules of art' which are not part of the official curriculum. According to two female instructors, two female students who had been raped by a male instructor at the EAP or by a student in another school, had to temporarily quit artistic education in order to receive various forms of support to be able to continue their studies.

A Threat to the Development and Recognition of Women's Creative Abilities

Women's workspace instability makes it more difficult for them to develop their creative abilities (Provansal, 2023). Some students end up working in a studio that does not fit their artistic practices. They are not supported by their studio head or they do not have access to adequate materials and tools.

As I have shown elsewhere (Provansal, 2024), women's sexualisation threatens their recognition as potential artists. It raises doubts about their success and obscures their artistic skills. For example, according to many graduates, if women are a majority at the EAP and in some studios of the school, it is because there are some 'pretty girl quotas'. The fact that some women are selected based on appearance affects how all women are perceived in the school. This expression delegitimises women's presence in the school. Women are not perceived as potential and legitimate colleagues, and since their artistic skills are not taken into consideration, they are less likely to be invited to collective exhibitions or to be supported by their instructors. A female instructor who used to teach in a preparatory program detailed the same mechanism at work in another school:

> I ended up blacklisting a school that I knew only took pretty girls, because I don't think that benefits anyone.[12] It doesn't benefit the pretty ones or the ugly ones. The ugly ones are eliminated from the competition. They don't get in. And the pretty ones get in, and during all their education they're under the suspicion that they got in because they're pretty, not because they're smart or brilliant.

The various forms of unwanted sexual attention limit women's possibilities to develop a singular artistic practice and a 'creative vision' (Wohl, 2021). For example, a twenty-eight-year-old graduate of the EAP explained how sexism and women's sexualisation constrained her artistic work on sexuality:

> I would have never seen myself discussing this with a teacher who has a seductive relationship with his female students, and who is very patriarchal in the way he operates, even paternalistic at times. When someone makes comments likes that, you're not going to develop themes, well I would not have felt at all comfortable being free about it.

Likewise, Anna Bull (in Chapter 6 of this book) shows how experiences of sexual harassment may hinder the creative freedom of women working on content related to sexuality in the UK screen industries. Some female instructors underlined how important it is to have more women so as to bring another perspective on female students' work on issues related to the body and sexuality:

> I warned the female students in general from the very first class. And

---

12 She decided to no longer train and encourage students to apply to this school.

it was a bit shocking for them. I'd say to them, it's possible that at some point some of you will want to do nude performances. But think carefully, because the way you see yourself in relation to your body during the performance and the way an outsider's gaze—and I mean a very male gaze, because my team was very masculine—receives these images is not at all the same thing. And you don't yet have the codes because you're very young. I think they were a little offended by what I was saying, but I think it was important because this nudity thing is perhaps a little less frequent in portfolios today, but ten years ago it was crazy. In other words, after a month of preparatory program, all my students were naked. And there are teachers behind this, too. There are teachers who recommend it.

Interviewer: Who encouraged it?

Oh yes, who encouraged it, who said that's how you get into a school, that's how you really expose yourself. It's total manipulation.

Limited Access to Professional Networks and Work Opportunities

Women's sexualisation affects their interactions with instructors and invited gatekeepers in the school. As mentioned before, they are expected to be responsible for containing men's sexuality and they have to manage the trouble of unwanted sexual attention. Like women opera singers and Japanese musicians (see Chapter 2 and Chapter 3 in this book), female students are caught between 'allowing seduction', with the risk of threatening the legitimacy of their reputation, and 'avoiding seduction', with the risk of losing some relational resources and being marginalised (Buscatto, 2021). It makes it more difficult to have strong and lasting relations with their instructors. By maintaining distance from their professors, they might miss professional opportunities and relational resources, and they are not part of the few students with whom professors informally share the rules of art.

Finally, sexist prejudices have an effect on women's access to professional opportunities. For example, women have long been excluded from student jobs at the EAP because they were considered to be physically weaker than men. Yet, several respondents, men and women, noticed that most of the tasks did not require physical strength. These jobs provide opportunities to become familiar with the professional conventions of the contemporary art world and to build professional networks. The devaluation of 'feminine' artistic practices limits the possibilities of artistic creation. Stereotypes related to motherhood also threaten the recognition of women's commitment to artistic careers and limit the support they can receive from professors. Assigning women to motherhood is a way to limit the professional future of female students.

Conclusion

While most studies mainly focus on the effects that gender-based violence has on working women (McLaughlin et al., 2017), in this chapter I have studied the effects of gender-based violence on women's careers with a focus on artistic education, which is a first step in distinguishing between amateurs and professionals. This case study reveals that gender-based violence does not disappear in contexts where women are a majority. As in other art fields such as opera or theatre (see Chapter 2 and Chapter 7 in this book), the various forms of gender-based violence experienced by female art students are part of routinised work practices and shared representations in art schools, which work to obscure and silence them.

Gender-based violence is both an expression of gendered inequalities in the art world and one of the social processes perpetuating them. First, gender-based violence limits women's field of possibilities in terms of artistic practice. Second, it hinders female students' professionalisation by restricting their access to the professional norms and networks of the contemporary art world. Without unhindered access to the rules of art and professional networks, some women ultimately experience less control over their artistic careers.

Finally, even if it was not the focus of this chapter, one should note that the commitment of some women to preventing and fighting gender-based violence in art schools has an impact on their own artistic careers when they are subjected to moral harassment by an aggressor, when they do not have time left for their artistic work, or when they have to cope with the mental burden imposed by this form of academic care.

References

Ahmed, S. (2021). *Complaint!* Duke University Press. https://doi.org/10.1215/9781478022336

Armstrong, E. A., Hamilton, L., & Sweeney, B. (2006). Sexual assault on campus: A multilevel, integrative approach to party rape. *Social Problems, 53*(4), 483–499. https://doi.org/10.1525/sp.2006.53.4.483

Belghith, F., Ferry, O., Patros, T., & Tenret, E. (2021). *Repères* 2020. Observatoire national de la vie étudiante. https://www.ove-national.education.fr/wp-content/uploads/2021/01/Brochure_Reperes_2020.pdf

Bereni, L., Lépinard, E., & Lieber, M. (2003). Contre le harcèlement et les violences sexuelles dans l'enseignement supérieur: Quelles réponses politiques et institutionnelles? *Nouvelles Questions Féministes, 22*(1), 134–137. https://doi.org/10.3917/nqf.221.0134

Briquet, C. (2019). De la banalisation des violences de genre en école d'ingénieur.e.s. *Les Cahiers du Genre,* 1(66), 109–128. https://doi.org/10.3917/cdge.066.0109

Brook, O., O'Brien, D., & Taylor, M. (2020). *Culture is bad for you. Inequality in the cultural and creative industries.* Manchester University Press. https://doi.org/10.7765/9781526152152

Brown, E., Debauche, A., Hamel, C., & Mazuy, M. (Eds). (2020). *Violences et rapports de genre. Enquête sur les violences de genre en France.* Ined Éditions. https://doi.org/10.4000/books.ined.14719

Buscatto, M. (2021). *Women in jazz. Musicality, femininity, marginalization.* Routledge. https://doi.org/10.4324/9781003177555 (Original work published 2007)

Buscatto, M., Cordier, M., & Laillier, J. (Eds). (2020). Sous le talent: le genre, la classe, la 'race'. *Agone,* Special issue, 65.

Cardi, C., Naudier, D., & Pruvost, G. (2005). Les rapports sociaux de sexe à l'université: Au cœur d'une triple dénégation. *L'Homme & La Société, 4*(158), 49–73. https://doi.org/10.3917/lhs.158.0049

CLASCHES (2014). L'action du CLASCHES. *Les Cahiers du CEDREF,* 19. https://doi.org/10.4000/cedref.724

Connell, R. W. (2005). *Masculinities* (2nd ed.). Routledge. https://doi.org/10.4324/9781003116479 (Original work published 1995)

Crenshaw, K. (1991). Mapping the margins: Intersectionality, identity politics, and violence against women of color. *Stanford Law Review, 43*(6), 1241–1299. https://doi.org/10.2307/1229039

Crowley, J. E. (2021). Sexual harassment in display work. The case of the modeling industry. *Gender & Society*, 35(5), 719–745. https://doi.org/10.1177/08912432211036890

Delage, P., Lieber, M., & Chetcuti-Osorovitz, N. (2019). Lutter contre les violences de genre. Des mouvements féministes à leur institutionnalisation. *Cahiers du Genre*, 1(66), 5–16. https://doi.org/10.3917/cdge.066.0005

DEPS. (2023). *Observatoire de l'égalité entre femmes et hommes dans la culture et la communication, édition* 2023. Ministère de la Culture. https://www.culture.gouv.fr/espace-documentation/statistiques-ministerielles-de-la-culture2/publications/Collections-d-ouvrages/Observatoire-de-l-egalite-entre-femmes-et-hommes-dans-la-culture-et-la-communication/observatoire-2023-de-l-egalite-entre-femmes-et-hommes-dans-la-culture-et-la-communication

DGCA. (2018). *Brochure enseignement supérieur création artistique*. Ministère de la Culture.

Frenette, A., Dowd, T. J., Skaggs, R., & Ryan, T. (2020). *Careers in the arts: Who stays and who leaves? Strategic national arts alumni project special report*. Indiana University, Strategic National Arts Alumni Project. https://snaaparts.org/findings/reports/careers-in-the-arts-who-stays-and-who-leaves

Galodé, G. (1994). Les écoles d'art en France: Évolution des structures d'offre et des effectifs. *Cahiers de l'IRÉDU*, 57. https://iredu.ube.fr/wp-content/uploads/2010/03/Cahier57.pdf

Galodé, G., & Michaut, C. (2003). Les études artistiques: hétérogénéité des écoles supérieures d'art, pratiques étudiantes et réussite scolaire. In G. Felouzis (Ed.), *Les mutations actuelles de l'Université* (pp. 317–340). Presses Universitaires de France.

Gonthier-Maurin, B. (2013, June 27). *La place des femmes dans l'art et la culture*. Rapport d'information fait au nom de la délégation aux droits des femmes du Sénat. https://www.senat.fr/rap/r12-704/r12-7040.html

Gromada, A., Budacz, D., Kawalerowicz, J., & Walewska, A. (2016). *Little chance to advance? An inquiry into the presence of women at art academies in Poland*. Katarzyna Kozyra Foundation. https://katarzynakozyrafoundation.pl/wp-content/uploads/2019/08/Little_Chance_to_Advance.pdf

Hanmer, J., & Maynard, M. (Eds). (1987). *Women, violence and social control*. Palgrave Macmillan. https://doi.org/10.1007/978-1-349-18592-4

Hattery, A. J. (2022). (Re)imagining gender-based violence as a strategy for enforcing institutional segregation and reproducing structural inequalities. *Gender & Society*, 36(6), 789–812. https://doi.org/10.1177/08912432221128665

Hirsch, J. S., & Khan, S. (2020). *Sexual citizens: Sex, power, and assault on campus*. W. W. Norton & Company.

Kelly, L. (1987). *The continuum of sexual violence.* In J. Hanmer & M. Maynard (Eds), *Women, violence and social control* (pp. 46–60). Palgrave Macmillan. https://doi.org/10.1007/978-1-349-18592-4_4

Kelly, L. (2016, March 1). The conducive context of violence against women and girls. *Discoversociety.* https://archive.discoversociety.org/2016/03/01/theorising-violence-against-women-and-girls/

La collective d'enseignantes, & H·Alix Sanyas. (2023). Violences sexistes et sexuelles en École d'art: Comment agir? *GLAD!,* 14. https://doi.org/10.4000/glad.6888

Les Mots de Trop (2021, June 28). Enough is enough. Art & design students lead the charge to expose the abusive underbelly of France's education system. *Futuress.* https://futuress.org/stories/enough-is-enough/

Les Mots de Trop. (2022). *Guide d'auto-défense pour étudiant.es en art.* https://lesmotsdetrop.fr/download/EDITION_web.pdf

Manifesto XXI. (2024, June 26). *Tribune. Pour un #MeToo du monde de l'art. Manifesto XXI.* https://manifesto-21.com/tribune-pour-un-metoo-du-monde-de-lart/

McLaughlin, H., Uggen, C., & Blackstone, A. (2017). The economic and career effects of sexual harassment on working women. *Gender & Society,* 31(3), 333–358. https://doi.org/10.1177/0891243217704631

Mediapart. À l'air libre. (2024, February 12). *Émission spéciale #MeToo cinéma français avec Judith Godrèche, Anna Mouglalis, Charlotte Arnould, Anouk Grinberg, Manda Touré, Marie Lemarchand, Noémie Kocher et Iris Brey* [Video]. YouTube. https://www.youtube.com/watch?v=MMtGu0CpKto&t=1s

Moeschler, O., & Rolle, V. (2014). *De l'école à la scène. Entrer dans le métier de comédien.ne.* Antipodes.

Moulin, R. (2009). *L'artiste, l'institution et le marché.* Flammarion. (Original work published 1992)

Prat, R. (2006, April 30). *Pour l'égal accès des femmes et des hommes aux postes de responsabilité, aux lieux de décision, à la maîtrise de la représentation.* Ministère de la Culture et de la Communication, DMDTS. www.culture.gouv.fr/Espace-documentation/Rapports/Mission-EgaliteS

Prat, R. (2009, May 21). *De l'interdit à l'empêchement.* Ministère de la Culture et de la Communication, DMDTS. www.culture.gouv.fr/Espace-documentation/Rapports/Acces-des-femmes-et-des-hommes-aux-postes-de-responsabilite-n-2-De-l-interdit-a-l-empechement

Provansal, M. (2023). *Artistes mais femmes. Une enquête sociologique dans l'art contemporain.* ENS Éditions.

Provansal, M. (2024). Precarious professional identities. Women artists and gender inequality within contemporary art. *L'Année Sociologique,* 74(1), 81–112. https://doi.org/10.3917/anso.241.0085

Robinson, H. (2021). Women, feminism, and art schools: The UK experience. *Women's Studies International Forum*, 85, 1–10. https://doi.org/10.1016/j.wsif.2021.102447

Schulz, G., Ries, C., & Zimmermann, O. (2016). *Frauen in Kultur und Medien. Ein Überblick über aktuelle Tendenzen, Entwicklungen und Lösungsvorschläge.* Deutscher Kulturrat. https://www.kulturrat.de/wp-content/uploads/2016/12/Frauen-in-Kultur-und-Medien.pdf

Schüz, H.-S., Pantelmann, H., Wälty, T., & Lawrenz, N. (2022). Dealing with sexual discrimination and violence in German universities: An inventory. *Open Gender Journal*, 6. https://doi.org/10.17169/ogj.2022.219

Simonetti, I. (2016). Violence (et genre). In J. Rennes (Ed.), *Encyclopédie critique du genre* (pp. 681–690). La Découverte. https://doi.org/10.3917/dec.renne.2016.01.0681

Sorignet, P.-E. (2010). *Danser. Enquête dans les coulisses d'une vocation.* La Découverte. https://doi.org/10.3917/dec.sorig.2010.01

The Countess. (2019). *The Countess report* 2019. https://files.cargocollective.com/c1501468/2019-countess-report.pdf

Vandenbunder, J. (2014). *La pédagogie de la création. Une sociologie de l'enseignement artistique* (Doctoral dissertation, University of Versailles-St-Quentin-en-Yvelines).

Wohl, H. (2021). *Bound by creativity. How contemporary art is created and judged.* The University of Chicago Press. https://doi.org/10.7208/chicago/9780226784724.001.0001

PART II
CREATING REPRESENTATIONS OF GENDER-BASED VIOLENCE IN ART AND CULTURE

Introduction

Part II consists of two chapters that explore how gender-hostile conditions of production impact and are reflected in women's artworks and other creative outputs. Drawing on case studies from the UK (screen industry) and Finland (photographic art), the chapters examine how women's creative practices and choices—for example, topic, perspective, form, and content—are shaped by their experiences in work environments where gender-based violence is normalised as part of industry culture.

In Chapter 5, Leena-Maija Rossi and Sari Karttunen focus on the Helsinki School, a Finnish photography training and branding initiative launched in the 1990s at one of the country's art universities. While the 'school' was presented as female-led, it was, in fact, designed and managed by male gatekeepers. In 2022, the celebrated project began to attract negative publicity when several former female students publicly accused key male figures of sexual harassment. These women also revealed how they had been encouraged to use their bodies, trauma and personal experiences as material in their artwork. At the same time, as Rossi and Karttunen note, the establishment of the 'school' required a unified 'formatisation' for marketing purposes, with an emphasis on large-scale works, technical rigour and a sense of coolness. The authors suggest that by placing expectations on the participating photographers, particularly the younger ones, the initiative shaped both the content and form of their work, with some images also taking on different meanings when viewed as part of the Helsinki School. The prominent representation of women gave the initiative a feminist and conceptual edge that was valued in the international art market, bringing up the economic dimension of gender-based violence.

In Chapter 6, Anna Bull examines the UK screen industry, focusing on women who create content on gender-based violence and sexuality while simultaneously struggling with harassment in their workplaces. Paradoxically, the industry also produces critical narratives about gendered violence but remains shaped by power structures that normalise such practices within its own professional culture. Bull's study draws on interviews with women working in the screen industry who have experienced or reported sexual harassment. She explores how workplace harassment affects their creative agency, influencing not only their career trajectories but also the ways in which gendered violence is represented in film and television. The chapter also considers whether producing content on gender-based violence increases women's vulnerability to harassment or provides them with a platform to challenge industry norms. By examining the interplay between creative work and lived experience, Bull sheds light on how gender-based violence influences both the working conditions and artistic choices of women in the screen industry.

Together, these chapters suggest that the conditions of gender-based violence prevalent in the arts and culture sector have a significant impact on women's creative agency and artistic production. The case studies underscore the need for further research to fully understand the multiple effects of these dynamics on women's creative practices and the representation of gender-based violence in artistic and cultural works.

5. The Helsinki School: Gendered Image Shaping and Gender-Based Violence in a Photography Branding Project

Leena-Maija Rossi and Sari Karttunen

Varieties of Gender-Based Violence in the Art Context

On the cover of a glossy photography book there is an image of a young woman, sunken in a bathtub so deep that we can only see the upper half of her head. The title of the book, printed on the cover, is *The Helsinki School, Vol. 4: A Female View*.[1] In the foreword the primus motor of the Helsinki School, curator, teacher and gallerist Timothy Persons writes:

> This book helps clarify why so many women have emerged as the leading figures from the Helsinki School. Each artist portrayed here is unique by her own making. However, they all share one common denominator and that is of experiencing the same educational model. (Persons, 2011, p. 7)

The Helsinki School was launched in the early 1990s as an educational, branding and marketing effort for photographic art at the University of Industrial Art and Design Helsinki. First wider in scope and using the title Gallery TaiK (the acronym for the Finnish name of the university, Taideteollinen korkeakoulu), the project later focused on cooperation with the Department of Photographic Art and came to be linked to its study programme. The title 'Helsinki School' started to spread after the German critic Boris Hohmeyer published an article in 2003, describing

---

1   The cover photograph is Aino Kannisto's *Untitled (White Tub)* (2008). It is the artist herself posing in the photograph.

how Persons saw the working methods of the Düsseldorf School of Photography—established by Hilla and Bernd Becher in the 1970s—as a model that could be applied in Helsinki (Hohmeyer, 2003).

In the above quotation from the book, Persons claims that women have played a significant role as key actors in the project, and indeed all eight artists who have been featured most frequently (appearing five times) across the six major Helsinki School volumes published by Hatje Cantz between 2005 and 2019 are women.[2] As mentioned, one of the books, and the related touring exhibition, is dedicated solely to women photographers. However, the founding members of the Helsinki School were all male,[3] and its educational model has been in male hands: all the professors in charge of it have been male. Given the power imbalance between the two genders, it was not entirely unexpected when, in early 2022, Finnish media reported on accusations of sexual harassment brought by several female students, with this allegedly perpetrated by the two male professors in charge of the School's educational and curatorial practices, Persons (until 2022) and Jyrki Parantainen (between 2006 and 2017) (Kartastenpää, 2022; Paananen, 2022a, 2022b). While the #MeToo movement reached Finland right after its global onset in October 2017 (Honkasalo, 2018), discussions of gendered misconduct in the arts have largely centred on film, music and theatre (see, e.g., Paanetoja, 2018; Pääkkölä et al., 2021). In this chapter, we delve into the complex interplay of the increasing female visibility and the pervasive male dominance that still prevailed at the beginning of the twenty-first century in the field of visual art in general, and at the Helsinki School in particular.

During the heyday of the Helsinki School—the 1990s and the early 2000s—the notion of the gender system as binary was still very strong in Finnish society, and pervaded art discourse as well. Publicly at least, most artists identified themselves at the time as either male or female, and in the case of the Helsinki School we thus find it legitimate to write about violence directed towards women in particular as gender-based

---

2   Tiina Itkonen, Ulla Jokisalo, Aino Kannisto, Sanna Kannisto, Sandra Kantanen, Anni Leppälä, Susanna Majuri and Riitta Päiväläinen. A total of 75 artists (36 women, 39 men) were represented in the six volumes published by the Helsinki School.

3   Curator and later Adjunct Professor Timothy Persons, Professor Jorma Puranen and Rector Yrjö Sotamaa (see Persons, n.d.).

violence. We are fully aware of the proliferation of gender terminology in this millennium, of the complexity of gender as a phenomenon and even of the binary in itself being a form of institutional violence. In this chapter, however, we use mostly the terms current in the Finnish context between the 1990s and the 2010s.

In her widely influential article written in the late 1980s, Liz Kelly (1987) suggested that various forms of violence against women, ranging from everyday sexism and harassment to rape and femicide, should not be conceived as isolated incidents but as forming an integrated whole in which they reinforce each other. Kelly's conception of a '*continuum* of violence' explains how seemingly minor forms of violence contribute to a culture of misogyny, enable more severe forms of abuse and maintain the normalisation of violence against women in society. This dynamic sustains gender-based violence as a systemic phenomenon. In our discussion, which focuses on the allegations of sexual harassment within, and the artistic imagery of, the Helsinki School, we connect Kelly's notion of a *continuum* with a wide concept of gender-based violence, one including homo- and transphobia. As we use the term, it encompasses various forms of violence that are directed at individuals based on their gender; such violence has a disproportionate impact on cisgender females, but is also directed at gay cisgender men, transgender women and men, and non-binary people at large (Karkulehto & Rossi, 2017). Gender-based violence can manifest in different forms, including physical, sexual and psychological. In its economic form, it encompasses financial control, deprivation of resources or economic exploitation (see, e.g., European Institute for Gender Equality, n.d.). Symbolic violence represented and reiterated through art and media fuels gender-based violence in its reinforcing stereotypes, normalising abusive behaviour and perpetuating unequal power dynamics pervasively through societal institutions and cultural norms. It legitimises straight cis men's dominance over women and gay and trans men, contributing to the acceptance and continuation of gender-based violence as a systemic phenomenon in society (see, e.g., Thapar-Björkert et al., 2016).

After presenting our data and methods, we will first provide a detailed description of the concept and practices of the Helsinki School. Then, analysing both written and visual material, we will investigate the various forms and instances of gender-based violence allegedly experienced by female students and artists within the School. Our chapter aims to demonstrate how gender-based violence in its entirety, including the gendered shaping of the images of female artists as well as their artworks, contributed to the persistence of male domination in the export and training project despite the number of female representatives and the high visibility given to them. Our analysis targets not only the representations of gender-based violence in the artworks produced by the Helsinki School but also the conditions attending the production of those representations.

Aims, Tools and Materials

This chapter continues the collaboration that we started in the early 2000s in the research project titled Polar Stars, funded by the Research Council of Finland. The project explored the internationalisation of Finnish photographic and video art.[4] Our interviewees, representing the field of Finnish photography of the time, drew attention to the selective access of students to the Helsinki School. Some also discussed extensive efforts aimed at shaping the students' artistic production, sometimes requiring them to exploit their own personal experiences. However, there were no indications of sexual harassment in the interviews, which were for the most part conducted in 2007. In this chapter, we update our research, and examine the export project from the perspectives of visual sociology and gender studies and through the lens of comprehensive gender-based violence.[5]

Our aim is to scrutinise how diverse forms of gender-based violence operated within the Helsinki School at the same time as it cultivated a public image centred around female artists. For this purpose, we have carried out both visual and textual analysis of the large-scale

---

4   In addition to the authors, the project involved Kati Kivinen, Anna-Kaisa Rastenberger and Juha Suonpää, and it was conducted at the Finnish Museum of Photography.

5   Our research project ran between 2005 and 2009, during which time the Helsinki School was gaining more international visibility. We dealt with the School in several of our publications (see, for example, Karttunen, 2009, 2010; Rastenberger, 2006, 2015; Rossi, 2012; Suonpää, 2011). The project group collaborated with Alain Quemin, a French sociologist of art, who conducted a visual sociological analysis of the first volume in the Helsinki School series (2005), and also considered representations of gender (Quemin, 2012, 2015).

photography books representing the School's artists and their works, published between 2005 and 2019 by Hatje Cantz, a well-known international art book publisher. All the volumes include introductory chapters by Persons, artist introductions and short texts by other art world practitioners. We also discuss on a detailed level the media material which exposed the gender-based abuse that allegedly took place within the export project. The visual representations of gender and sexuality are analysed via theory-informed close reading of the distinct ways of portraying young female bodies, often female members of the Helsinki School posing in the photographs themselves.[6] We ask whether the gendered image-shaping of both the photographs and the export project as a whole also represent a form of gender-based violence. The analysis of both textual and visual material is framed by critical feminist studies of visual culture and cultural work at large, and by feminist research on gender-based violence (Bronfen, 1992; Butler, 2004; Carter & Weaver, 2003; Cuklanz, 2000; Projansky, 2001).

From Stardom to Hardship

The Helsinki School developed out of a coaching project for photography students in the early 1990s at the University of Industrial Art and Design Helsinki, now known as the Aalto University School of Art, Design and Architecture. The curator, Timothy Persons, who held a position as Adjunct Professor, began to internationalise the photography programme together with Professor Jorma Puranen, a photographic artist, under the leadership of Rector Yrjö Sotamaa (Aalto University, n.d.; Paananen, 2022a).[7] A module of internationalisation studies was established in the Master's Programme in Photographic Art[8] in which a handpicked group of students was taught how to write an artist

---

6   We will not address representations of male bodies due to their scarcity in the Helsinki School books, and because these representations do not constitute gender-based violence in our reading.

7   Puranen (b. 1951) taught photographic art at Taik between 1978 and 1998, acting as professor between 1996 and 1998.

8   At that time this was the only Master's programme in photographic art in the country. Photographic art was defined and organised as a subfield of visual arts in Finland in the 1980s. The Association of Photographic Artists that was established in 1988 has currently over 450 members.

statement, taken to international art fairs and introduced to curators and collectors (Paananen, 2022a; Persons, 2014; Korpak, 2021). After reshaping the concept of the University's gallery, Persons established a physical gallery space in Berlin. The School also started to include former students and teachers at Taik, eventually increasing its membership to as many as several dozen artists. Persons himself has been involved with international networks, being, for instance, a member of the Board and the Honor Committee of Paris Photo (Paananen, 2022a; Paris Photo, n.d.-b), and has subsequently enabled the School's photographers to present their work internationally, especially in European venues.

The Helsinki School was largely celebrated as a brand, and a success story of internationalisation in the Finnish art scene (see, for example, Korpak, 2021; Mäcklin, 2021; Uimonen, 2012) until, in early 2022, it came into the public eye in a different light. The media began publishing allegations of abuse of power, sexual harassment of students, lack of transparency of operations and ambiguities in funding. The malpractices were first reported on *Long Play*, a web platform of critical journalism, in an article by an independent investigative journalist (Paananen, 2022a). The discussion immediately spread to the national mainstream media (for example, Kartastenpää, 2022) as well as various social media platforms. In the following days, several new allegations of sexual harassment against students were brought to public attention. *Long Play* soon published another article on the case (Paananen, 2022b). Aalto University launched an internal investigation into the matter, following which it terminated the programme, and Persons (b. 1954) retired after a slight reprimand made public by the University (Aalto University, 2022a, 2022b). As of 2022, The Helsinki School is no longer associated with Aalto University but rather continues its work as an entity associated with the Berlin gallery, now under the name 'Persons Projects' (The Helsinki School, n.d.). In the following, we draw on the published statements of the former female members of the Helsinki School when discussing different forms of gender-based violence and gendered structures of power in the field of visual art and art education.

Recurring Sexual Harassment within the Helsinki School

For the original article reporting on the malpractices, Karoliina Paananen, the *Long Play* journalist, had interviewed several people who had been chosen to be part of the Helsinki School (Paananen, 2022a). They described distinct power dynamics and processes of screening, pointing out how the Aalto photography students were first taken up as 'candidates' for some art fairs, later becoming members proper, and how the School divided the photography students hierarchically into two groups. Several former students also told Paananen (2022a) about being inappropriately approached during their studies, behaviour that could be framed as 'grooming'. In the present case, grooming consisted of the gradual manipulation of students in which boundaries are blurred and inappropriate behaviour is normalised, often leading to emotional or sexual exploitation under the guise of mentorship (compare Ramstedt, 2024, on similar cases in classical music). Persons had, for instance, asked one female student to an afterparty of an opening, but there was nobody else there—except Persons, who wanted to discuss the student's personal life, including a possible boyfriend. He also wanted to walk arm-in-arm from the restaurant in which they had met and, according to the student, told her that he wanted to 'kidnap her to his villa [...] to see some kittens'.[9] The student felt threatened by the suggestion. Many female students told the journalist how Persons had commented on their looks, pried into their personal lives and later discussed their private issues in front of other students.

Aalto University's handling of harassment cases was challenged in the *Long Play* article (Paananen, 2022a). The representatives of the University interviewed for the article either said that they had no part in running the Helsinki School, or emphasised that the School had benefited the University and Finnish photography at large. Only one of the teachers, a female professor, Marjaana Kella (whose own artwork had previously been presented within the frame of Helsinki School), openly questioned the practice of commercialising the

---

9   The quotations were initially in Finnish and have been translated by the authors for inclusion in the article.

students' work from early on.[10] She had also spoken to the Human Resources Department and the University's lawyer about two cases of harassment (Paananen, 2022a). Persons was given a formal warning for his inappropriate behaviour in 2018, but there was little confidentiality in the University process: if the students made their complaints under their own names, Persons found out who had complained about him and, according to the students, made angry and threatening phone calls to them. What is more, many students interviewed by Paananen (2022a) said they did not take their cases forward, because they worried about being able to finish their degree at the University and even about their future career.

Persons has been very influential in the European photographic scene (Paananen, 2022a; Paris Photo, n.d.-b) and arguably has had enough power to include as well as exclude photographic artists from that setting. Significantly, his role at Aalto as a teacher-cum-curator also provided him ample opportunities for the use and abuse of power (Paananen, 2022a). Persons himself, when interviewed for the *Long Play* article, denied the accusations of physical abuse, and even the fact that the University had given him an official warning in 2018. He only admitted that he had 'complimented' the students' looks, but had been told that 'one must not say such things nowadays' (Paananen, 2022a), obviously referring to the repercussions of the global #MeToo movement. The dean of the Aalto School of the Arts, Design and Architecture agreed in the article that Persons did wield considerable power, and that 'the use of power always includes the possibility of using it in a wrong way'. He also mentioned that collaboration between Persons and the University had come to an end, but cited financial reasons as the cause: the journalist reports the dean as saying 'No matter how great a job they [the Helsinki School] have done, we have to cut expenses' (Paananen, 2022a).

The female students' stories accord with Sophie Hennekam and Dawn Bennett's (2017) claim that sexual harassment pervades the creative industries to the extent that it becomes normalised, with many women accepting it as an inevitable aspect of their professional environment and career progression. Hennekam and Bennett define

---

10 Kella (b. 1961) acted as professor of photographic art between 2017 and 2020. She participated in two Helsinki School volumes (2005 and 2011).

work-related sexual violence as any form of unwelcome sexual conduct, comprising unwanted remarks, gestures, and physical contact, including situations where sexual favours are exchanged for employment opportunities. Their analysis takes into account the context, relying on an understanding of the specific social and economic organisation shaping the creative industries (compare Caves, 2000; Menger, 2014). Hennekam and Bennett (2017) identify four main factors that contribute to the prevalence and tolerance of sexual harassment in these industries: competition for jobs, industry culture, gendered power relations, and the importance of informal networks. The Helsinki School stories show all these factors at work.

Blurred Lines between Work and Personal Life

While informal networks are crucial for employment and career advancement in the creative industries, networking can reinforce existing power imbalances and exclusionary practices, leading to environments where sexual harassment may be normalised or overlooked to maintain professional relationships. The fluidity between work and personal interactions can blur the lines between acceptable behaviour and harassment, making it difficult for individuals to recognise and report misconduct. As Hennekam and Bennett (2017) note, taken together these dimensions shape the culture within the creative industries, influencing attitudes towards sexual harassment and perpetuating its prevalence within the workforce. These characteristics are prominent in the story of Eva Persson, one of the former students whose experiences of sexual harassment by Timothy Persons were detailed in the second *Long Play* article (Paananen, 2022b).

According to Paananen (2022b), while pursuing her photography studies, Eva Persson was also working at the Helsinki School's gallery. The work demanded a lot of travelling, and Persons and the student usually stayed in modest hotels in separate rooms. However, on one trip, Persons booked them a shared room in an expensive hotel, justifying this to the student on the grounds of saving money and promising to sleep on the floor. She recalled responding, 'I said that was fine, as long as I have the bed' (Paananen, 2022b). In the evening, Persons asked if they could sleep in the same bed after all, but the student refused. In the night, she woke up to find Persons crawling into her narrow bed and wrapping his arms around her. She recalled, 'When I asked what he was doing, he answered: "Just making myself comfortable"' (Paananen, 2022b).

Another time, Persson told the journalist (Paananen, 2022b), Persons invited Eva Persson to his country house, where he was staying with his children. The student agreed to the invitation, thinking it would be safe with the children present. At night, Persons came to the room where the student was staying and asked her to go outside with him. She refused, but Persons persisted. The student became frightened and thought it best to get up. Outside, Persons started to make passes at her, and she became paralysed. She recalled, 'I noticed I was defeated. I could not escape the situation; it was not possible. I could not make a scene [...] I did not say no, I did not fight. I gave up' (Paananen, 2022b). After this episode, the student worked with Persons as a gallery assistant for a while longer, but then changed to another field completely. She had not talked about her experiences before 2022, but decided to share them after Persons had claimed in the first *Long Play* interview that he had never approached any student sexually.

Another female student told Paananen (2022b) a story of a visit to Persons' country house as well: they ate, drank wine and the curator-teacher asked if they might go take a sauna and go swimming. Nothing happened in the sauna, but later, when the student had gone to sleep, Persons suddenly came to the room, climbed to her bed, and pressed his penis against her. The student got up and went to another room. Later she blamed herself for having been naive and did not tell anybody about the incident. She eventually gave up on photography as a field altogether. *Long Play* interviewed four other women who had quit photography and switched careers (Paananen, 2022b).

As mentioned, informal networks play a crucial role in establishing and advancing careers in the creative industries. Participating in these networks often leads to the boundaries between professional and personal life becoming blurred, especially in situations involving alcohol consumption. In the visual arts, exhibition opening parties and private showings represent just such situations. Eva Persson's work at the Helsinki School's gallery included establishing relationships with the art world. She told Paananen (2022b) that on one occasion, when a party was thrown for art influencers in a prestigious Helsinki residence, Persons invited the student to a room where he was having a conversation with a Swedish museum director. The student presumed the purpose of the meeting was networking, but when she went in, Persons asked her to show her breasts. The student said that she was unable to say anything in the situation, so she just left the party. In this incident, Persons could be interpreted as demonstrating his position of power to both the student and the visiting museum director (see, for example, Wilson & Thompson, 2001); at the same time, he completely objectified the student. The case also illustrates the common mechanism whereby women are reduced from their professional role to their gender role (see, for example, Saresma et al., 2020).

Toleration Fuelled by Multiple Factors

Hennekam and Bennett (2017) note that their research participants often found themselves in 'gendered dependency situations' in the creative sector. Referring to research concerning other industries, the authors state that sexual harassment arises from men's economic power over women and that dependency situations enable sexual exploitation and coercion. Hennekam and Bennett see this as consistent with the fact that women tolerate more intrusive types of sexual harassment from higher-status males. Eva Persson's working relationship with Persons is an example of such gendered dependency. Power and economic imbalances foster a cycle of tolerated harassment. Observing the acceptance of sexually charged behaviour can lead female students to perpetuate such conduct, sustaining an environment in which harassment is accommodated.

The statements from female students in the Helsinki School align with previous studies that have identified various reasons why harassment often goes unreported and fails to be revealed (see also Chapter 2 and Chapter 7 in this book). Victims often doubt their experiences, unsure where normal behaviour ends and intentional harassment begins; Gunilla Carstensen (2016) refers to this ambiguity as a 'grey zone'. Women, particularly those socialised in industries where harassment is normalised and job security is tenuous, may opt for individual discretion out of concern for career repercussions. Hennekam and Bennett (2017) cite a number of reasons for this behaviour. These include fear of revenge, reluctance to be perceived as a victim, concern about being labelled overly sensitive. Moreover, women may be sceptical regarding the likelihood of the harasser facing consequences, have limited awareness of their rights and lack adequate access to external support. Organisational or occupational characteristics and power imbalances may further inhibit reporting.

The investigative articles published by *Long Play* on the Helsinki School case shed light on several structures that perpetuate violence against women, both within art education and in the art world at large. The female students told the journalist that they had experienced sexual harassment on the part of male teachers; male students did not tell similar stories. Because of the male professors' positions of power in the art world, the female students felt that they could not jeopardise their careers by making their experiences public. Homosocial male bonding (see, for example, Sedgwick, 1989) further protected the leaders of the Helsinki School from accusations of malpractice. The instances of violence identified range from physical acts to more subtle forms, and the *continuum* formed by these incidents can easily be interpreted as exemplifying the intersectional symbolic violence that older, influential heterosexual men exercise over younger women. This is proven by the threatening atmosphere, in which the students kept quiet due to fear for their academic progress and further career. This atmosphere was repeatedly reported in both *Long Play* articles, which were based on several student interviews (Paananen, 2022a, 2022b).

Maria Isabel Menéndez-Menéndez (2014) has criticised cultural industries and their discourses for legitimising certain power relations and for subtle practices that contribute to the reproduction of symbolic violence against women. For instance, competitive structures and outright sexual harassment may be tolerated in an art university if people at the top level of the hierarchies insist that 'the benefits are bigger than the harm done', as was the case in the Helsinki School (Paananen, 2022b). It is crucial for symbolic violence (see also Karkulehto & Rossi, 2017) that the members of the dominant group believe that their own domination is legitimate (Menéndez-Menéndez, 2014).

Familial Industry Culture Favouring Gender-Based Violence

In her chapter in this book (Chapter 8), Alice Laurent-Camena writes about people in cultural scenes forming relationships resembling family ties, and about these 'families' not wanting to wash 'their dirty linen in public' (see also Chapter 3 in this book). The members of the Helsinki School have similarly described their community as a family, or as a succession of generations. It is performatively repeated in several texts concerning the Helsinki School that the uniqueness of the School's educational method lies in the interaction between different generations of artists, where both explicit and tacit knowledge is passed on from one generation to the next. As Hilla Kurki, a member of the Helsinki School, said in a 2016 interview (Virri, 2016): 'Maybe it's a dysfunctional family, but all families are dysfunctional'. Interestingly, this observation was published several years before the allegations on malpractices became public and before #MeToo became a global movement.

The way a family closes its ranks became evident when soon after the first *Long Play* article appeared, former photography professor Jyrki Parantainen published an op-ed piece in *Helsingin Sanomat*, the largest subscription newspaper in Finland, together with two other senior Helsinki School artists, Elina Brotherus and Sandra Kantanen. In their joint piece, they defended the School and maintained that 'friendships, open criticism, argumentation and differing opinions are part of the same parcel; harassment of any kind is not' (Brotherus et al., 2022). Brotherus, who has spoken in public about the importance of feminist practices and role models in the art world (for example, Paris Photo, n.d.-a), did not acknowledge the claims of her younger female colleagues regarding the Helsinki School, but rather allied herself with Parantainen to refute their accusations. The joint letter-to-the-editor by Brotherus, Kantanen and Parantainen may also be recognised as an example of the way the older generation of the Helsinki School, bound as they were in their day to Persons, the leader of the School, have in turn come to exercise power over the younger artists or students. This kind of complicity is not to be taken as voluntarism, but rather as a complex effect of the domination process: the acts of obedience and submission, in no way acts of full awareness, are acts of knowledge (of a structure) and recognition (of a legitimacy) (Menéndez-Menéndez, 2014).

Gendered Paradox of Male Artists' Power and Intentions

In the second *Long Play* article, several female whistleblowers not only told more stories about Persons but also denounced Parantainen for approaching students in an inappropriate manner and having started relationships with students during the years he was teaching at Aalto University.[11] The narratives describe him seeking physical contact with female students in bars and at school parties and, for instance, kissing students without any warning (Paananen, 2022b). These behaviours do not come as a surprise, given that it has been a characteristic of Finnish photography schools' 'industry culture' for professors and students to interact in a non-hierarchical manner and often spend time together outside the institution. Parantainen did not respond to the *Long Play* journalist's phone calls and messages at first, but eventually sent an email explaining that in his view the time teachers and students spent together was 'consensual' and that 'the claims about relationships and "kisses" were rumours and interpretations' (Paananen, 2022b).

In his own photographs selected for the Helsinki School books, Parantainen depicts cityscapes or people, mostly women or girls. His works showing female characters often prompt reflection on gender-based violence. One example is *57 Optional Spots to Crack the Bone* (2004) from the *Dreams and Disappointments* series that was featured in Volume 5. In the photograph, a young woman leans her hands on the edge of a stainless steel sink in a white-tiled men's restroom, with the urinals visible in the background. She is wearing a shiny, nude sleeveless party dress, with a neckline revealing her cleavage. Her party purse lies on the sink. Water is flowing from the tap, but the woman pays no attention to it, instead gazing earnestly, perhaps desperately, to her right, outside the frame. The woman's black mascara is smudged, and her hair is dishevelled. Each of the fifty-seven potential fracture points of bones is marked on the female figure with a small nail, connected by a thread to another nail outside the figure. The combination of nails, wire and number markings lends the photograph a scientific touch.

---

11   Parantainen was Professor of Photographic Art at Aalto University's School of Arts, Design and Architecture between 2010 and 2017 and its predecessor University of Arts and Design Helsinki between 2006 and 2010. He started his teaching career there in the early 1990s.

According to Parantainen himself, his series *Dreams and Disappointments* aims to direct the audience toward the reassuring possibility of a happy ending (Silva, 2008). In Winter 2024, *57 Optional Spots to Crack the Bone* was for sale at Artsy, where it was described as depicting a friend of the artist as a young bride to be, with all her doubts and fears prior to her wedding ceremony.[12] However, when analysed through the lens of gender-based violence, the frozen narrative of Parantainen's photograph appears to depict a moment of crisis and an underlying threat of violence faced by the young woman. Artsy also contextualises this twenty-year-old artwork as reflecting 'the turbulent times and general lack of awareness of domestic violence that was just becoming a major issue back in 2004' (Artsy, n.d.). Given the recent revelations concerning the Helsinki School, the idea that meaning-making within this context leads to a "happy ending" appears increasingly untenable. The tension between the testimonies of female whistleblowers and the artistic intentions articulated by a male professor creates a striking paradox.

Gendered Image Shaping: Women's Aesthetic Labour

Not only in the performing arts but also in such art forms as the visual arts, the practitioners' physicality and bodily capital, 'aesthetic labor' (Mears, 2014) or 'display work' (Mears & Connell, 2016) may assist in gaining visibility in the art market and access to its informal networks. In the case of the Helsinki School, female bodily capital also emerges as a resource to be used in photographs. For instance, the branding effort has to some extent utilised the bodily capital and aesthetic labour of its female members. In the first *Long Play* article, one of the students said that Persons had suggested she 'get inspired by another female artist, who posed naked in her works' (Paananen, 2022a). Female students have also been expected to engage in emotional labour by drawing on their personal traumas in their artmaking (Paananen, 2022b). For instance, in *The Female Point of View* (2011), Milja Laurila's childhood trauma is referenced when discussing her work (see also Chapter 6 in

---

12 See https://www.artsy.net/artwork/jyrki-parantainen-57-optional-spots-to-crack-the-bone

this book).

Nude photographs are indeed not uncommon in the six Helsinki School volumes, although not all of them are self-portraits. Elina Brotherus (b. 1972) does a lot of nude studies, but there is little sexual reference in her photographs. She often works alone and photographs herself using a cable release. The photographs are taken from afar, she often has her back turned towards the viewer or looks straight out of the photograph, facing the viewer in a direct and unabashed manner. In a feminist art historical frame, her photographs may be conceptualised as pictures of non-eroticised nakedness rather than sexualised nudes (see, for example, Nead, 1992). Some of her pictures, nonetheless, make references to the *Venus pudica* type of classic art historical pose (Vänskä, 2005), which contains contradictory references: in covering their pubic area with their hand, the women in the old paintings and sculptures simultaneously direct the viewer's attention to it. The same arguably happens in the photographs by Brotherus. In her interviews she has insisted that she is not interested in representing female sexuality (see, e.g., Hujanen, 2018), and does not care if the human figure is a man or a woman. Yet she has also made a series of photographs in which two male painters are painting her posing naked as a model, quite obviously hinting that she is conscious of the masculinist tradition of the heterosexual male gaze (Mulvey, 1989). Through this series, and many others, Brotherus clearly establishes that she herself is in control of the process and representation in her images. Accordingly, she participates in the already long *continuum* of feminist photography, and feminist art at large, emphasising female agency (see, for example, Reckitt & Phelan, 2001; Reilly & Nochlin, 2007). Having ambitiously constructed a strong agency of her own in the art world, she has also lent her images to the gendered image shaping among other women artists who 'have emerged as the leading figures from the Helsinki School' (Persons, 2011, p. 7).

Several female artists associated with the Helsinki School appear to have been strategically used both for crafting the collective image of the School and enhancing the market success of the branding effort, implying an economic form of gender-based violence. The project involved not only young students but also established photographic artists, ones who already had extensive experience in international collaboration and exhibition activity and many of whom were female (for example, Elina Brotherus, Ulla Jokisalo and Marjaana Kella). As Anna-Kaisa Rastenberger (2006) noted, inclusion of such established artists in the Helsinki School concept was crucial for the credibility of the entire brand and presumably beneficial for obtaining public funding as well. Many of the participating female artists have dealt with personal, intimate issues, giving the branding effort a feminist edge and theoretical foothold, contributing to the School's endeavour to present itself as conceptually oriented. Nevertheless, it should be observed that, in its interpretive framework, *The Helsinki School, Vol. 4* (2011) does not offer a critical contemporary feminist approach to photography but chooses terms that take us back to the 1980s and to the simple gender binary, a violent system in itself. The photographers whose work is presented in *Vol. 4* supposedly self-identified as women at the time, and we have not observed any gender-queer or non-binary identifications or representations within the Helsinki School.

Women as Victims, Women as Powerless in Photographs?

Aino Kannisto (b. 1973) is another of the Helsinki School's core photographers who has focused throughout her career on photographing herself. Unlike Brotherus, she does not present herself totally naked; instead she changes her clothes and the settings of her photoshoots, and produces images that look like film stills (evoking such predecessors as Cindy Sherman and Nan Goldin). With these frozen moments she invites the viewers to fabricate narratives around the 'stills', that is, to ask, What happened before the image was taken, and what will happen afterwards? In the light of the recent allegations concerning gender-based harassment, it is interesting to look at some of Kannisto's photographs as somewhat symptomatic of the tensions that have arisen within 'the School' since. For instance, in several photographs in the series *Hotel Bogota* (2013), the female 'protagonist' can be read as anticipating something sexually violent or unpleasant to happen, or has already been attacked, either sexually or otherwise.[13] In one of the images, her figure is seen lying on the bed on her stomach,

---

13   See https://www.personsprojects.com/artists/aino-kannisto?x=works/hotel-bogota

wearing only a blouse and black garters, her arms laying impassive on her sides, her face looking apathetic. In another 'still' she is lying on her back on the floor, and the viewer is looking at her from above, through a balustrade. Has the woman been pushed down the stairs? Her eyes are open, but the stare is vacant; she has tousled hair on her lifeless face. The suggested narratives and atmospheres of the images are grim, oppressive or ominous at worst, joyless and serious at best; it is quite clear that at least some of Kannisto's photographs represent gender-based violence, its anticipation or aftermath, which can ultimately be death. Moreover, there are no signifiers of strong agency, only ones of ambiguity and frozen waiting.

There is one shared pattern in many of the photographs of the Helsinki School's female artists: whether they pose themselves in their images or use other models, in many of the photographs the women turn away their gaze or hide their faces from the viewer. For example, this is the case in the images of Aino Kannisto, Anni Leppälä, Susanna Majuri, and Heli Rekula. Alain Quemin (2015) also draws attention to the absorptive mode of the Helsinki School portraits, adding that the subjects' eyes often remain hidden. Rekula (b. 1963), who works as senior lecturer at Aalto University, only participated in two Helsinki School books (2005, 2007). Rekula has often posed nude in her own photographs, and critically studied corporeal malleability, submission and exposure in her work. In the Helsinki School volumes, however, she has used other models as well, and some of the images are quite straightforward references to either gender-based violence or poses for sexual services. Quemin (2015) mentions Rekula as one of the few Helsinki School artists in whose works issues of gender are brought up critically. For instance, in Rekula's photograph *Desire (Pain)*, 2004, we can see the head and shoulders of a red-haired young woman; she is shot in profile, turning a (heavily made-up) black eye towards the viewers, wearing a neck brace and a very low-cut décolleté black dress. Two other photographs, *Stage I* and *Stage II*, from 2006, are shot on a bed with an extremely tall, padded beige headboard; they depict an isolated figure of a woman bending over or sitting naked in profile so that we cannot see her face, only her long blond hair/wig. Both poses are easy to read as signifiers of sexual availability, even though the beige and white surroundings and bright lighting distinguish them from stereotypical pornographic conventions. In the context of Rekula's own work, these photographs read as feminist statements, but within the sterile context of the Helsinki School, this interpretation does not feature prominently. The images are aesthetically quite clinical, and fit the signature cool aesthetic known as 'international clean', associated with the Helsinki School's books and exhibitions at its prime (cf. Heikka, 2004; Uimonen, 2007).

Art Education and Branding Supporting Practices of Gender-Based Violence

In this chapter, we have examined the diverse forms of gender-based violence connected to the Helsinki School—an educational, branding and marketing effort at the University of Industrial Art and Design Helsinki, which became part of Aalto University in 2010—throughout its entire period of activity, from the 1990s to the 2020s. We have been asking whether the gendered image-shaping of the photographs created by the artists participating in the project and the School's educational practices and marketing measures combine to form a *continuum* of gender-based violence. In public, the Helsinki School was celebrated as a unique promotional and educational effort—until winter 2022, when the media exposed ambiguities in economic matters and accusations of sexual harassment.

In our reading, the School presents an example of the ways in which not only straightforward physical sexual harassment but also more subtle forms of symbolic violence are facilitated and allowed to prevail in the creative sectors. We have identified several factors working to sustain this kind of multi-level gender-based violence in the case of the Helsinki School. To start with, there was intense competition for visibility and career prospects among the students and even senior artists, both nationally and globally. The harassing practices could continue because the School was built upon gendered dependency relations and male bonding. Moreover, the School's culture was imbued by the importance of informal networks and the construction of an idea of one big, multi-generational family. These factors became obvious when close reading the media material provided by the investigative journalism of the *Long Play* platform. While several female artists have been portrayed as prominent figures within the Helsinki School, recent discourse has highlighted the number of female students who have abandoned their studies and pursued different careers due to gender-based violence that occurred in the course of the branding scheme.

We have also analysed some photographs published in the Helsinki School books produced by the curator-promotor-educator Timothy Persons. The visual appearance of the School has been described as 'international clean' by journalists and art professionals (see, for example, Heikka, 2004; Uimonen, 2007), and there are not many photographs whose content would raise immediate 'interest' in terms of gender-based violence. 'International clean' refers to a polished style that prioritises technical precision. While the works are large-scale and visually striking, the term subtly hints that the focus on form may overshadow emotional depth or narrative engagement. Rastenberger (2006) notes that the subjects of the images are dominated by empty spaces, as well as coolly aesthetic portraits of individuals and objects. Heikka (2004) observes content-related blind spots in the Helsinki School works, connecting this to the logic of market forces. As the aim is to appeal to both non-commercial (museums) and commercial (collectors) audiences, serious disruptions are avoided. The themes are rather 'apolitical' within the context of contemporary art, and if they are explicitly political—including gender issues—their aesthetic is allusive and cool, Heikka observes. In our interpretation, such 'formatisation' taking place within the School may also fall under gender-based violence, as it shapes the image of female artists and affects the form, content and interpretation of their artworks. When taking a closer look at the Helsinki School volumes, we found photographs that may be interpreted as representing, through their fictional narratives, either premonitions or the aftermath of physical violence. In the context of the gendered image shaping and hierarchy of the School, investigated through the lens of gender-based violence, these images begin to resemble bruises on the surface of what has been described as 'international clean'.

References

Aalto University. (n.d.) *The Helsinki School. Aalto University shorthand stories.* https://aaltouniversity.shorthandstories.com/the-helsinki-school/index. html

Aalto University. (2022a, February 16). *Helsinki Schoolin toiminnasta aloitettu selvitys.* https://www.aalto.fi/fi/uutiset/helsinki-schoolin-toiminnasta-aloitettu-selvitys

Aalto University. (2022b, June 7). *Selvitys Helsinki Schooliin liittyvistä epäasiallisen kohtelun sekä taloudellisten epäselvyyksien väitteistä on valmistunut.* https://www.aalto.fi/fi/uutiset/selvitys-helsinki-schooliin-liittyvista-epaasiallisen-kohtelun-seka-taloudellisten

Artsy (n.d.). Jyrki Parantainen. 57 *Optional Spots to Crack the Bone,* 2004. *Artsy.* https://www.artsy.net/artwork/jyrki-parantainen-57-optional-spots-to-crack-the-bone

Bronfen, E. (1992). *Over her dead body: Death, femininity and the aesthetic.* Routledge.

Brotherus, E., Kannisto, S., & Parantainen, J. (2022, February 15). Helsinki Schoolia kohtaan esitetty kritiikki on hämmentävää. *Helsingin Sanomat.* https://www.hs.fi/mielipide/art-2000008614771.html

Butler, J. (2004). *Precarious life: The powers of mourning and violence.* Verso.

Carstensen, G. (2016). Sexual harassment reconsidered: The forgotten grey zone. *NORA—Nordic Journal of Feminist and Gender Research,* 24(4), 267–280. https://doi.org/10.1080/08038740.2017.1292314

Carter, C., & Weaver, C. K. (2003). *Violence and the media.* Open University Press.

Caves, R. (2000). *Creative industries: Contracts between art and commerce.* Harvard University Press.

Cuklanz, L. (2000). *Rape on prime time. Television, masculinity, and sexual violence.* University of Pennsylvania Press. https://doi.org/10.9783/9780812204001

European Institute for Gender Equality (n.d.). Forms of violence. *EIGE.* https://eige.europa.eu/gender-based-violence/what-is-gender-based-violence/forms-of-violence

Heikka, E. (2004). Neitseestä tuotteeksi: Valokuvan kansainvälistymisen lyhyt historia. *Kaltio,* 60(6), 254–263.

Hennekam, S., & Bennett, D. (2017). Sexual harassment in the creative industries: Tolerance, culture and the need for change. *Gender, Work & Organization,* 24(4), 417–434. https://doi.org/10.1111/gwao.12176.

Hohmeyer, B. (2003). Aufbruch im hohen Norden. *art—Das Kunstmagazin,* 9, 18–20.

Honkasalo, V. (2018). Mitä jää #MeToo-kampanjan varjoon? *Sukupuolentutkimus–Genusforskning*, 31(1), 23–26. https://sukupuolentutkimus.fi/wp-content/uploads/2018/04/st-1-2018-puheenvuoro.pdf

Hujanen, M. (2018, August 4). Elina Brotherus: 'Elän vapaan naisen elämää vailla sovinnaisuuksia'. *Eeva.* https://www.eeva.fi/jutut/elina-brotherus-elan-vapaan-naisen-elamaa-vailla-sovinnaisuuksia

Karkulehto, S., & Rossi, L.-M. (2017). Johdanto: Lukemisen etiikkaa ja politiikkaa—sukupuolen ja väkivallan risteyksessä. In S. Karkulehto & L.-M. Rossi (Eds), *Sukupuoli ja väkivalta. Lukemisen etiikkaa ja politiikkaa* (pp. 9–24). SKS.

Kartastenpää, T. (2022, February 9). Long Play: Valokuvan vientihankkeen Helsinki Schoolin taustalla on epäselvyyksiä, Aalto-yliopisto lopettaa rahoituksen. *Helsingin Sanomat.* https://www.hs.fi/kulttuuri/art-2000008600153.html

Karttunen, S. (2009). *'Kun lumipallo lähtee pyörimään': Nuorten kuvataiteilijoiden kansainvälistyminen 2000-luvun alussa.* Taiteen keskustoimikunta.

Karttunen, S. (2010). From photographers to artists working with lens-based media: Helsinki as a cradle of training. *Next Level, 20,* 73–84.

Kelly, L. (1987). The continuum of sexual violence. In J. Hanmer & M. Maynard (Eds), *Women, violence and social control* (pp. 46–60). Palgrave Macmillan. https://doi.org/10.1007/978-1-349-18592-4_4

Korpak, H. (2021, October 7). The jive and the flip side. *Kunstkritikk—Nordic Art Review.* https://kunstkritikk.com/the-jive-and-the-flip-side/

Mears, A. (2014). Aesthetic labor for the sociologies of work, gender, and beauty. *Sociology Compass,* 8(12), 1330–1343. https://doi.org/10.1111/soc4.12211

Mears, A., & Connell, C. (2016). The paradoxical value of deviant cases: Toward a gendered theory of display work. *Signs: Journal of Women in Culture and Society,* 41(2), 333–359. https://doi.org/10.1086/682922

Menéndez-Menéndez, M. I. (2014). Cultural industries and symbolic biolence: Practices and discourses that perpetuate inequality. *Procedia—Social and Behavioral Sciences,* 161, 64–69. https://doi.org/10.1016/j.sbspro.2014.12.011

Menger, P.-M. (2014). *The economics of creativity. Art and achievement under uncertainty.* Harvard University Press.

Mulvey, L. (1989). *Visual and other pleasures.* Palgrave.

Mäcklin, H. (2021, September 17). Helsinki School on suomalaisen valokuvataiteen merkittävimpiä ilmiöitä. *Helsingin Sanomat.* https://www.hs.fi/kulttuuri/art-2000008259618.html

Nead, L. (1992). *The female nude: Art, obscenity and sexuality.* Routledge. https://doi.org/10.4324/9780203135471

Paananen, K. (2022a, February 8). Ruskeita kirjekuoria, häirintää ja miljoonatuki yliopistolta—näin suomalaista valokuvaa viedään maailmalle. *Long Play*. https://www.longplay.fi/lyhyet/ruskeita-kirjekuoria-hairintaa-ja-miljoonatuki-yliopistolta-nain-suomalaista-valokuvaa

Paananen, K. (2022b, March 3). Helsinki Schoolin johtohahmot pyrkineet suhteisiin opiskelijoiden kanssa—entiset valokuvauksen opiskelijat kertovat ahdistelusta ja painostamisesta seksiin. *Long Play*. https://www.longplay.fi/lyhyet/helsinki-schoolin-johtohahmot-pyrkineet-suhteisiin-opiskelijoiden-kanssa-entiset

Paanetoja, J. (2018). *Harassment and other inappropriate treatment in the film and theatre industry: Analysis report*. Publications of the Ministry of Education and Culture, Finland. http://urn.fi/URN:ISBN:978-952-263-586-0

Paris Photo. (n.d.-a). *Elles X Paris Photo—Elina Brotherus. Paris Photo*. https://www.parisphoto.com/en-gb/elles/artistes/elina-brotherus.html

Paris Photo. (n.d.-b). Selection committees. *Paris Photo*. https://www.parisphoto.com/en-gb/exhibitor/selection-committees.html

Persons Projects. (n.d.) Aino Kannisto. Hotel Bogota. *Persons Projects*. https://www.personsprojects.com/artists/aino-kannisto?x=works/hotel-bogota

Persons, T. (n.d.). Introduction.*The Helsinki School*. http://www.helsinkischool.fi/history/history

Persons, T. (2011). Introduction. In T. Persons (Ed.), *The Helsinki School, Vol. 4. A female view* (pp. 6–7). Hatje Cantz Verlag.

Persons, T. (2014). Introduction. In T. Persons & A. Zak Persons (Eds), *The Helsinki School. From the past to the future, Vol. 5* (pp. 7–11). Hatje Cantz Verlag.

Persons, T. (Ed.) (2005). *The Helsinki School. Photography by Taik*. Hatje Cantz Verlag.

Persons, T. (Ed.) (2007). *The Helsinki School. New photography from Taik*. Hatje Cantz Verlag.

Persons, T. (Ed.) (2009). *The Helsinki School, Vol. 3. Young photography from Taik*. Hatje Cantz Verlag.

Persons, T. (Ed.) (2011). *The Helsinki School, Vol. 4. A female view*. Hatje Cantz Verlag.

Persons, T., & Zak Persons, A. (Eds) (2014). *The Helsinki School,Vol. 5. From the past to the future*. Hatje Cantz Verlag.

Persons, T., & Zak Persons, A. (Eds) (2021). *The Helsinki School. The nature of being, Vol. 6*. Hatje Cantz Verlag.

Projansky, S. (2001). *Watching rape. Film and television in postfeminist culture*. New York University Press.

Pääkkölä, A.-E., Käpylä, T., & Peltola, H.-R. (2021). Populaarimusiikkitoiminnassa koettu sukupuolittunut epäasiallisuus. *Musiikki,* 51(2), 55–82. https://doi. org/10.51816/musiikki.110848

Quemin, A. (2012). Kansalliset ja kansainväliset erityispiirteet Helsinki Schoolin taiteilijoiden teoksissa. In P. Rajakari (Ed.), *Pohjan tähdet. Suomalaisen valokuvan ja liikkuvan kuvan kansainvälistyminen* (pp. 184–199). Suomen Valokuvataiteen museo.

Quemin, A. (2015). La culture et ses clichés: Analyse sociologique des œuvres de l'École de photographie d'Helsinki. *L'Année sociologique,* 65(1), 148–168. https://doi.org/10.3917/anso.151.0148

Ramstedt, A. (2024). *Classical music, misconduct, and gender. A feminist study on social imaginaries and women musicians' experiences of gender inequality in Finland* (Doctoral dissertation, University of Helsinki).

Rastenberger, A.-K. (2006). The Helsinki School—Täysi oppimäärä brändäyksessä. *Kulttuurintutkimus,* 23(4), 13–26.

Rastenberger, A.-K. (2015). *Tietoa, valtaa ja toimintaa – suomalaisen valokuvataiteen kansainvälistyminen. Käsitteiden kautta järjestyvä valokuvataiteen kenttä 1990–2000-luvuilla.* Suomen valokuvataiteen museo.

Reckitt, H., & Phelan, P. (Eds) (2001). *Art and feminism.* Phaidon.

Reilly, M., & Nochlin, L. (Eds) (2007). *Global feminisms: New directions in contemporary art.* Merrell.

Rossi, L.-M. (2012). Pohjoisen tähtiä: Vientiponnistusten tuloksia vai vuorovaikutuksen prosesseja? In P. Rajakari (Ed.), *Pohjan tähdet. Suomalaisen valokuvan ja liikkuvan kuvan kansainvälistyminen* (pp. 6–11). Suomen Valokuvataiteen museo.

Saresma, T., Pöyhtäri, R., Kosonen, H., Haara, P., & Knuutila, A. (2020). Poliittisten toimijoiden kokema vihapuhe sukupuolittuneena poliittisena väkivaltana. *Sukupuolentutkimus,* 33(4), 18–38. https://journal.fi/sukupuolentutkimus/ article/view/159607

Sedgwick, E. Kosofsky (1985). *Between men: English literature and homosocial desire.* Columbia University Press.

Silva, S. (2008, September 21). Jyrki Parantainen. *Nihilsentimentalgia: A Blog about photography by Sofia Silva.* https://nihilsentimentalgia. com/2008/09/21/%E2%95%91-jyrki-parantainen-%E2%95%91/

Suonpää, J. (2011). *Valokuva on IN.* Suomen valokuvataiteen museo

Thapar-Björkert, S., Samelius, L., & Sanghera, G. (2016). Exploring symbolic violence in the everyday: Misrecognition, condescension, consent and complicity. *Feminist Review,* 112(1), 144–162. https://doi.org/10.1057/ fr.2015.53

The Helsinki School. (n.d.) About. *The Helsinki School.* http://www. helsinkischool.fi/

Uimonen, A. (2007, June 1). Nuorilla on tunteet mukana. Lapsuus ja oman elämän käsittely tulevat näyttelyssä vahvasti esiin. *Helsingin Sanomat.* https://www.hs.fi/kulttuuri/art-2000004487206.html

Uimonen, A. (2012, November 10). Nosturibaletista museokelpoiseksi. *Helsingin Sanomat.* https://www.hs.fi/kulttuuri/art-2000002578962.html

Virri, S. (2016). Kallis koulu. *Aino,* 4. https://ainolehti.fi/aino/kallis-koulu/

Vänskä, A. (2005). Why are there no lesbian advertisements. *Feminist Theory,* 6(1), 67–85. https://doi.org/10.1177/1464700105046976

Wilson, F., & Thompson, P. (2001). Sexual harassment as an exercise of power. *Gender, Work & Organization,* 8(1), 61–83. https://doi.org/10.1111/1468-0432.00122

6. Creating Content about Gender-Based Violence and Sexuality while Being Subjected to Sexual Harassment: Experiences of UK Screen Industries Workers

Anna Bull

Introduction

Since the 2017 #MeToo movement—building on Tarana Burke's 2006 campaign[1]—screen industries content about gender-based violence has increased in volume, visibility and complexity (Banet-Weiser & Higgins, 2023; De Benedictis et al., 2019). At the same time, evidence has emerged revealing the extent of sexual harassment that occurs within the industries that produce this content, with, for example, 11% of women working in the UK screen industries having been subjected to sexual harassment at work in the past year (Film and TV Charity, 2022). As such, it is highly likely that a significant minority of screen industries workers are creating content about gender-based violence while also being subjected to such experiences at work.

A range of questions follow from this observation. How do these working conditions affect women's and gender and sexual minorities' creative freedom in producing such content? Does producing content about gender-based violence—or indeed sexuality more generally— affect the risk of experiencing sexual harassment at work? Conversely,

---

[1]   In 2006, African American activist Tarana Burke set up Me Too as a movement
        to address sexual violence, enabling young women of color to share their stories
        (Brockes, 2018).

 https://doi.org/10.11647/OBP.0436.06

questions can also be raised about how this content is acting back on workplace gender politics. For example, is this new wave of content about gender-based violence influencing workplace conditions in ways that affect the gendered order in this industry? Now that complex, nuanced post-#MeToo representations are being produced (Banet-Weiser & Higgins, 2023) does this mean that conditions of production are allowing women creative freedom to produce?

In order to explore these questions, this chapter examines the intersection between representations of gender-based violence in the UK screen industries and the gendered culture of workplaces in which this content is produced. It draws on a study of eighteen workers in the UK screen industries who had been subjected to, or involved in reporting, sexual harassment or violence at work since 2017, focusing on a subset of these accounts in which interviewees described producing content relating to sexuality, gender-based violence or harassment—across journalism, factual entertainment and drama/comedy—at the same time as negotiating sexual harassment or violence within the workplace in which this material was being produced. It explores how the conditions of cultural production in the UK screen industries are affecting representations of gender-based violence, and conversely how these representations are acting back on conditions of production.

This discussion contributes to wider debates around gender inequalities in the screen industries (Gill, 2014; O'Brien, 2019; Wreyford, 2018); women's creative agency (Battersby, 1994; French, 2018; O'Brien, 2019); as well as conversations around 'creative freedom' (Saha, 2017) in cultural production, such as whether the presence of more women in the industry, especially senior women, affects the ways in which they are represented. Anamik Saha argues that even when racialised minorities are present in the cultural workplace, they may not have creative freedom to produce the content they choose in the ways that they want (Saha, 2017). A similar point has been made about women's experiences of cultural production; Anne O'Brien (2019) describes the 'masculinist routines' in the Irish screen industries that shape normative ways of producing content. Indeed, UNESCO recommendations for addressing gender inequalities in the cultural and creative industries propose that 'initiatives aiming to uphold freedom of expression, artistic freedom and the social and economic rights of artists must factor in gender-related threats to these freedoms and rights' (Conor, 2021, p. 42).

To explore these questions, this chapter first briefly introduces literature on gender-based inequalities and violence in the creative industries and in the screen industries specifically. After outlining methods and context, the chapter introduces three ways in which content relating to gender-based violence or sexuality intersected with workplace cultures of sexual harassment.

Gender-Based Violence and Harassment in the Arts and Cultural Industries

Recent studies have explored the ways in which gender inequalities in the arts and cultural industries have created a context in which gender-based violence can occur (Buscatto et al., 2021; Hennekam & Bennett, 2017; Keil & Kheriji-Watts, 2022; Scharff, 2020; Willekens et al., 2023). These have tended to focus on how conditions of work and study in the arts and cultural industries enable gender-based violence and harassment, for example through competition for work (Hennekam & Bennett, 2017; Willekens et al., 2023); industry culture, and informal networks (Hennekam & Bennett, 2017; Kleppe & Røyseng, 2016); precarity (Keil & Kheriji-Watts, 2022; Scharff, 2020); gendered power relations (Bull, 2016, 2024; Buscatto et al., 2021; Hennekam & Bennett, 2017); artistic ideals legitimising poor behavior (Kleppe & Røyseng, 2016); recruitment processes (Kleppe & Røyseng, 2016); and sexualised and/or gender-biased cultures (Bull, 2016; Buscatto et al., 2021; O'Brien, 2019).

In the screen industries specifically, Anne O'Brien (2019, p. 55) describes how the workplace culture of screen production in her interview-based study in Ireland was characterised by gender biases which could 'become more overt occasions of outright discrimination against women' including in the form of sexual harassment. She also describes how 'masculinist routines of production', including the 'perspective applied' and the 'practices of narration and direction', shaped the kinds of content it was possible to produce (p. 21). She is sympathetic to the idea (heavily debated in screen studies) that women have a gendered 'sensibility' in the creation of content that makes them write/direct differently to men. This is evident in their interest in women's lived realities, interior emotional lives and psychological complexity. Her study also describes specific practices that women in her study used to create content outside of the normatively masculine industry hierarchies, for example directing in less authoritative and more collaborative ways. In these ways, she argues that the aesthetic, and feminised modes of producing content, can be sites for resistance to the masculinist gender norms of the industry.

O'Brien's study does not explicitly discuss the production of content relating to gender-based violence. This is, however, an area of cultural production in which it is particularly important to question masculinist routines of production and gender-biased cultures. Elsewhere, critical debates around representations of gender-based violence have explored how such violence can be depicted in ways that avoid dehumanising women but still raise awareness (Berridge & Boyle, 2023), or whether women and other sexual violence survivors should even watch such content, even when it is produced by women (Harrison, 2023). Lisa French (2018, 2021) argues that women's 'sensibility' includes the 'resonant themes' that women choose to write about, as well as how women's lived experience shapes the work they create. Women, queer, transgender and non-binary people are more likely to be subjected to gender-based violence and harassment than heterosexual cisgender men. It is therefore important for women—and minorities—to have creative freedom in making content that depicts it.

In news media, there is evidence that depictions of gender-based violence have increased in volume and changed in tone since the 2017 #MeToo movement (De Benedictis et al., 2019). Whether women's presence in the newsroom plays a role in this shift is unclear (Simons & Morgan, 2018) but there is evidence, as described in journalism in India for example, that the macho culture and masculine values of a gender-unequal workplace contribute to creating a 'journalistic doxa' around sensationalist and superficial news coverage of sexual violence (Sreedharan & Thorsen, 2023). In television and film more generally, as Sarah Banet-Weiser and Kathryn Claire Higgins (2023) demonstrate, post-#MeToo there is an increased complexity in (some) stories around gender-based violence. More generally, in the UK screen industries, the #MeToo movement led to significant ruptures and some initiatives to address gender-based violence, although these remain insufficient (Bull, 2023).

However, this work has not explored the intersection between cultures that enable sexual harassment in the screen industries and the content on gender-based violence and sexuality that is produced. Studies that explore sexual harassment in the screen industries have often used survey-based methods (French, 2014; North, 2016; Wilkes et al., 2020; Willekens et al., 2023) which do not necessarily allow these interconnections to become visible, although a Norwegian survey of 3626 journalists and editors found that 26% of respondents who had experienced sexual harassment reported that it had impacted their journalistic work (Idås et al., 2020). However, Marta Keil and Katie Kheriji-Watts (2022, p. 15), in recommendations for the European cultural sector, argue that 'increased understanding of what contributes to violence and inequity is leading some to think differently about art'. In this book, Provansal's as well as Rossi and Karttunen's chapters (Chapter 4 and Chapter 5) argue that sexual harassment and abuse inhibit women's creativity and creative outputs. This chapter builds on these discussion to analyse how experiences of gender-based violence in the workplace shaped the creative content being produced, as well as how content on gender-based violence acts back on the gendered workplace cultures.

Methods and Context

This chapter draws on accounts from five women from a study of eighteen interviewees working or studying in the UK film and television industry, who had all experienced and/or spoken up about sexual harassment and violence at work since December 2017 (Bull, 2023). The screen industries include film, TV, animation, video games and special effects production (VFX). Within this broader sector, this study focused on film and television workers, which includes both 'above the line' workers—those responsible for the creative development, production, and direction of a film or TV show—as well as 'below the line' workers—technical crew members. For both groups, working conditions in the film and television industry labor market involve short-term contracts and precarity, long working hours, and accepted norms of 'putting up with bad practice for fear of being seen as a troublemaker' (Swords & Johns, 2023, p. 5). These working conditions are argued to be a crucial factor in the gender inequalities in the industry (Coles & Eikhof, 2021; Eikhof & Warhurst, 2013).

There is a well-developed research and policy agenda around diversity in the screen industries, with gender diversity a key focus (Eikhof et al., 2019). There are high levels of horizontal and vertical segregation across the screen industries in general (O'Brien, 2019), and in the UK context, similarly to elsewhere, women are under-represented in senior positions, and as well as in particular roles such as directing and screenwriting (BFI Statistical Yearbook 2021; Creative Diversity Network, 2023; Directors UK, 2018; Ofcom, 2022). There is recent evidence that gender inequalities within the UK screen industries are increasing (Creative Diversity Network, 2023). However, research on the UK screen industries has not yet explored sexual harassment as a cause or consequence of gender inequalities (Eikhof et al., 2019).

For this study, interviewees were recruited through opportunistic sampling via social media, industry organisations, and an item in the industry publication *Broadcast Now*. Interviews were carried out by the author of this chapter, who is trained and experienced in supporting survivors of sexual violence.

The semi-structured interviews included a question, where relevant to interviewees' roles, about whether the sexual harassment in their workplace affected their creative agency. Five interviewees were in roles where they had creative agency and had produced content related to sexuality or gender-based violence. It is these accounts that are analysed below. Other interviewees either did not work in roles where they had creative input into the content (for instance they were runners or crew in non-creative roles) or they were not working on creating content relating to gender-based violence or sexuality. The five interviewees whose accounts are discussed here were all white British women, one of whom indicated an identity as bisexual. They had been in the industry between three years and several decades. Three interviewees worked in journalism and the other two in drama and factual entertainment. While organisations representing trans workers as well as racially minoritised people within the industry were involved with recruiting participants, this did not lead to the inclusion of any trans or non-binary participants, and only two people of colour participated (whose accounts are not within the remit of this chapter's discussion). Those who participated in the research, and whose accounts are discussed here, therefore reflect the whiteness of the UK screen industries; and also are likely to reflect those who feel most confident to speak out (especially to a white researcher) about their experiences of harassment or violence. The discussion is not intended to be generalisable, but rather describes some of the ways in which content and workplace culture interact and explores new directions for thinking about the questions raised above.

Data analysis involved a thematic analysis of the whole dataset as well as creation of narrative summaries of each interview. The data relating to 'creativity and content' was analysed for the discussion below. This material included all mentions of creativity or discussion of the content being produced. From this data, accounts from interviewees who were producing content unrelated to sexuality or sexual harassment/violence were omitted. The initial, deductive analysis examined how workplace experiences of sexual harassment and violence shaped the content that was produced, in order to interrogate questions of 'creative freedom' raised by Saha (2017) and O'Brien (2019). However, it became clear that the relationship was more complex than this, and therefore further inductive codes were added. The three themes discussed below were arrived at from a systematic analysis of the material relating to 'creativity and content' from across all interviewees who were working on content relating to sexuality or sexual harassment/violence.

Ethical review of the study design was carried out by the University of York Department of Education Ethics Committee. Interviewees were given the opportunity to edit their interview transcripts, and to comment on the final draft of the report and this chapter. All names given below are pseudonyms, and minimal detail of roles/sub-sector/identity are given in order to aid confidentiality.

Interactions of Workplace Culture and Content

The wider study on which this chapter draws outlined how gender inequalities in the UK screen industries contributed to creating workplace cultures that enabled or worked against sexual harassment and violence (Bull, 2023). The workplaces or settings where sexual harassment or violence took place were almost all described as being gender unequal, in different ways. Six overlapping types of workplace culture relating to gender inequality were identified, including both horizontal and vertical segregation (Acker, 1990; Hirdman, 1990; O'Brien, 2019), as well as cultures where gendered harms were invisibilised; supportive cultures despite gendered inequalities; and finally actively anti-sexist cultures. In addition, in some workplace cultures other hierarchies, inequalities or risk factors contributed to enabling sexual harassment (for example, hierarchies between 'talent' and crew).

Below, I focus on the intersection between workplace cultures where sexual harassment occurred and the content relating to gender-based violence that was produced across three themes, as described above. The first theme outlines ways in which workplace cultures influenced the content produced. The second theme explores examples where content related to gender-based violence and sexuality acted back on workplace culture and women's agency in different ways, both positive and negative. Finally, the third theme describes examples where there was a stark contradiction or disjuncture between workplace culture and content.

How Culture Influenced Content

The first theme examines how workplace cultures influenced content relating to gender-based violence. One example of this is how sexual harassment experiences and a culture that normalised sexual harassment within the workplace could impede women's creative freedom. Abby, in her twenties, worked as a development producer, a role that involved developing and pitching script ideas. She described her company as having a toxic workplace environment and had been subjected to sexual harassment by a senior male colleague and by a peer, as well as from men outside her company. The impacts of this harassment she described as 'heavy, relentless and exhausting' as well as time-consuming. I asked whether she thought that these experiences had affected her creative freedom; she was clear that they had. She explained that:

> In order to get anything I want to get made, made, or for us to invest in
> it, or for us to pay for it as a company, in order for me to work with the
> people I want to work with and who I think will bring us business, I
> have to pitch to the person who described me the way that he described
> me [referring to a repeated incident of sexual harassment]. He's the one
> with the money bag and the one who makes the ultimate call on pretty
> much everything. [...]

Having previously been targeted for humiliating sexualised comments from this senior man, Abby was wary of pitching work ideas that included sexualised content for fear that they could lead to further sexual harassment. Indeed, women subjected to sexual harassment sometimes describe feeling complicit in what happened (Bull & Page, 2021). Avoiding pitching sexualised content was therefore a self-protective mechanism against the idea that she had invited or encouraged this behavior.

Abby was particularly interested in working on content related to sexuality and sexual identity, so she persisted with doing so. But there was a further reason that such ideas were complicated to pitch in this workplace:

> If I did and when I do [pitch content related to sexuality]—because that's what I'm interested in—I have to sort of grit my teeth through it, because there will be a virtue signaling response like, 'Brilliant, that sounds amazing, yeah, we need more stories like that', and I'm like, [...] 'Oh my god, if he stands up and takes credit for this, I'm going to die inside'. So, creatively, that does sometimes put a block on me.

The awareness that her senior colleague might take some of the credit for her ideas was extremely galling to her, as this would let him appear progressive and supportive of women's stories in contrast with the reality where he would verbally harass her. This situation required a complex balancing act of weighing up her desire to work on the material she was interested in, against the risk of sexual harassment and the possibility that credit for this content would go in part to this man.

By contrast with this example of workplace culture impeding women's creative freedom, there also existed counter-cultural possibilities where women could make the content they wanted to— together. In her study of the Irish screen industries, O'Brien (2019, p. 119) describes how women sometimes operated outside of industry hierarchies, for example working with other women in collaborations that would allow them to create a different kind of workplace culture, for example with 'relational' rather than hierarchical modes of leadership. Kate, an experienced journalist, described taking this approach to put together all-women teams to produce content on gender-based violence. For example, with the same two women producers:

> We've done seven or eight films on rape, we've done domestic violence,
> we've done child sex abuse; those tend to be all-women teams and
> that's great. And there's always been a degree of conspiratorial phoning
> around: 'Hey, are you free? When are you going to be free? I'm going to
> pitch this; can we work on it together?'

As such, Kate could (sometimes) pull together an all-women team with
whom she wanted to make this content. However, this possibility was
less open to more junior women such as Abby who didn't yet have Kate's
networks or experience. Age and experience therefore contributed to
women's ability to resist creatively. However, this space for creative
resistance was still very limited by wider gendered conditions of
production, even for women such as Kate.

Across both Kate's and Abby's experiences, gendered workplace
cultures affected the content it was possible to make safely. While
previous literature has debated whether there is a female 'sensibility' in
film aesthetics (French, 2018; O'Brien, 2019), such a discussion assumes
that the conditions of cultural production allow women to work in ways
that will allow such a 'sensibility' to be realised. The accounts from Abby
and Kate (as well as other chapters in this book) reveal the conditions
that impede—as well as allow—any potential gendered sensibility to
emerge in the creation of content on sexuality and gender-based violence.
Abby is unable to fully explore the creative directions she would like
to, and if she does, any success of her work might end up legitimising
the feminist credentials of her harassing boss. By contrast, Kate—being
more experienced—can sometimes put together the team she wants to
work with. These examples shed light on an under-discussed topic in
relation to gender inequalities in creative labor: how sexual harassment
shapes women's creative voices.

How Content Acted Back on Culture

As well as workplace cultures shaping content relating to sexuality
and gender-based violence, the content itself could act back on those
producing it, sometimes in unexpected ways. The first example of
how gender-based violence content acted back on workplace cultures
was through helping interviewees to recognise or get support for their
experiences. Roz, who worked in factual entertainment, described

how being involved in creating such content could equip women with knowledge that helped in labelling and recognising their own experiences. She was experiencing sexual harassment and gendered bullying from her boss, which included 'weird, sort of sexual comments' as well as remarks undermining her work, for example telling her, 'I think we're paying more for you than what you're worth'. As she explained:

> the irony of it is the scripts that we were writing are about intimate partner homicides and so, often these forensic psychologists are talking about this kind of coercive, controlling relationship where the men, not always, but [usually] the men are sort of constantly tapping away at [women's] confidence.

As part of her work for this series, they drew on expert knowledge from criminologists or forensic psychologists. Roz was:

> learning more and more through this program about coercion and control and knocking people's confidence constantly, the effect that that can have on someone. I was writing these scripts not really understanding what these psychologists were saying until suddenly I felt like my confidence was so low that it wouldn't have taken much to knock me over.

Roz eventually realised that the behaviors they were analysing for the program she was making were related to what she was experiencing from her boss. In this way, the content that she was producing on gender-based violence—alongside sessions with a private therapist who she found to cope with the harassment—helped her to make sense of what was happening.

Working on content related to gender-based violence could also open conversations in this area between colleagues. For Abby, introduced above, having worked on content in this area meant that she had discussed her previous experiences of gender-based violence with a female colleague. Later, when she was groped at a work social event, her colleague noticed her reaction and took her aside to check if she was ok. As Abby described, their previous work together on a program about sexual violence had created a shared understanding of this issue which enabled her colleague to support her after the assault. Previous discussions of sexual violence in the workplace made it more possible for her to draw on such support. This topic therefore became less 'unspeakable', adapting Rosalind Gill's (2014) argument that gender inequalities are unspeakable, in contrast with accounts of the screen industries from earlier studies (North, 2016).

A second way in which the content acted back on the culture was through catalysing interviewees to act on their experiences of sexual harassment in the workplace. Vanessa was a journalist making a story about sexual harassment. At the same time as this was occurring, she was being subjected to sexual harassment from her boss. As she describes:

> When I found out that he was doing it to another woman, I was like, 'Oh crap. This is a pattern of behavior'. Not only that, but I found out about it in the weeks before our own investigation into that very subject was about to be aired. And me and my colleague were very aware we had a responsibility to do something about it because you can't spend two years uncovering the very same issues or criticising the behavior of other people and bystanders as well, and then do the exact same thing yourself. So, that's why we were like, 'Okay, we need to do something'.

The expertise she and her colleague had learned from working on this story—as well as from their previous work on gender-based violence—informed their decision to act, as well as how they tried to get action taken in their workplace (attempts that were, however, ultimately futile and damaging to themselves (Bull, 2023). In this way, the content they were producing acted back on the workplace culture. If other journalists react in similar ways to Vanessa and her colleague, such experiences could be contributing to wider shifts in workplace cultures. Sara De Benedictis et al. found a high level of press coverage of sexual harassment and violence in the UK during the six months after #MeToo (2019). The increasing amounts of content on this topic being produced post-#MeToo suggest that there is the potential for widespread resistance to workplace sexual harassment due to others finding themselves in the same position as Vanessa of reporting on this issue while being aware of it occurring in their own workplaces.

These more positive accounts of the ways in which gender-based violence content acted back on workplace cultures can be contrasted with ways in which the content sometimes facilitated the perpetration of sexual harassment. Creating content relating to sexuality—which could include exploring 'grey areas' around consent—could create an uncomfortable or potentially unsafe workplace environment by requiring sexualised conversations that occurred without any oversight or ground rules. For actors, the rise of 'intimacy coordinators' post-#MeToo for choreographing sex scenes (Sørensen, 2022) has been hailed as a hugely positive step for creating safer workplace environments on set or on stage (although, as Chapter 2 in this book reveals, sexual harassment and violence can still occur despite the presence of those in such roles). However, as Abby noted, there is no parallel role for those working on pre- or post-production sexualised content. She described how generating ideas could involve highly sexualised conversations, personal disclosures or being asked about sexual experiences. She described how her work involves discussing stories, including stories about characters' sexual relationships, with colleagues, which can draw on their own experiences. These conversations involve 'incredibly personal and open conversations' (echoing Bleuwenn Lechaux's discussion, in Chapter 7 of this book, about the openness demanded from actors). However, Abby noted that 'part of the problem with that is that there's no training for anyone to be able to have those conversations' and there are 'people who would take advantage of that' for example by asking questions that 'are not appropriate for a workplace but just about appropriate considering the context of the conversation you're having'. These 'grey areas' can be uncomfortable for some people:

> So, there's this kind of informal environment in a lot of meetings that makes for some uncomfortable conversations for young women to be around, and like me personally, I have always been incredibly comfortable talking about those things [...] but I know for a fact that there have been people—young women—sat in meetings who have been talking about, you know, sex acts and personal anecdotes [...] and I know they have been uncomfortable, and I don't even have the tools to make sure that that doesn't happen, or to debrief them afterwards about that, other than to say, 'Are you okay?'

In this situation, discussion of sex and sexuality is required for the job role. Kirsten Dellinger and Christine Williams, in their study of work cultures at two US magazines that publish material about sex and sexuality, argue that what constitutes sexual harassment varies according to organisational culture; sexualised behaviours have different meanings in different contexts (Dellinger & Williams, 2002). Nevertheless, it is clear that in Abby's workplace, which was characterised by gender relations of power with senior roles dominated by men (Bull, under review; Connell, 2006) sexualised discussions could contribute to an intimidating environment. Such instances are captured by the UK legal framework, within which someone sharing information about their sex life or talking about sex in acts constitutes sexual harassment if it creates a humiliating, degrading or offensive environment for anyone present (Equality and Human Rights Commission, 2017).

In order to create a safer environment for these discussions, Abby thought that if an initiative along the lines of intimacy coordinators was proposed in her workplace to address this risk,

> I think you would find a lot of resistance to it if that was something that was suggested or recommended for development, because people would very easily be able to say, 'Well, we need to be able to have these open conversations. We need to be able to let the writer say what they want to say [...]—it's a safe space'. We weaponise safe space language.

The informal working environment that Abby describes within her workplace was also commented on by other interviewees in this study (see also Conor et al., 2015, p. 10). Similarly, the screen industries more widely are characterised as valuing people who are 'fun' (Swords & Johns, 2023). Abby's experience shows how this informality creates an environment where sexual harassment is enabled by normalising the sharing of intimate personal details, but also by pre-empting any objections through arguing that this sharing is required by the creative or artistic process, as has also been documented in theatre (Kleppe & Røyseng, 2016). The informality—and the value that is placed on it—also potentially acts as a way of resisting putting in place any protocols to avoid sexual harassment occurring. The irony is that 'safe spaces' or 'safer spaces' initiatives usually involve setting ground rules in order to enable people from different positionalities to participate in a particular discussion in ways that allow for difference (UCL, 2020). However, here Abby shows this terminology being 'weaponised' to do the opposite—to argue that there is no need for such care.

There was also evidence that gender-based violence content could be used directly to carry out sexual harassment. Journalist Kate noted that she had previously worked successfully and safely with an all-male team on a story about rape, but it was clear that this was not something that could be taken for granted:

There's a guy in our industry, lauded, [...] and as far as I can tell from having done one film [that he was working on], he has a pornographic interest in women being executed, tortured and raped and that's why he makes the films. [...] I sat in edit with him when he basically became aroused by an execution sequence, about how wonderful it was, how fantastic it was, and could we find more and could we do more about women being beheaded and were there women hanging from cranes and what else did they do to women? And he's still making films like that.

In fact, similarly to Abby's experience above, this situation could in itself constitute sexual harassment as it might reasonably have the effect on someone in Kate's position of creating a degrading and humiliating environment (Equality and Human Rights Commission, 2017). But as this material formed part of the content that Kate and her colleague were creating, it would have been extremely difficult to label such an experience as harassment, let alone raise concerns about it. As such, this situation was normalised as part of the requirements of the job.

Kate's and Abby's experiences reveal how content on gender-based violence or sexuality was being created without any codes of conduct or conversations about workplace safety. These conditions of production are high-risk environments for sexual harassment, but this risk is entirely unrecognised, with no safeguards in place. More positively, Roz and Abby were involved in producing content that helped them to recognise their experiences and get support when they were targeted for violence or harassment. However, not all identities are equally depicted in the content that is being produced. As De Benedictis and colleagues (2019) note, while there is a higher volume of media content relating to gender-based violence being produced post-#MeToo, it tends to centre 'the experiences of celebrity female subjects who are predominately White and wealthy'. This means that there are more cultural resources for certain groups to recognise and label their experiences than others, compounding the perceived impact of #MeToo as supporting white, middle-class women rather than other groups (Fileborn & Loney-Howes, 2019). More generally, the increase in production of such content means there is an even greater need to interrogate its impacts on those making it.

Disjunctures between Content and Culture

Finally, for some interviewees working in journalism, there was a stark disjuncture between content and culture, where the content they were producing belied the experiences of sexual harassment that were occurring during its production. For two of the journalists in this study, in the workplace where they were speaking up about or being subjected to sexual harassment, they were also being encouraged to produce content on this topic. Vanessa, introduced above, was a journalist working on an investigation about sexual misconduct. I asked if her boss—who was sexually harassing her and others—was supportive of that investigation. Vanessa explained that he had commissioned the investigation himself:

> On the night where he took me back to his hotel room, he commissioned that investigation the next morning. [...] Yeah, it's really confusing. We went for drinks at the time, and he kept on saying like, 'Oh, these guys are truly disgusting. They're terrible. I'm not like that'. I was like, 'It's so similar. How do you not see it?'

Vanessa—who collaborated with one of the few other women in her workplace on this story—didn't describe her creative freedom being impeded by this situation. In fact, her boss saw himself as a champion of women, and was supportive of the investigation on sexual harassment that Vanessa was working on. In this, her experience can be contrasted with Abby's as described above who found that having to pitch to, and report back to, a sexually harassing boss affected the content she produced. What is similar across both situations, however, is that the senior man responsible for the harassment was receiving some of the credit for Vanessa's and Abby's work.

Sarah, also a journalist, found a similar contradiction between the culture in the newsroom and the content that was being reported on. In Sarah's workplace, there had been calls for staff to report harassment, but then when they did so they found themselves silenced, and in her case losing her job and career and obliged to sign a non-disclosure agreement. She contrasted this silencing with her employer's aggressive seeking-out of stories on sexual harassment in other sectors:

> I'll tell you what's changed [since #MeToo]. They hunt down the stories because they know that the stories are appealing, that there is a zeitgeist. But has it changed anything in the newsroom? [...] I mean,

> look, how could it get much worse? [...] if the truth was known about this newsroom, the damage to them would be so huge and you're just like, 'Can none of you see this?'

In these instances, by contrast with the examples in the previous section, the content was emphatically not 'acting back' to influence the culture of the workplace in which it was being produced. The hypocrisy of cultural organisations failing to deal with sexual harassment while producing more and more content about it should not come as a surprise; various authors have documented sexual harassment in news organisations (North, 2016; Barton & Storm, 2014) and it would be surprising if this culture had changed simply because more media content in this area was being produced. Nevertheless, the weight of the contradiction between culture and content is stark, and confirms that there is no necessary relationship between workplace culture and cultural content.

Conclusion

This chapter has described the ways in which five interviewees who had experienced or reported sexual harassment or violence at work since 2017 described producing content relating to gender-based violence or sexuality in workplaces where sexual harassment was occurring. It has outlined three ways in which the interaction between content and workplace culture occurred. First, workplace culture influenced the content by impeding women's creative freedom through creating a humiliating, degrading environment where they felt less able to talk about issues relating to sexuality in the workplace, and where senior men perpetrating harassment could take the credit for content in this area. Another way in which workplace culture influenced content was through women creating counter-cultures by collaborating in order to produce content relating to gender-based violence.

By contrast, content relating to gender-based violence also acted back on interviewees and their workplace cultures in several ways: through helping interviewees to recognise or get support for their experiences; through catalysing them to take action on their experiences of sexual harassment in the workplace; but also through creating an uncomfortable or potentially unsafe workplace environment by requiring sexualised conversations that occurred without any oversight or ground rules; or through gender-based violence content being used to carry out sexual harassment. Finally, for some interviewees there was a stark mismatch between the material on gender-based violence they were being commissioned or encouraged to produce as part of the post-#MeToo zeitgeist, and the sexual harassment and silencing on this issue that they were experiencing within their own workplaces.

These findings reveal a complex picture of how cultural production and content relating to gender-based violence and sexuality are intersecting in the UK screen industries. There is clearly not a one-way or deterministic relationship between workplace culture and creative content; while Abby found that the sexual harassment she experienced at work 'put a block' on her creatively, for Vanessa her sexually harassing boss saw himself as a supporter of women and indeed enabled her to work on acclaimed content revealing sexual harassment in other industries. Instead, the intersections between workplace culture and content relating to gender-based violence are multiple and non-linear. The content itself can create increased opportunities for sexual harassment to occur but can also serve as a cultural resource for women to talk about this issue and label their experiences. Even in the final theme, which revealed a stark disjuncture between workplace cultures that enable sexual harassment and critical content being produced on this topic, a relationship between the two existed in the minds of women experiencing the contradiction, and this contradiction might be able to be used as a creative resource for their future work. In presenting this analysis it is important to note the narrow set of social profiles of women's experiences covered in this study. While interviewees had a wide range of levels of experience and ages, their whiteness and in some cases, their class privilege, affected how they felt able to respond to the situations they found themselves in. Nevertheless, all of the women—regardless of their class, race or other forms of privilege—felt harmed by the experiences they had had.

This discussion raises questions around what safer conditions of cultural production that better enable creative freedom for women would look like. The wider study that this chapter draws on found that in the UK screen industries it was rare for employers to take an actively anti-sexist approach to workplace culture (Bull, 2023). Similarly, O'Brien describes the ways in which women in the Irish film industry could thrive despite the biased structures and culture, for example by resisting the individualised male-genius director/auteur tradition (2019, chapter 5). One step forward would be to draw on the model of intimacy coordinators, as well as practices developed by gender-based violence organisations and sex educators on holding safer spaces, to devise guidance for areas of cultural production where risks are heightened. In this study, such areas include script and production development (as outlined in Abby's experience) and editing (as in Kate's experience). Some examples discussed above could also fall within the remit of workplace health and safety protocols, as editing violent content could be triggering to those with post-traumatic stress disorder developed as a result of gender-based violence. Working with such content should also require strategies—which already exist in other workplaces—for 'holding' the space to be able to work safely with difficult material, or to allow people to try out risky stories. It should also be possible for survivors of gender-based violence, if they choose to, to refuse to look at material depicting such violence, as Rebecca Harrison argues (2023). For such protocols to be effective, however, a significant shift in culture is clearly still needed, moving beyond attitudes that minimise sexual harassment and violence (Bull, 2023) towards taking this issue seriously.

There is one final way that content about gender-based violence may be influencing gendered workplace cultures that this chapter has not discussed. This is whether the post-#MeToo focus on gender-based violence in cultural and media production challenges what O'Brien (2019, p. 67) calls the 'gendering of content'. O'Brien (2019), Natalie Wreyford (2018) and Louise North (2014) in the screen industries, screenwriting and journalism respectively, have all described the gendering of genre hierarchies, whereby men get to cover high-profile stories or work on the most prestigious genres of film/television, while women are assigned to 'soft' news or 'women's genres' such as romance or the family. However, gender-based violence appears now to be a prestigious, high-profile content area; it is no longer a 'soft' topic but it is still unarguably a 'women's' topic. The 'genre' of gender-based violence may therefore be disrupting the gender/genre hierarchies that the authors above have described. As such, content in this area may be contributing to a culture where women are given more opportunities; indeed Vanessa's break into broadcast journalism came through the story on sexual harassment described above—but then the experience of sexual harassment and reporting it forced her out of this career. Overall, if content about gender-based violence is to challenge these genre-gender hierarchies, it needs to be produced in conditions of safety that support women's and other survivors' creative freedom to tell these stories in complex and varied ways.

References

Acker, J. (1990). Hierarchies, jobs, bodies: A theory of gendered organizations. *Gender & Society*, 4(2), 139–158. https://doi.org/10.1177/089124390004002002

Banet-Weiser, S., & Higgins, K. C. (2023). *Believability: Sexual violence, media, and the politics of doubt*. John Wiley & Sons.

Barton, A., & Storm, H. (2014). *Violence and harassment against women in the news media: A global picture*. International Women's Media Foundation. https://www.iwmf.org/wp-content/uploads/2018/06/Violence-and-Harassment-against-Women-in-the-News-Media.pdf

Battersby, C. (1994). *Gender and genius: Towards a feminist aesthetics*. Women's Press.

Berridge, S., & Boyle, K. (2023). Representing reality: Introduction to part 2. In K. Boyle & S. Berridge (Eds), *The Routledge companion to gender, media and violence* (pp. 99–115). Routledge. https://doi.org/10.4324/9781003200871-21

BFI Statistical Yearbook 2021. (n.d.). https://core-cms.bfi.org.uk/media/24979/download

Brockes, E. (2018, January 15). #MeToo founder Tarana Burke: 'You have to use your privilege to serve other people'. *The Guardian*. https://www.theguardian.com/world/2018/jan/15/me-too-founder-tarana-burke-women-sexual-assault

Bull, A. (2016). Gendering the middle classes: The construction of conductors' authority in youth classical music groups. *The Sociological Review*, 64(4), 855–871. https://doi.org/10.1111/1467-954X.12426

Bull, A. (2023). *Safe to speak up? Sexual harassment in the UK film and television industry since #MeToo*. Screen Industries Growth Network, University of York. https://screen-network.org.uk/wp-content/uploads/2023/10/Safe-to-Speak-Up-full-report.pdf

Bull, A. (2024). Classical music after #MeToo: Is music higher education a 'conducive context' for sexual misconduct? In R. Reitsamer & R. Prokop (Eds), *Higher music education and employability in a neoliberal world* (pp. 99–115). Bloomsbury Publishing. https://doi.org/10.5040/9781350266995.ch-007

Bull, A. (Under review). *How gender inequalities enable sexual harassment in the UK screen industries: A qualitative study of experiences since #MeToo*.

Bull, A., & Page, T. (2021). Students' accounts of grooming and boundary-blurring behaviours by academic staff in UK higher education. *Gender and Education*, 33(8), 1057–1072. https://doi.org/10.1080/09540253.2021.1884199

Buscatto, M., Helbert, S., & Roharik, I. (2021). L'opéra, un monde professionnel hanté par les violences de genre. *Les Cahiers de la Société québécoise de recherche en musique*, 22(1–2), 49–67. https://doi.org/10.7202/1097857ar

Coles, A., & Eikhof, D. R. (2021). On the basis of risk: How screen executives' risk perceptions and practices drive gender inequality in directing. *Gender, Work & Organization*, 28(6), 2040–2057. https://doi.org/10.1111/gwao.12701

Connell, R. (2006). Glass ceilings or gendered institutions? Mapping the gender regimes of public sector worksites. *Public Administration Review*, 66(6), 837–849. https://doi.org/10.1111/j.1540-6210.2006.00652.x

Conor, B. (2021). *Gender & creativity: Progress on the precipice*. UNESCO. https://unesdoc.unesco.org/ark:/48223/pf0000375706

Conor, B., Gill, R., & Taylor, S. (2015). Gender and creative labour. *The Sociological Review*, 63(1), 1–22. https://doi.org/10.1111/1467-954X.12237

Creative Diversity Network. (2023). Writers, directors and producer directors: A six-year overview of Diamond data 2016/17 to 2021/22. *Diamond Reports*. https://creativediversitynetwork.com/diamond/diamond-reports/writers-directors-and-producer-directors-report/

De Benedictis, S., Orgad, S., & Rottenberg, C. (2019). #MeToo, popular feminism and the news: A content analysis of UK newspaper coverage. *European Journal of Cultural Studies*, 22(5–6), 718–738. https://doi.org/10.1177/1367549419856831

Dellinger, K., & Williams, C. L. (2002). The locker room and the dorm room: Workplace norms and the boundaries of sexual harassment in magazine editing. *Social Problems*, 49(2), 242–257. https://doi.org/10.1525/sp.2002.49.2.242

Directors UK. (2018). Who's calling the shots? Gender inequality among screen directors working in UK television. *Directors UK*. https://directors.uk.com/news/who-s-calling-the-shots

Eikhof, D. R., Newsinger, J., Luchinskaya, D., & Aidley, D. (2019). And … action? Gender, knowledge and inequalities in the UK screen industries. *Gender, Work & Organization*, 26(6), 840–859. https://doi.org/10.1111/gwao.12318

Eikhof, D., & Warhurst, C. (2013). The promised land? Why social inequalities are systemic in the creative industries. *Employee Relations*, 35(5), 495–508. https://doi.org/10.1108/ER-08-2012-0061

Equality and Human Rights Commission. (2017). *Sexual harassment and the law: Guidance for employers*. EHRC. https://www.equalityhumanrights.com/sites/default/files/sexual-harassment-and-the-law-guidance-for-employers.pdf

Fileborn, B., & Phillips, N. D. (2019). From 'me too' to 'too far'? Contesting the boundaries of sexual violence in contemporary activism. In B. Fileborn & R. Loney-Howes (Eds), *#MeToo and the politics of social change* (pp. 99–115). Palgrave Macmillan. https://doi.org/10.1007/978-3-030-15213-0_7

Film and TV Charity. (2022). *Mental health in the film and TV industry after COVID.* Film+TV Charity. https://filmtvcharity.org.uk/assets/documents/Reports/ Looking-Glass-Report-2021.pdf

French, L. (2014). Gender then, gender now: Surveying women's participation in Australian film and television industries. *Continuum*, 28(2), 188–200. https://doi.org/10.1080/10304312.2014.888040

French, L. (2018). Women in the director's chair: The 'female gaze' in documentary film. In B. Ulfsdotter & A. B. Rogers (Eds), *Female authorship and the documentary image* (pp. 9–21). Edinburgh University Press. https:// www.jstor.org/stable/10.3366/j.ctt1tqxt8w.7

French, L. (2021). *The female gaze in documentary film: An international perspective.* Springer International Publishing AG. https://doi.org/10.1007/978-3-030- 68094-7

Gill, R. (2014). Unspeakable inequalities: Postfeminism, entrepreneurial subjectivity, and the repudiation of sexism among cultural workers. *Social Politics: International Studies in Gender, State & Society*, 21(4), 509–528. https:// doi.org/10.1093/sp/jxu016

Harrison, R. (2023). I won't look: Refusing to engage with gender-based violence in women-led screen media. In K. Boyle and S. Berridge (Eds), *The Routledge Companion to Gender, Media and Violence* (pp. 611–621). Routledge.

Hennekam, S., & Bennett, D. (2017). Sexual harassment in the creative industries: Tolerance, culture and the need for change. *Gender, Work & Organization*, 24(4), 417–434. https://doi.org/10.1111/gwao.12176

Hirdman, Y. (1990). *The gender system: Theoretical reflections on the social subordination of women.* Maktutredningen.

Idås, T., Orgeret, K. S., & Backholm, K. (2020). #MeToo, sexual harassment and coping strategies in Norwegian newsrooms. *Media and Communication*, 8(1), 57–67. https://doi.org/10.17645/mac.v8i1.2529

Keil, M., & Kheriji-Watts, K. (2022). *#MeToo in the arts: From call-outs to structural change.* Shift Culture. https://www.ietm.org/system/files/publications/ SHIFT%20Gender%20and%20Power%20Relations%20Report%202022.pdf

Kleppe, B., & Røyseng, S. (2016). Sexual harassment in the Norwegian theatre world. *Journal of Arts Management, Law & Society*, 46(5), 282–296. https://doi. org/10.1080/10632921.2016.1231645

North, L. (2016). Damaging and daunting: Female journalists' experiences of sexual harassment in the newsroom. *Feminist Media Studies*, 16(3), 495–510. https://doi.org/10.1080/14680777.2015.1105275

O'Brien, A. (2019). *Women, inequality and media work*. Routledge. https://doi.org/10.4324/9780429434815

Ofcom. (2022). *Equity, diversity and inclusion in TV and radio*. Ofcom. https://www.ofcom.org.uk/__data/assets/pdf_file/0029/246854/2021-22-report-diversity-in-tv-and-radio.pdf

Saha, A. (2017). *Race and the cultural industries*. Polity Press.

Scharff, C. M. (2020). From 'not me' to 'me too': Exploring the trickle-down effects of neoliberal feminism. *Rassegna Italiana di Sociologia*, 60(4), 667–691. https://doi.org/10.1423/96111

Simons, M., & Morgan, J. (2018). Changing media coverage of violence against women. *Journalism Studies*, 19(8), 1202–1217. https://doi.org/10.1080/1461670X.2016.1266279

Sørensen, I. E. (2022). Sex and safety on set: Intimacy coordinators in television drama and film in the VOD and post-Weinstein era. *Feminist Media Studies*, 22(6), 1395–1410. https://doi.org/10.1080/14680777.2021.1886141

Sreedharan, C., & Thorsen, E. (2023). Journalism, sexual violence and social responsibility. In K. Boyle and S. Berridge (Eds), *The Routledge Companion to Gender, Media and Violence* (pp. 174–184). Routledge.

Swords, J., & Johns, J. (2023). Deepening precarity—the impact of COVID-19 on freelancers in the UK television industry. *Cultural Trends*, 33, 624–640. https://doi.org/10.1080/09548963.2023.2247375

University College London. (2020, April 27). Creating safe spaces for students in the classroom. *Teaching & Learning*. https://www.ucl.ac.uk/teaching-learning/publications/2020/apr/creating-safe-spaces-students-classroom

Wilkes, M., Florisson, R. & Carey, H. (2020). *The looking glass: Mental health in the UK film, TV and cinema industry*. The Film and TV Charity. https://filmtvcharity.org.uk/wp-content/uploads/2020/02/The-Looking-Glass-Final-Report-Final.pdf

Willekens, M., Siongers, J., & Lievens, J. (2023). Threatening men, threatened women and vice versa: Job and status-related risk factors for experiencing sexual harassment in the media and cultural sectors. *The Social Science Journal*, 1–13. https://doi.org/10.1080/03623319.2023.2232625

Wreyford, N. (2018). *Gender inequality in screenwriting work*. Palgrave Macmillan. https://doi.org/10.1007/978-3-319-95732-6

PART III
CHALLENGING GENDER-BASED VIOLENCE IN ARTISTIC WORK

Introduction

The first two parts of this book aim at identifying the ways gender-based violence is produced, perpetuated and legitimised over time as well as how gender-based violence strongly affects women's reputations as worthy artists as well as their abilities to be trained, to be recruited or to create in their own right. The third part attempts to unveil how gender-based violence might be challenged in artistic and cultural worlds. Denouncing and countering gender-based violence is made difficult, and often even impossible, for victims as well as witnesses due to the asymmetrical power dynamics in favour of (often male) aggressors. However, victims and witnesses, even more so since the beginning of the #MeToo movement, sometimes succeed in developing a range of tactics to navigate these practices, targeting both the emergence of gender-based violence and the fabric of its underlying power relations. Even if those tactics do not yet succeed in questioning the gender order and do not transform the gender hierarchies and social dynamics in place, they do weaken this same gender order and give potential victims room to prevent some sexist and sexual violence from occurring and to even get some recurring offenders to be outed and condemned.

In Chapter 7, Bleuwenn Lechaux examines sexual harassment in New York theatre. She shows that, even though sexual harassment is ingrained in everyday professional practices, more and more often, theatre professionals use both informal methods and more formalised tools to fight sexual harassment: speaking out with other colleagues; sharing stories in support groups and through digital tools; using intimacy coordinators in order 'to create an atmosphere in rehearsal that allows everyone to feel safe to do these very vulnerable things'; mobilising unions, or sometimes even lawyers, to protect victims and to help change the current professional practices allowing for sexual harassment to happen. Even if still limited in their impact, some of those tactics do change the very content of theatrical activities and prevent the occurrence of some unconsented remarks or gestures.

In Chapter 8, focusing on the male-dominated French electronic dance music world, Alice Laurent-Camena shows how, since the #MeToo movement and the spreading of egalitarian norms, some recent public denunciations have led to an ousting of repeat offenders. She first studies denunciations as rumours. Since denials of violence are strong, and the costs of speaking up are high, most denunciations are low-key and circulate among potential victims and witnesses to try to prevent the exposure of female colleagues to male predators. Such denunciations may gain legitimacy when testimonies multiply and are supported by established artists, preferably men. Then, the blame shifts from victims to the accused. But no public stand is taken yet, so as to keep things 'in the family'. Finally, even if rarely, some denunciations become public when audiences and whole professional networks are involved. Although this results in an exclusion of the accused, new obstacles for future claims are produced. Overall, the shared egalitarian ethos of electronic music and the political fight against gender-based violence do not seem to shake the gender order of this art world.

7. Playing Is Not Consenting: Sexual Harassment in New York Theatre[1]

Bleuwenn Lechaux

During an interview conducted in October 2017, a female playwright recounted an offer of assistantship made to her by an artistic director years earlier, when she was studying at the prestigious Juilliard School.[2] After declining his invitation to dinner, she emphasised that she'd always wondered about the real reasons why she hadn't gotten the job:

> Were you only offered that role, that opportunity, because he wanted to sleep with you? So you can't win for losing. Even if you're right and he did it just to get sex, somebody can turn around and say you still don't deserve that position. So, you don't know where you stand. And you can't move forward. (J.P., fifty-one years old, 2017)

Reflecting on this excerpt, and listening once more to the full interview with this playwright, it's not just the residual psychological cost to survivors that stands out, but also the way in which skills, careers and professional content are structured by gender relations. In contrast to media content that reflects the unprecedented nature of the #MeToo movement but tends to extract or dissociate sexual violence from its context of production, in this chapter, I show how routine theatre practices are at the core of this type of violence and, as a consequence,

---

1   This text is a translation of: Lechaux, B. (2022). Jouer n'est pas consentir: Le harcèlement sexuel dans le théâtre new-yorkais. In C. Cavalin, J. Da Silva, P. Delage, I. Despontin-Lefevre, D. Lacombe & B. Pavard (Eds), *Les violences sexistes après #MeToo* (pp. 129–143). Presses des Mines. Minor adjustments have been made to this version.

2   The Juilliard School is a private and prestigious performing arts conservatory in New York City.

    https://doi.org/10.11647/OBP.0436.07

represent obstacles to reporting and condemning wrongdoings. Some professional organisations and public authorities are nevertheless working to address these difficulties alongside the significant awareness-raising work that has been carried out—by women essentially—for many years.

Based on field research conducted in 2015 and 2017 among some twenty female New York theatre professionals, and before and during the reverberations of the 'Weinstein affair', I use a political-sociological lens to show that the sexual harassment that occurs in these art worlds is anchored in established ways of working. Indeed, the organisation and content of professional activities daily perpetuate practices of subordination. In keeping with the research conducted by Catharine A. MacKinnon (1979), sexual harassment is thus analysed here as being inscribed on a *continuum* of gender inequality.

Methodology

I went to New York in October 2017 as part of a decade-long investigation of activism among theatre professionals and, since 2015, an exploration of the trajectories and careers of women working in the theatre sector. It was during this time that the 'Weinstein affair' broke and female interviewees would often bring up the subject of sexual harassment unprompted. Though, this narrative profusion should not overshadow its prior mention, when, during my 2015 research stay, I spoke with several interviewees about the 'scandal' that had occurred within the Wooster group (addressed in the second part of this chapter). This was a delicate subject to broach because, as several people mentioned, the scandal was a sensitive issue that was '*very* complicated' to discuss in the performing arts sector. Whereas this 'affair' received relatively limited media coverage and gave rise to only short accounts, cautious in their conclusions, the series of 'scandals' and 'revelations', notably in the theatre and film industries, unleashed outpourings in the interviews conducted in 2017. Indeed, my interlocuters were likely speaking publicly for the first time about things they had only previously addressed in the context of informal *speak-outs*. This because, they told me, everybody knew what was going on but nobody did anything about it. In an interview with a female director in 2017, she talked about a Facebook article she had read that very morning about a famous actor sexually harassing the seventeen-year-old sister of one of her friends, and then about another friend who had also been sexually harassed by this actor. She came to the conclusion that the 'dam was bursting' and that there wouldn't be any 'good men' left after this deluge of revelations.

The fieldwork I conducted in 2015 and in 2017 over a total duration of seven weeks, together with several interviews carried out in 2020 (by videoconference, due to the COVID-19 pandemic), allow us to explore, through their life stories, the careers—and the discrimination that may have marked them—of twenty-eight New York theatre professionals.[3] Beyond the Weinstein affair, the approach adopted, including repeat interviews with some of them over several years, encouraged the verbalisation of experiences of discriminatory practices. Lastly, far from being the result of an abstract theorisation, the interweaving of sexual harassment on the one hand and other forms of discrimination or, more broadly, professional inequalities specific to the theatre on the other, is the result of research informed by empirical findings. In this respect, the methodological framework developed over the course of previous investigations on the activism of female theatre professionals and the functioning of the related arts worlds—in particular the 126 semi-structured interviews conducted between 2007 and 2010 in Paris and New York as part of my doctoral thesis research—provide a useful foundation for analysing sexual harassment and understanding its structural foundations.

Before exploring how sexual harassment is embedded in New York theatre, I first discuss both the working conditions and gender inequalities that structure New York theatre, as well as outline the legal framework governing sexual harassment in the United States. The second part of this contribution looks at theatrical activity as a

---

3   Each quotation is followed by brackets providing details on the interviewee's profession or position and age at the time of interview.

crucible of gender-based violence in professions whose hierarchies only sharpen the inequalities they already perpetuate. Within an 'embodied job',[4] the exposure and denunciation of sexual harassment are all the more hindered by the fact that the body is not only a work tool, but also the medium of interactions that involve gender relations in their physical intimacy. There are a range of strategies in place to deal with these practices, targeting both the emergence of sexual harassment and the fabric of its underlying power relations. Some of these tools can be applied outside the performing arts sector, whereas others—the focus of the third part of the chapter—have been designed with the specific characteristics of the performing arts in mind.

New York Theatre Worlds and the Framing of Sexual Harassment in the US

In New York, the difference between Broadway, off- and off-off-Broadway refers to geographical zones, aesthetic movements, the number of seats in theatres (respectively 500, between 100 and 499, and less than 100 seats), and to a hierarchy of professional recognition, objectified by salary grids, differentiated legal frameworks and levels of consecration (Broadway being the most prestigious space). In terms of working conditions, Brídín Clements Cotton and Natalie Robin (2024) highlight this sector's generally precarious employment conditions. Namely, consisting of 'a prevalence of extremely underpaid work in the [US] theatrical production field. Many theatrical production employers pay workers, especially designers and assistants, as independent contractors on a fee-based structure that allows them to avoid minimum wage requirements. Workers are not encouraged to track their hours (or at times even encouraged not to) and are often expected to be available for last-minute engagements such as unscheduled meetings or additional rehearsals' (Cotton & Robin, 2024, p. 96).

As this chapter analyses the ways in which power relations form the crucible of sexual harassment, it is important to provide some data on

---

4   I coin this term with reference to Joan Acker's work, specifically her notion of 'disembodied job', which 'symbolises th[e] separation of work and sexuality' (Acker, 1990, p.151).

sex ratios in the artistic direction of performances. To this regard, the 'Historical Perspectives' project, led by Derek Miller and covering the period from 1920 to the present, gathers information about Broadway. It shows that while there has been a general trend towards greater feminisation of directing from the 1990s onwards, parity remains elusive. Indeed, this steady observed rise resulted in only a quarter of plays or musicals being directed by women by 2020. In an effort to remedy the lack of data on the theatre worlds (statistics being mostly devoted to the functioning of Broadway), 'Women Count' reports look at trends in recruitment in off- and off-off-Broadway theatres since 2014. According to the Women Count VI report, the rate of playwrights identified as female or non-binary has oscillated around parity for produced plays: 43% in 2019/20 and close to 60% in 2021/22. The number of female directors in both study seasons (with no non-binary playwrights among the studied productions) rose from 44% in 2019/20 to 54% in 2021/22. Thus, as also noted by Cotton and Robin (2024, p. 95) relative to a 1998 study on women directors and playwrights commissioned by the New York State Council on the Arts stating that the off-off-Broadway participation of women had increased over time, 'it [is] not a lack of women directors and playwrights but a lack of access to the most notable and high-paying jobs'.

A full understanding of the context framing sexual harassment in the United States then requires an examination of its specific legal jurisdiction. As Abigail Saguy (2003, p. 10) shows, within a common-law system such as that underlying the US legal system, and without any specific federal law governing sexual harassment, 'American feminists and lawyers have had to make a legal case in U.S. courtrooms that sexual harassment violates an existing statute. For strategic and intellectual reasons, they chose to build sexual harassment jurisprudence on Title VII [of the Civil Rights Act of 1964]', defining it as a form of employment discrimination on the basis of sex. 'This, in turn, has compelled them to stress certain aspects of the harm of sexual harassment, such as group-based discrimination and employment consequences, and downplay others, such as sexual violence and behavior outside of the workplace' (Saguy, 2003, p. 10).

The legal framework for sexual harassment as workplace discrimination is especially evident in the role of the Equal Employment

Opportunity Commission (EEOC) in the filing of charges (the EEOC is the federal agency responsible for the enforcement of laws prohibiting discrimination in the workplace).[5] Specifically, charges can either be filed directly with the employer (who is then responsible for investigating what happened), or with the EEOC in the absence of any reporting/investigating procedure at the place of employment or when the employer is the harasser. Once a complaint has been filed with the EEOC, the latter informs the employer and conducts an investigation that has several possible outcomes. In the first instance, mediation can be used to try to resolve a dispute. If a solution cannot be found between the two parties and the charge has been filed against a private sector employer, then the EEOC can bring the case before the federal court. The EEOC can also decide to dismiss the charge, but the option of going to court remains available and a right to sue letter can be obtained even before the Commission has completed its investigation.

Two types of sexual harassment are defined: (i) *quid pro quo* (something that is offered in exchange for something else, such as sexual favours for professional opportunities), and (ii) unwelcome verbal and physical sexual conduct in the workplace that creates a 'hostile or offensive working environment'.[6] The latter formulation is of particular scientific interest to the present contribution. Indeed, this specific framework for sexual harassment poses certain challenges where the performing arts are concerned. Not only does this sector lack a strict definition of 'workplace' since rehearsals take place both inside and outside performance spaces, but professional stakes remain high in places that prima facie appear 'non-professional', such as cafés, restaurants or private spaces in which professional networks are created. Furthermore, the classification of discrimination under Title VII is determined by company size (over fifteen employees).[7]

---

5   The EEOC was created one year after the adoption of the Civil Rights Act.
6   The Supreme Court's 1993 decision in *Harris v. Forklift Systems, Inc.* expanded the definition of sexual harassment to include the creation of a hostile environment (Saguy, 2003). A violation of Title VII of the Civil Rights Act is therefore considered to have occurred when there is evidence of the existence of such an environment in the workplace, marked by intimidation, insulting remarks, or ridicule of the targeted person.
7   Nevertheless, recently implemented regulations in New York City extend the scope of application.

Sexual Harassment as a Product
of Professional Practices

John D. Skrentny's research on the entertainment industry points to the existence of practices that are legally sanctionable, but not sanctioned. Skrentny (2013, pp. 200–201) writes of 'acceptable discrimination', a 'cultural allowance for discrimination': 'The culture may say "yes" even when the law says "no"'. The specific features of theatre practices and related artistic content may hinder people from speaking out against and reporting psychological and physical violence. Particularly so in these professions, characterised by hierarchies that sharpen the gender asymmetry already contained therein (see also Chapter 6 in this book).

To begin, an emotional intensity characterises physical proximity in relations onstage. In interviews, the lexical field of touch permeates the accounts of female respondents, or as one female actor put it: 'we all touch each other, hug each other' (female actor, H.G., seventy years old, 2015). In some theatre pieces, intimacy is increased by the subject matter of the scenes, as underlined by a female stage director:

> The subject of what we are working on is deeply emotional and deeply physical and deeply sexual [laughter] [...]. We're dealing with human emotions and people, actors have to strip down to their underpants and get onstage and kiss each other when they don't really know each other. (female stage director, K.R., forty-eight years old, 2017)

At the very minimum, actors are implicitly required to use their 'real' emotions for theatrical purposes. As a female artistic director of a theatre institution underlined, 'the private is really present on the stage because you use your emotions' (M.C., fifty years old, 2015). As a result, as a female stage director put it, 'it's not too surprising that we come up against these problems. I think we are expected to be vulnerable to each other. In the workplace.' In interviews, this emphasis on the emotional is also evoked as that which drew somebody to a career in the arts: an early tapping into the essence of the theatrical project and thriving off a role. There is also admiration, even a fascination with charismatic directors (usually interpreted as male) who are seen as immensely talented, as reflected in an interview with a female playwright: 'That's the idea we have, that of the young male genius who is *obsessed* with his work' (J.P., 2017). The theatrical project gradually becomes the most important thing in the person's life, as they devote themselves to their passion, give themselves over to it. Once the sacrifice has been embraced, the theatrical project becomes all-consuming and takes over everything.

Then, both the temporal and spatial concentration and extension of professional practice thwart the attempt to qualify behaviours as sexual harassment. First, rehearsals and shows intensify the closeness between people working on the same project, and it is implied that this physical complicity between two people enhances artistic performance. The crossover between the personal and the private is even more pronounced when on tour. A female actor described this aspect in the following words:

> When you're in a play, the company becomes your family, at least for a time, taking emotional primacy over anything else, because it's where you spend all your time, and often the drama in the play works out in real life. (H.G., seventy years old, 2015)

Next, what happens offstage in 'society' events, rehearsal spaces or aftershow parties plays a crucial role in careers, professional practices and the creation of networks. Although these offstage spaces may be considered to be professional places, or if not professional, then at least of professional interest, their extensive boundaries make it all the more complicated to define the spatial scope of the second form of sexual harassment outlined above, that of employer (here, mainly a theatre owner or a producer) liability for a 'hostile working environment':

> Because, if it didn't happen in the context of a rehearsal or a performance, then it seems that it's a personal matter, something that has to do with the police [...]. There are things that a theatre union can protect you from, and that doesn't extend to your apartment. (female actor, L.P., fifty-eight years old, 2015)

Another obstacle to sexual harassment becoming a professional issue lies in the value placed on physical beauty, which translates into a stereotyped conception of physical attractiveness that is defined as a 'skill'. This is not exclusive to the stage, but something that the industry values paroxysmally. Several 'scandals' (including *Miss Saigon* in 1991 on Broadway) have revealed the potential incompatibility between the struggle against discrimination (and the possible existence of discrimination in hiring prohibited by Title VII of the Civil Rights

Act) and the preservation of 'artistic freedom' protected by the First Amendment to the American Constitution, opening the way to the legal endorsement of exceptions to discrimination. Several of my female interlocutors spoke of bad experiences as actors when they were given roles that reflected the director's vision of physical attributes that were supposedly 'necessary' for a character. The perpetuation of these stereotypes is also rooted in assumed audience expectations, which are continually being fed.

How the construction of artistic desire is shaped professionally and, more broadly, socially, thus begs further reflection. Far from responding to a deliberate individual choice, the ability to 'create theatrical desire' is considered to be a major professional asset in getting parts and, consequently, establishing a reputation as an artist. 'Playing the game' means wanting to be wanted. A female director emphasised what is expected of female actors in the following words:

> Sexuality. Because they look sexy, because they seem sexy onstage. These are legitimate reasons to hire people. (K.R., forty-eight years old, 2017)

The criteria guiding professional choices are indexed to the forms of identity essentialism they help to reproduce: people seek in women the naturalist bias that is projected onto them, thus helping to reproduce or even reinforce the gender order.

That women are expected to produce what is expected of them is more broadly rooted in professional practices. For example, female playwrights are encouraged to write easily accessible scripts that supposedly reflect 'women's tastes'. One female playwright highlighted the effects of this social expectation of aesthetic conformity:

> That old classic, this whole thing when they go chick lit and all the serious writers are males. You can say two things. You can say, 'You perceive our work to be frivolous', but you can also say 'You've been specifically looking to publish women who've written women's novels'. (J.P., fifty-one years old, 2017)

Professional practices are thus doubly biased. First, in an awareness that narrative complexity is not what is mostly expected from their writing and second, in a perpetuation of female stereotypes that they are required to portray. Both ultimately justify a discrimination that is highly damaging to their professional careers. At play here is the paroxysmal mechanism of the 'self-fulfilling prophecy' and an ensemble of individual discriminations that all feed into one another.

Moreover, insofar as hypersexualised behaviours are quasi-normalised and have become integrated into an ordinary work reality (on this question, see also Chapter 2 and Chapter 4 in this book), the question of what defines appropriate conduct arises once again. In an article in the *New York Times* in 2015, Artie Gaffin, a stage manager with thirty years of experience on Broadway wrote (Healy, 2015):

> I work on a highly sexualised musical, 'Cabaret', where there has always been a certain amount of offstage ass-slapping and nipple-tweaking; Most people have thick skin or they know it's all in fun, not personal.

On the subject of their own or others' intimate relationships, some interviewees exercised caution when expressing their opinion about a clear threshold not to be crossed and the line between consent and harassment. In this regard, a female stage director commented:

> This idea of a casting couch has been around for a long time and we have intimate relationships in the theatre. I mean, the person that was my colleague with whom I started the theatre company, is now my husband. So [laughter], this... the moment of transition from being friends to being boyfriend and girlfriend, it could have been a moment where I reported sexual harassment. I suppose. But it wasn't, because we actually liked each other and wanted to be boyfriend and girlfriend. (female stage director, K.R., forty-eight years old, 2017)

As seen, in organisational terms, responsibility for sexual harassment lies with the employer, and the characterisation of discrimination under Title VII applies only to companies of over fifteen employees. However, many theatre institutions are smaller than this, and the interviewees often lacked knowledge about the law and the relevant authority to contact for this type of discrimination. Moreover, even if those sexually harassed were well informed about the law, it would not be enough to put a stop to it in the performing arts sector. To understand how sexual harassment happens in these worlds, the artistic content associated with it must be embedded in professional power relations. It is through this cognitive process that sexual violence can be understood as the result of an instrumentalisation of artistic practices for domination purposes.

Beyond the legal integration of sexual harassment into a broader set of discriminations, my study, conducted in 2017 while the Weinstein affair was unfolding, also highlights the issue of sexual harassment as violence integrated into a *continuum* of occupational discriminations, themselves shaped by the gender order. Broadly, sexual harassment reflects a structurally asymmetrical situation that replicates pre-existing relationships of domination. Given the gendered relationships of domination within the theatre, it is not surprising that occupational content and occupational functioning become detrimental to women. This is reflected in the words of one female director:

> Sexual harassment is another stage of misogyny, where in the case of... I shouldn't say misogyny, but of power dynamics. It's just another step of one person exerting power over another person. Because of their gender. Or because of their sexuality. Or their age. Or whatever. (K.R., forty-eight years old, 2017)

The emergence of violence depends on gender-structured professional hierarchies and positions of prestige (e.g., male directors/female actors; male employers/female employees; see also Chapter 2, Chapter 3 and Chapter 5 in this book). Aware of these inequalities, a Black playwright and director recounts his own moral dilemma when, in 2001, he interviewed several times to become a film producer's assistant at a major film and television production and distribution company. His comments reflect both the professional opportunity he perceived and his desire not to contribute to the sexual violence that the company was actively covering up:

> At the end of my fourth interview, the young woman said: 'OK, last question before you meet X [the film producer]: are you willing to do absolutely anything to become a Y's [major film and television production and distribution company's] executive?' And I was like twenty-five, and I said, 'no'. And for years, I kept thinking, 'If I'd said yes, I would have gotten the job', but now I know I'm very lucky I didn't get the job. (F.T., forty years old, 2015)

Sexual harassment is thus part of a career-shaping system of power that can be both a boost through the promise of integration into professional networks, or a hindrance through the possibility of harming a reputation. The subordination that this professional order contains is accentuated by a principle that guides the inner workings of art worlds: subjective choice (hiring or not hiring a female actor, for example), which makes for relatively arbitrary recruitment. Since the primary criterion for hiring is 'to serve a character', obtaining sexual favours can become a bargaining chip. With no safety nets and in a highly competitive market, the implicit or explicit threat of unemployment can function as a professional regulation tool. It should moreover be added that dual positioning in a career (beginning/end of career), often correlated with statutory position (job insecurity/security), and in a professional sub-space (fringe/mainstream theatre), makes reporting possible to various degrees: it can encourage people to speak out publicly or, on the contrary, jeopardise the very possibility of identifying the issue and the likelihood of a complaint being successful. [8]

Taken together, these relationships of domination represent a barrier to reporting possible manipulations of theatre standards as actual domination, as documented in an interview with the female artistic director of a professional theatre organisation:

> I had a friend, this was a long time ago, she was in a show with a very, it was a very well-known director. And so she was new in the field, and he was demonstrating something, and he slapped her across the face to *demonstrate*. She lost... like it was... he knocked her off her feet. And she was like, 'What do I do? I'm gonna get fired. Who are they gonna believe?' He's, it was... horrible. And he did it in the name of 'I'm going to demonstrate something', and he slapped her across the face, like threw her off balance, it was hard, everybody heard it, but she had no power in that room. None at all. (M.C., fifty years old, 2015)

Notably, the fictitious alibi can be used as a defence strategy. Indeed, when Ben Vereen was accused of sexual misconduct, he explained that he wanted to create an environment that replicated the themes addressed in 'Hair', a 1969 musical that includes full-frontal nudity (Puente, 2018).

Moreover, the progressiveness supposedly inherent in 'open' sexuality, which takes the form of an injunction, is reminiscent of that of the gendered cost of sexual liberation observed in France (Lechaux & Sommier, 2018). An activist from the Guerrilla Girls On Tour collective stated in an interview I conducted with her in 2017:

---

8   There exist significant differences between Broadway, off-Broadway and off-off-Broadway. If a theatre production takes place on Broadway, then it falls within the scope of discrimination under Title VII of the Civil Rights Act and benefits from the social protection offered by a union such as Equity, which in 2018 represented over 51,000 actors and stage managers in the United States.

And in the arts, people feel that they always have these certain liberties, like 'We can approach women, we can do plays with sexuality and we have to be very open'.

Being open can, however, be tantamount to getting pushed around. From this point of view, a culinary metaphor, which came up several times in an interview with a female actor, equates to a disembodiment, allowing the person who is assaulted to be considered a consumable commodity:

> In all of these reports of these cases of sexual harassment, the person who's doing it absolutely does not recognise the other person as a person [...]. That's not a human interaction, that's hunger. That's what you do at midnight in your refrigerator. When you can't stand it anymore and you eat three quarts of ice cream. The ice cream, those women are the ice cream. (female actor, H.G., seventy-two years old, 2017)

Gender dissymmetry, and in particular confining female characteristics to outdated stereotypes—which then need to be adhered to in order to 'succeed'—is so embedded in the rules of the game that not being wanted ends up meaning not being competent. The actor continued:

> And the idea that somehow women are dangerous, untrustworthy and *ask* for it. That's the great defense. 'Well, she was wearing a short skirt'. So then what you're saying to me is that men are incapable of controlling themselves, that besides everything else, we have to look out for them, we have to protect them from themselves, which is what that argument is. So that all of the responsibility is ours.

Women are then faced with a double constraint: the fact of having to anticipate how much seduction is required professionally (by playing the game) means that they also bear the social responsibility for an assault.[9]

Fighting Sexual Harassment

To fight sexual harassment, theatre professionals use both informal methods and more formalised tools, some of which aim to change

---

9   On seduction as a constraint for women in everyday working relationships within the art worlds, see notably Buscatto, 2009.

the very content of theatrical activities and prevent the occurrence of unconsented remarks or gestures.

At first, the struggle is low-key: women tell their stories and bear witness in speak-outs or consciousness-raising groups, which are often 'single-sex'. The speech that circulates there, and which can consist of 'rumors' (see Chapter 8 in this book), is a political action in its own right (Delage, 2017) insofar as it acts on the gender system. These instances give credit to women's voices and help to circulate information on 'reputations' for preventive purposes, as underlined by a female playwright:

> And honestly, that's what we've always been doing by whispering to each other, 'That guy's a sleaze, don't go there'. 'If you say no to him he'll be rude, but just say no, you won't lose your job'. Or 'If you say no you will lose your job'. That information has always been passed around. (J.P., fifty-one years old, 2017)

Support groups can then become more formalised, fulfilling the purpose of healing survivors' wounds, notably through the intervention of psychologists. The legitimacy of speaking out as a collective action has been strengthened with the emergence of the #MeToo movement—even if we know that women talk long before they are listened to.

Furthermore, the use of digital tools such as Callisto, an application launched in 2015 for reporting sexual assault and that matches presumed victims, is seen as a way of overcoming a threefold difficulty. This digital tool aims, first off, to break victims' isolation, whose fragmentation is exacerbated by the multitude of professional structures that employ them and short employment contracts, leading to the decollectivisation of forms of combatting sexual harassment. Secondly, the application avoids a situation in which any one person bears the financial and psychological costs and consequences of reporting an assault. Lastly, it allows for 'strength in numbers', thereby making a person's report more credible and robust, and increasing the likelihood that they will be believed and not suspected of lying about a practice denounced as discriminatory. This technology is mainly used in universities, but in March 2018, playwright Julia Jordan, among others, organised a meeting to see if it could be transposed to the theatre industry. In practice, the victim writes an account of the assault and the application keeps a record of it over a long period of time, such that when another victim names the same aggressor, a Callisto agent can offer to put them in contact to discuss how they might wish to follow up on their respective experiences (file a complaint, contact the press, sue).

This discreet matching also aims to give more weight and credibility to the action and, as such, mitigates the potentially harmful effects on an artist's reputation after speaking out. In addition, the keeping of a digital record and the repetition of reports help to diminish, at least in the university setting, the risk of the identity of a harasser being concealed behind the generational renewal of student cohorts, erasing traces of aggression and consequently leading to their reoccurrence:

> So to be able to say it, 'There're thirty other women who said it', 'Oh yes, you know what, when we were doing the fight scene', or 'When we were doing that love scene, he actually put his hand inside my panties'. And all of a sudden, there are twenty people who say, 'You know, during that scene, he was grabbing my breast', and he's like, 'That was an accident, I just brushed her'. You know, all of a sudden, it paints a different picture [...]. You can change people to do the right thing. Shame is a powerful human thing. (J. P., fifty-one years old, 2017)

Other tools aim to mitigate the risks involved in performing arts practices by offering a guarantee of preserving emotional safety through learning what we might call "stage consent." One such example is Intimacy Directors International, a non-profit organisation providing training on safe rehearsal and performance practices during scenes of intimacy. They have five pillars: context, consent, communication, choreography and closure. Based on these pillars, each scene of intimacy is discussed beforehand between the parties involved in order to reach a mutual understanding and agreement about its development and exclude any improvised gesture that might surprise or offend one of the parties. Martial analogies permeate several of the interviews conducted, notably used to emphasise the unacceptable nature of violence of any kind. In the words of one playwright, the fictional alibi should no more apply to a fight scene than to a sex scene:

> If an actor on stage is playing a fight scene, and he's supposed to be acting out a strangulation, and someone is actually strangled and hurt, then nobody's going to say 'I was too much in character', they'd think you're crazy and you can't act anymore because you're crazy. It's the same with sex. (R.B., fifty years old, 2017)

During the interview, she mentioned having recently become aware of this training, and expressed her interest in using it, much like choreography for fight scenes, in order 'to create an atmosphere in rehearsal that allows everyone to feel safe to do these very vulnerable things'.

As much as my research highlights the process of 'cumulative disadvantage' (Blau & Otis, 1967) that activates and perpetuates discrimination against women, it also reveals the actions aimed at fighting both the occurrence of such discrimination and the inequalities that underpin it. Acknowledging that there is an overlap between different forms of gender discrimination, some initiatives focus on fighting the glass ceiling as a means of preventing sexual assault. Unions have also stepped up their efforts to fight sexual harassment. In February 2018, Actors' Equity Executive Director Mary McColl published a column in *Variety* magazine recommending that employers seeking to reduce harassment hire women in leadership positions. Often then, the struggle against sexual harassment is not waged in isolation from the *continuum* of inequalities on which it lies. For instance, the above-mentioned playwright, Julia Jordan, is not only among the founders of the Lilly Awards,[10] but also one of the leaders of the Count,[11] helped draft the Statement of Principles on Harassment,[12] and is the originator of the study conducted by Emily Sands at Princeton.[13] In an interview conducted in 2017, she mentioned how difficult it was, before 2017, to get unions to address the issue of sexual harassment. By contrast, the Weinstein scandal has led to the implementation of many of the conditions she had previously proposed to union leaders.

Moreover, reinforcement of state and municipal laws (New York State and City) is expected to accompany the aforementioned professional provisions. The New York State budget bill for 2019 requires employers to take a series of measures to address and prevent sexual harassment. On April 11, 2018, the New York City Council passed the Stop Sexual

10   The organisation was founded in 2010 to honour and reward the work of women in the American theatre.
11   See https://the-lillys.org/the-count-2
12   Drawn up in December 2014 by a group of theatre professionals in consultation with attorney Norman Siegel.
13   Emily Sands' thesis (2009) establishes econometric measures demonstrating the existence of prejudicial discrimination against female playwrights in American theatre.

Harassment in NYC Act, explicitly stating that protections against sexual harassment extend to all employees. Here, the application is broader than that provided under Title VII of the Civil Rights Act, at least concerning the specific discrimination of sexual harassment, and thus also applies to small theatre collectives. On June 27, 2018, in the wake of #MeToo and ahead of the formal obligation to comply with state and municipal legislation, the Broadway League (the national trade association of Broadway) proposed a training course in partnership with the Actors Fund 'specifically related to and focused upon employer responsibilities'. In January 2018, the Off-Broadway League trade association formed a sexual harassment task force and began working towards adopting an anti-harassment policy and code of conduct for its members, in addition to plans to hold training in the months that followed.

However, legal measures alone are not enough to put a stop to conduct that is embedded in the gender order described above. The use of tools aimed at countering sexual harassment comes up against the same obstacles that determined the latter's emergence. That is, a gender-structured job market and strong personalisation of hiring power—linked to the subjectivity that guides artistic choices—where the fragile definition of rules framing interactions seems to depend on individual willingness. Collectively undetermined, the delimitation of boundaries of what is acceptable and what is condemned then hinges on how the leader of an artistic project perceives their professional role:

> When I'm working on very physical work, I will often just check in with people. Like, 'Does that feel okay? Do you feel...' Because part of [the work] is about being physically safe and that's something that I have to be really on top of. [...]. Actors will not complain. They will not stop things because they don't want to cause problems. So I feel like I'm very aware of needing to just tell them over and over again, 'Don't do anything that doesn't feel safe, stop things if you don't feel safe'. You have to let people know that there's space for that. (R.M., fifty years old, 2017)

The relationship of trust forged within an artistic collective can nevertheless give rise to conflicts of loyalty when accusations of violence arise. This was the case in what became a major scandal involving the Wooster Group theatre company, reported in a *New York Times* article entitled 'Sex and Violence, Beyond the Script' (Healy, 2015), about actor Scott Shepherd's physical assaults of his then-partner, actor Marin Ireland, during the London rehearsals of the play *Troilus and Cressida*. Though highly sensitive, the public scandal did lead to a collaboration between lawyers and theatre professionals, one result of which was the drawing up of 'statements of harassment'. After a meeting on December 4, 2017 in the Public Theater in New York City to discuss tools for combatting sexual harassment 'post-#MeToo', Marin Ireland and civil liberties lawyer Norman Siegel launched the Human Resources for the Arts project on January 16, 2018, the aim being to create a *pro bono* mediation system (with a mediator not working in the theatre worlds), in particular for microaggressions.

Conclusion

Making an issue visible does not automatically mean that it will be addressed. Though, the exposure of criminal offences has pushed the issue of sexual harassment to the top of the public agenda, accelerating the implementation of measures to stop it. While procedures for fighting sexual harassment have been formalised (the Callisto project and tool, intimacy direction through choreographic techniques, *pro bono* mediation), legal measures nevertheless seem to be of little help in worlds where hiring practices remain governed by the uncertainty and arbitrariness of subjective artistic choices. From this point of view, and within the limits of the law in the fight against discrimination in theatre (as also highlighted elsewhere, see Lechaux, 2021), sexual harassment is no exception.

Faced with the *continuum* of gender-based inequalities, the struggle against sexual harassment must be accompanied by actions targeting all the professional practices that perpetuate endemic violence daily (Saguy, 2018). This arises as early as the training period for apprentices in artistic workplaces, where the 'constraints of the vocation' prevail and the necessary endorsement of the master already sets up a professional interest in subordination (Trachman, 2018, p. 139). Gender-based violence is also deeply embedded in local contexts, upon which the possibilities and modalities of denunciation depend (see Chapter 8 in this book).

References

Acker, J. (1990). Hierarchies, jobs, bodies: A theory of gendered organizations. *Gender & Society*, 4(2), 139–158. https://doi.org/10.1177/089124390004002002

Blau, P. M., & Otis, D. (1967). *The American occupational structure*. John Wiley & Sons.

Buscatto, M. (2009). Femme et artiste: (dé)jouer les pièges des 'féminités'. In I. Berrebi-Hoffmann (Ed.), *Politiques de l'intime* (pp. 265–280). La Découverte.

Clements Cotton, B., & Robin, N. (2024). *Theatre work: Reimagining the labor of theatrical production*. Routledge. https://doi.org/10.4324/9781003330394

Delage, P. (2017). *Violences conjugales: Du combat féministe à la cause publique*. Presses de Sciences Po. https://doi.org/10.3917/scpo.delag.2017.01

Healy, P. (2015, March 15). Sex and violence, beyond the script. *The New York Times*. https://www.nytimes.com/2015/03/15/theater/sex-and-violence-beyond-the-script.html

Lechaux, B. (2021). Distinguer sans discriminer? Le combat paradoxal du théâtre new-yorkais. *Critique Internationale*, 93(4), 115–136. https://doi.org/10.3917/crii.093.0118

Lechaux, B., & Sommier, I. (2018). Quand le 'je' s'oppose au 'nous' (et vice versa). In O. Fillieule, S. Béroud, C. Masclet, I. Sommier, & Collectif Sombrero (Eds), *Changer le monde, changer sa vie: Enquête sur les militantes et les militants des années 1968 en France* (pp. 513–544). Actes Sud.

MacKinnon, C. A. (1979). *Sexual harassment of working women*. Yale University Press. Puente, M. (2018, January 5). Broadway star Ben Vereen accused of sexual assault during production of 'Hair'. *USA Today*. https://eu.usatoday.com/story/life/2018/01/05/broadway-star-ben-vereen-accused-sexual-assaultduring-production-hair/1007489001/

Saguy, A. C. (2003). *What is sexual harassment? From Capitol Hill to the Sorbonne*. University of California Press. https://doi.org/10.1525/9780520936973

Saguy, A. C. (2018). Europeanization or national specificity? Legal approaches to sexual harassment in France, 2002–2012. *Law & Society Review*, 52(1), 140–171. https://doi.org/10.1111/lasr.12313

Sands, E. (2009). *Opening the curtain on playwright gender: An integrated economic analysis of discrimination in American theater* (Undergraduate senior thesis, Princeton University, Department of Economics).

Skrentny, J. D. (2013). *After civil rights: Racial realism in the new American workplace*. Princeton University Press. https://doi.org/10.23943/princeton/9780691159966.001.0001

Trachman, M. (2018). L'ordinaire de la violence: Un cas d'atteinte sexuelle sur mineure en milieu artistique. *Travail, genre et sociétés*, 40, 131–150. https://doi.org/10.3917/tgs.040.0131

8. From Rumours to Calling Out: Denunciations of Gender-Based Violence in Electronic Dance Music in France

Alice Laurent-Camena

The complexity here is—and I think it's not just related to sexual violence—it's an environment where everything is brushed under the rug.[1]

Thomas (DJ and music producer, aged thirty-four—2023)[2]

I tell myself that at some point it's going to calm down but obviously it's not. It's... hell. Every week something new comes out.

Marc (DJ and artistic director, aged thirty-five—2022)

Introduction

How can these two artists, both relatively well established in the networks of cooperation of the French electronic 'art world' (Becker, 1982), make such contradictory statements relative to denunciations of gender-based violence? During extensive fieldwork in France, this tension emerged time and again. During our conversation, Thomas used the word 'omerta' to describe the situation, a term originally associated with a code of silence in secret societies. Marc instead described the frequency with which he heard reports of violent colleagues as a 'hecatomb'. Such a label is symbolically charged. It conveys the idea of numerous acts of violence committed by fellow artists, but also the idea that the thereby

---

1   All quotes were collected in French and translated by the author.
2   To preserve confidentiality and without affecting the analysis, the names of interviewees have been changed, as well as minor details regarding their socio-demographic profiles.

    https://doi.org/10.11647/OBP.0436.08

denounced artists face a dramatic ending (to their careers, in our case). I found myself constantly caught between two empirical observations: abusers in this art world are denounced in the name of gender equality, but testimonies of violence are concurrently silenced. I explore this seemingly paradoxical tension, which, upon deeper analysis, reveals the ambivalence of social change regarding gender relations.

On the one hand, this social world is rife with gender-based violence, which, following Liz Kelly's conceptualisation (1987), can be analysed as part of a *continuum*. My research reveals that female and LGBTQ artists are very likely to encounter violence throughout their careers. These violent experiences span a variety of contexts, all linked to the interviewees' activities as DJs: as frequent partygoers, in their day-to-day professional activities and in conjugal relationships with other members of the scene.[3] The concept of 'gender-based violence'—contrary to the phrasing 'sexist and sexual violence' that prevails in the art world— enables us to conceive violence as rooted in gender relations and as exacerbated manifestations of gender inequalities (Brown et al., 2020). That is, these forms of violence should be understood not as isolated incidents but as elements reminding individuals of the hierarchical and dichotomous 'gender order' (Connell, 1987) in place, as well as ordinary forms of practice of this order enabling its maintain.

On the other hand, fighting gender-based violence is a major political theme in the French electronic music world. Since the transnational #MeToo movement,[4] several cases have emerged within this professional space. As documented in the previous chapters of this book, media coverage is but the tip of the iceberg when it comes to gender-based violence and its embedment in specific social contexts. The most widely publicised case concerning the French electronic music world broke in May 2020. The four denounced members of the Parisian collective *Qui Embrouille Qui* saw their careers come to an abrupt halt despite their

---

3   Nearly all of the interviewees is or has been in a conjugal relationship with other professionals (artists or 'backup personnel') during their career. This endogamy has similarly been observed in other art worlds, such as that of jazz (Buscatto, 2021).

4   At the end of 2017, close to a hundred women used this hashtag to speak up against film producer Harvey Weinstein. The transnational developments of the #MeToo movement are considered unprecedented, in particular in France, where recent works analyse and question its impact (see, for instance, Cavalin et al., 2022).

central positions in the artistic networks of the time. Yet, how can this environment, a male-dominated professional world operating around informal networks and reputations, be the site of denunciations that 'work'? That is, of denunciations leading to sanctioning—by exclusion—of the alleged authors of violence? This chapter seeks to answer this question.

In addressing denunciation as a sociological object, I draw on the work of Luc Boltanski et al. (1984), who situate the latter as social process on a *continuum* between the denunciation of an individual and the denunciation of an injustice (here, gender-based violence as a whole). According to this theoretical framework, a denunciation corresponds to a 'system of places' bringing into play a whistle-blower (or denunciator), a victim, an accused, and a recipient (e.g., the public) of the denunciation who judges what has been reported. In this 'actancial system,' a denunciation can only be received as normal and valid—from a sociological perspective—if it leads to a 'generalisation' process. To be considered rightful, claims and testimonies must be linked to values shared by the public. As set forth by Boltanski, the social positioning of the different actors distributed in this system of places has some importance, though is far from the only determinant of the success of a given denunciation.[5] The French electronic music world offers a heuristic case to explore the effects of denunciations of a specific gendered form of injustice, and what these effects tell us about the gendered organisation of a given social world.

The art world under consideration here is relatively homogeneous as far as the denunciation of violence as a gender-based form of injustice is concerned. 'Sexist and sexual' forms of violence are described in exactly these terms, in ordinary discourse as well as in official statements, and are widely considered a social problem. This is, firstly, because overall

---

5   It would be a stretch to say that Boltanski's theory is crafted with a gendered lens. Still, his article 'La dénonciation', co-written with Yann Darré and Marie-Ange Schiltz, presents several empirical elements regarding denunciations of gendered forms of injustice, analysed in parallel to other causes that have gained some (ambivalent) legitimacy at the political level, such as racism. The authors also mention that women, like other social categories (the elderly, members of the working class, etc.), tend to lack the 'authority' to defend another individual (Boltanski et al., 1984, p. 32). They do not, however, push this specific argument further, gender being treated as an illustration among others of their theory, more than a sociological object of inquiry in itself.

sensitivity to violence has changed over the last decade in the French context (Brown et al., 2020)—a sensitivity that has continued to evolve in the wake of the #MeToo movement (Cavalin et al., 2022). Secondly, this art world, though still largely male-dominated, is widely touched by the spreading of egalitarian norms in the workplace (Bereni & Jacquemart, 2018). With regard to gender-based violence, these norms manifest in multiple ethical charters aimed at preventing the occurrence of violence in party spaces. Meanwhile, norms related to gender equality are expressed through the art world's 'egalitarian ethos', a concept Isabelle Clair (2011, p. 80) employs to describe how an ideal of gender equality spreads in ordinary practices, while at the same time reaffirming the idea of differentiation and 'complementarity between sexes'. [6] Here, I use this egalitarian ethos as a tool to investigate how the 'professional ethos' of individuals involved in the art world is enriched by this dimension, conveying the general idea of an environment 'naturally' sensitive to social inequalities,[7] though without fundamentally disturbing its gendered organisation.

In order to go beneath the 'egalitarian surface coating'[8] (Cavalin et al., 2022) of denunciations of violence in a general sense, it is useful to thoroughly analyse the different *practices of denunciation* at play. For, if multiple artistic groups post on social networks or display slogans in clubs such as 'all forms of violence and discrimination are banned', what actually happens when peers are singled out and accused of violent behaviours? I argue that public denunciations resulting in professional sanctions (i.e., exclusion from the musical scene) must necessarily be situated relative to all the other forms of denunciation that do not have this degree of social validity. I present three categories, or stages, in an itinerary of denunciations: rumour, internal denunciation and eventually public denunciation—or what interviewees referred to as 'calling out'. At each stage, a set of obstacles tends to delegitimise the claims in question.

---

6   This theoretical proposition is based on her study of young people's sexual and
     conjugal relationships in France.
7   In his thesis, Andreas Rauh Ortega (2018, p. 59) identifies a similar naturalisation of
     egalitarian ideas in Great Britain: 'Mythical ideals about community and sociality in
     EDM [Electronic Dance Music] are associated with notions of a common pursuit of
     pleasure and egalitarianism'.
8   *'Vernis égalitaire'* in French.

A club-centred, precarious and male-dominated art world

Electronic dance music covers a 'myriad of subgenres' (Attias et al., 2013, p.2) from 'techno' to 'house' or 'drum and bass', and a wide range of events—legal or otherwise, free or paid access, in clubs or outdoor venues (Picaud, 2023). One of its core features is music played by a DJ (who is considered an artist) in front of an audience, engaging people in dancing. Electronic music is therefore intertwined with local party spaces and practices. In France, these practices are mainly the purview of young adults, while venues, especially clubs, are concentrated in urban areas. Artists themselves typically first encounter electronic music through partying before engaging in amateur DJing or music producing and then possibly making a career out of it. Indeed, there is an absence of institutions conditioning entry into this art world. Contrary to other artistic spaces considered in this book (see, e.g., visual arts as analysed in Chapter 4 and Chapter 5 in this book), no dedicated school or diploma are relevant to its members. Rather, entry and holding a position depend primarily on informal processes. Like most art worlds, electronic music is a precarious and competitive environment (Jouvenet, 2006). DJs draw their income from gigs in specialised clubs and festivals and tour each weekend from city to city, in France or in neighbouring countries. The vast majority are not renowned outside the art world and can be considered 'ordinary' artists (Perrenoud & Bois, 2017). Some make additional money as support personnel (Becker, 1982) for fellow musicians. They may organise or curate parties, 'manage' the career of a more settled DJ or work as sound technicians. Others supplement their income with less prestigious jobs such as bartending.

Furthermore, this art world is male-dominated. Though quantitative data is difficult to produce, there is a clear predominance of male artists on stage; in twelve major Parisian clubs in 2018, 90% of the artists performing were male and 10% female (Picaud, 2020). In the case of French electronic music festivals over the course of 2013–2023, 70.5% of the considered live acts were by male artists, 19.9% by female artists, 0.7% non-binary artists and 6.7% mixed genders.⁹ From an organisational standpoint and following Joan Acker (1990), this art world can likewise be considered male-dominated: gender being embedded in the ways activities are organised and hierarchised, starting with the construction of technicity and artistic talent as masculine attributes (see Attias et al., 2013; Thornton, 1995).

Methods

This study is based on three years of ethnographic immersion from 2020 to 2023 among eighty electronic musicians (between the ages of twenty-three and fifty-four) in five different French cities. In addition to shadowing them in their day-to-day professional activities, I carried out in-depth interviews with fifty-one of them, chosen in light of the artistic networks I progressively identified during fieldwork. Of these interviewees, twenty-six identify as male and twenty-five as female, all of them cisgender at the time of the study.¹⁰ During interviews, I did not directly ask about gender-based violence, with the exception of a single and broadly formulated question at the end of our conversation. The goal of this strategy was to leave space to assess who speaks about violence, how and when.

A first probable consequence of this approach is that the (already numerous) accounts of violence reported are potentially underestimated. Nonetheless, it allows us to inductively construct (Glaser & Strauss, 1967) the question of denunciation as a sociological object. A first empirical clue was the fact that most women spoke of experiences of violence that they (or some of their close colleagues) had experienced during their careers. Meanwhile, the discourse of male interviewees

---

9   A little over 2% were 'non-identified' in terms of gender of the performer(s). The full extent considered consists of seventeen festivals and 3,158 acts over this decade. The survey is conducted annually by 'female:pressure', a worldwide network active in promoting women and gender minorities in electronic music.

10 Only one of these men identifies as gay while seven of the interviewed women identify as bisexual, lesbian or queer—though not all of them are 'out' in the workplace. This distribution was not intentional, nor was it meant to be representative of the population of electronic music artists. Nevertheless, the relative absence of gay or queer men and the significant presence of non-heterosexual women helps to situate how gender and sexuality intertwine in denunciations of violence in male-dominated and heterosexual-centred environments.

relative to 'sexist and sexual violence' mostly revolved around its general condemnation, on the relaying of 'internal rumours'[11] and moral remarks on the 'importance' or the 'limitations' of calling out as a form of social justice in the art world.

With specific regard to the denunciation of gender-based violence, my analysis refers to twenty-two cases encountered during fieldwork: seven denunciations as rumours, ten internal denunciations and five public denunciations. I identified these cases during fieldwork and furthered their analysis by collecting press and public online statements, when relevant. Of these, twenty concern men accused of violence towards women and two involve women accused of violence against women.[12] These cases are not meant to be representative but rather to contribute to a better understanding of denunciation processes in this art world. They are furthermore grounded on the broader empirical data I collected on the subject: artists' testimonies of violence during interviews and ordinary discourses regarding denunciation practices, on the part of both men and women.

Denunciation as a Rumour: A 'Code of Silence'?

Sexual and Professional Reputations at Play: The 'Borderline Guy'[13]

It's true that some behaviours are tolerated, behaviours that aren't at all healthy. And then, there's where you draw the line with what should be denounced, what's really—well, what you can reproach. Because there are still people who behave—well, badly. But you don't actually say anything to them. Because it's a party. But in fact, they do it all the time. [...] And everyone kind of excuses it. (Dana, DJ, aged thirty—2021)

---

11 In varying degrees of detail, depending on the position of the denunciator and the denounced in the art world's hierarchies, and on the ethnographic relation with each interviewee.

12 This does not mean that men (cisgender or transgender, 'passing' for heterosexual or not) are not subject to gender-based violence in art worlds. On the contrary, and as suggested by Mathilde Provansal (Chapter 4), further research on the interplay between specific forms of violence and hierarchies among masculinities (Connell, 1995) would be fruitful for a more global understanding of gender-based violence.

13 The term 'borderline' was used by interviewees, mostly in its shortened form 'border'. The expression refers to an individual whose actions (in particular their sexually-charged interactions with peers or members of the public) are considered questionable though tolerated.

I heard multiple remarks during fieldwork similar to Dana's thoughts on denunciation. The terms 'omerta' or 'code of silence'[14] were frequently evoked when reflecting on the possibility of denouncing violent behaviours attributed to colleagues. Strikingly, they are also mobilised in other artistic contexts, such as the French opera (see Chapter 2 in this book). In a literal sense, they indicate a commitment to secrecy. Yet, a certain paradoxical tension characterises denunciation as rumour: even though untold, rumours seem to be 'everywhere'. As some interviewees put it: 'You always hear stories—stories about borderline guys' (Jeanne, DJ and producer, aged twenty-six), or 'As I'm starting to know some people, I've started hearing stories. [About] guys still doing their job. Club promoters, festival promoters, artists, all three. Everywhere' (Loic, DJ and producer, aged twenty-five). An attentiveness here to rumours as denunciations in and of themselves is grounded in gender studies and feminist scholarly works on gender-based violence.[15] In taking these initial clues and hints seriously, the ethnographer can begin to link recurring elements to a broader pattern—the *continuum* that denunciations of gender-based violence follow in a given art world.

First of all, though rumours largely concerned the sexual reputations of men, they were far from being systematically formulated in negative terms. The accused is most often categorised as someone who 'likes to flirt'. For example, one of my interlocutors asked a member of her collective to stop working with a particular artist at an upcoming event coordinated by the group. She had witnessed his 'sexist behaviour' at another festival organised by peers. Her colleague argued, 'He's not a bad guy, he just likes to party'.[16] Despite her request, the DJ in question attended the event and was assigned a shared room with a female staff member.[17] Though, rumours can also have a negative connotation, where

---

14   'Loi du silence' in French.

15   On this subject, see in particular *Complaint!* by feminist scholar Sara Ahmed and her reflections on how 'complaints are not heard and how we are not heard when we are heard as complaining' (Ahmed, 2021, p. 3).

16   This same individual had already been accused of violence by a woman in another city, two years prior to this exchange.

17   These sorts of accommodation arrangements are frequent, especially in the case of small collectives and organisations that must often navigate tight budgets when promoting in specialised clubs. They are also based on the idea that artists of the same collective are 'family' who can share amongst them a room or beds. However, as confided by different female interviewees, they represent a potential context for

the individual in question is described as 'borderline' or 'edgy'. These expressions are as recurrent as they are revealing. Here, 'borderline' doesn't refer to the personality disorder but to someone whose actions are borderline permissible in a given social context. The individuals under study thus euphemistically use a term that materialises a disputed boundary between attitudes considered unsavoury but tolerated and actions considered unacceptable because socially associated with violence.

While rumours relate to the accused's sexual reputation (not fundamentally threatened by these 'illegitimate' claims), the victim's reputation also comes into play. Take, for example, Manon, a young DJ who began to play in parties in her hometown when she was eighteen. As is common in medium and large-scale French towns, she began her career by progressively becoming part of local collectives, composed mostly of older male DJs and music producers. She was sexually harassed by a member of one of these groups,[18] but also experienced how men's negative sexual reputations do not necessarily tarnish their professional reputations:

> Everyone knew that the guy who said those things about me was a misogynistic bastard. And when I saw Dean [a colleague who had witnessed the harassment in question] a couple of years later, he was like 'Ah! But everyone knew! And he's even been charged for sexual assault'. Except that since guys always have each other's backs, nobody voices anything when something problematic is said. When the guy was calling me a slut everywhere he went, nobody agreed with him but nobody confronted him. Everyone continued to validate his totally outrageous comments about women. (Manon, DJ, aged twenty-four—2022)

A second characteristic of denunciation as rumour concerns the caution with which accusations are relayed. By definition, rumours are only heard in informal spaces and between people who know each other sufficiently well to exchange this confidence. When two individuals are discussing a situation, the identity of the victim (who is not yet completely considered as such) is kept quiet, all the more so when there

---

sexual forms of gender-based violence.

18 This harassment included shaming her technical skills in public and nicknaming her 'the bitch' (*la salope* in French).

is a sociologist in the room.[19] I started hearing rumours more explicitly at the end of my fieldwork, primarily during interviews. As I had carefully separated the different artistic networks I followed and studied, I was even privy to rumours denouncing some of my male interviewees.[20] These circumstances—though uncomfortable at times in terms of fieldwork relations and the moral dilemmas I faced as a feminist (Clair, 2016)—were an important indicator of data saturation.

The 'Killjoy': Obstacles to the Social Validation of the Denunciation as Rumour

This caution in the way denunciations are passed on as rumours is tied to the different costs incurred for victims and whistleblowers. If gender-based violence is embedded in the way art worlds operate (see Chapter 7 and Chapter 2 in this book), the possibilities and modalities of denunciation are also embedded in these contexts and shaped by the constraints they impose. Here, three levels of obstacles intertwine.

Firstly, at the subjective level, speaking up against a colleague presupposes that the victim considers the offence 'serious enough':

> Frankly, I hesitated a lot about [a promoter who harassed her by text message]. To not talk about it publicly, because nothing serious happened, I didn't feel in danger. I wasn't alone with him in a hotel room, you know. I didn't experience any trauma. It's just that... I think it's very edgy. In my opinion, the guy must be *really borderline* [emphasised]. (Naomi, DJ and producer, aged twenty-six—2022)

Naomi did end up telling her closest female colleagues about her exchanges with this promoter—the denunciation then circulating in 'preventive' mode, much like the 'whisper circles' described by

---

19   For this reason, I ultimately considered only seven of the rumour cases for which I had gathered sufficient material. My claim that denunciations as rumours are potentially numerous is grounded on the different testimonies of violence reported individually by artists during interviews.

20   Specifically, the names of three different male interviewees came up in accusations. Two were mentioned to me at the rumour stage, one had started to evolve towards the internal denunciation stage. In all three cases, the individuals giving me the information did not know that the denunciated men were also in my study, reflecting the importance of ensuring anonymity and partitioning fields and fieldwork relations when dealing with sensitive data.

Bleuwenn Lechaux in the New York theatre world (Chapter 7 in this book). Notably, rumours tend to be accepted as more legitimate when they are passed on between women. For instance, an interviewee shared with her friend the attraction she felt to a fellow DJ, to which her friend responded in a confidential tone: 'Girl, you wouldn't believe how many skeletons he has in the closet'.

Naomi's reservations regarding a more public form of denunciation are also linked to a second level of obstacles to denunciations. Namely, the competitive, precarious and network-based work environment characteristic of such art worlds:

> And the thing is, this guy offered me [an invitation for a podcast series]. So yeah, as he's really got some power... Of course, I could! But I mean, I would never dare snitch on him[21] like that. Because the guy's really powerful, although he's really borderline! I mean, if he's capable of saying stuff like that to me, what's it like with girls he works with [on a regular basis]? Who have been with him backstage? (Naomi—2022)

One can very easily be cast aside in this endogamous and competitive world, as happens in other art spheres such as in jazz (Buscatto, 2021), opera (Chapter 2 in this book), the visual arts (Chapter 4 and Chapter 5 in this book), theatre (Chapter 7 in this book) or the Japanese music industry (Chapter 3 in this book). In the French electronic music world, the main employment networks operate around the artists themselves. Indeed, most DJs are also party organisers, promoters and discographic label curators, and therefore the actual or future employers of their peers. At the same time, the hierarchical dimension of professional relationships is very implicit, reinforced by the important role of socialising and the ways in which a range of festive practices are fully integrated as professionally appropriate behaviours. To quote Sarah Thornton (1995, p. 91), electronic music artists can be analysed as 'professional clubbers'. They are expected to consume (at least some) alcohol and to follow the temporal logic of the club, which requires them to stay in the venue and interact with peers throughout the night, intertwining work and leisure. In this context, denouncers sometimes fear being categorised as killjoys: 'Maybe I'm the one who's too uptight' (Manon, DJ, aged twenty-

---

21 'Je n'oserais jamais le balancer' in French. The expression conveys the idea of denouncing someone to the police or more largely to some kind of authority.

four—2022). In this social world, the figure of the 'feminist killjoy', as coined by Sara Ahmed (2010), is particularly salient. Not only do these complaints go against 'a social order, which is protected as a moral order, a happiness order' (Ahmed, 2010, p. 2), they also go against emotional (Hochschild, 2001) and embodied forms of labour expected in certain artistic practices (see also Chapter 3; Chapter 5; and Chapter 7 in this book). In this profession, one is expected to perform playfulness and joy both when in the DJ booth and with colleagues.

A third political and moral level of obstacles can be captured through the notion of 'egalitarian ethos' (Clair, 2011). Given the progressive values that circulate in the electronic music world, embedded in a salient sense of community and an appropriation of feminist ideals, the denegation[22] of gender-based violence is strong:

> Because it's an alternative atmosphere, because there are lots of people who are politically committed in various ways, you would think that... What should normally follow from that is more awareness and less violence. But no! Nobody can escape violence, that's the way it is. There's no escaping it [inhales sharply]. And the fact that we struggle to even imagine it, well... When it happens, it creates an image of what's going on that's *just not real* [emphasised]. (Maya, DJ, producer and radio show curator, aged thirty-four—2023)

Indeed, nearly all interviewees situate themselves as politically 'leftist' or 'radical leftist' and mobilise the term 'feminist' to define their personal and political views on gender equality. Here, a comparison with other left-wing political spaces is useful. Like in the German libertarian-left wing groups studied by Emeline Fourment, 'The very possibility that gender-based violence can be perpetrated [in this case, by an artist against a peer] calls into question the progressive identity of the group' (Fourment, 2017, p. 110).

Many art worlds are also spaces where people maintain not only day-to-day professional but also friendly, romantic or sexual relationships—indeed, the artistic project often absorbs most of the interviewees'

---

22 In an article focusing on French Universities, Coline Cardi, Delphine Naudier and Geneviève Pruvost (2005, p. 51) analytically distinguish between the 'denial' of gender relations (i.e., completely discarding the fact that gendered forms of injustice can take place) and their 'denegation'. Denegation is a form of double-speak: arguing the absence of discrimination, while acknowledging that some abuses of power can occur on the margins.

spheres of sociability (see also Chapter 4; Chapter 5; and Chapter 7 in this book). This explains the important number of experiences of violence at the intersection of the conjugal and professional I came across during fieldwork. It also helps to understand the strong denegation of specifically sexual forms of violence when they concern members of the electronic music scene, seen as a 'family' and its spaces as 'home'. Sexual violence accordingly turns into a taboo subject, as often observed in closed social groups such as families (Dussy, 2013). Reactions of male artists to violent events are illustrative in this regard:

> On the dancefloor, around 3 AM, Isa (DJ and producer, aged twenty-seven) grabs my arm and looks at me with a terrified expression on her face: 'Can we go outside? Stay with me'. She takes my hand and leads me towards the exit; we end up sitting on the pavement opposite the club. She warns me: 'I'm having an anxiety attack, but I'll be fine'. A man 'groped [her] arse' earlier in the evening and she's now having a 'paranoid attack', wondering if she's been drugged. [...] The stage manager joins us. They know each other well, he's a local DJ too. He reassures her by saying: 'Don't worry, you're at home, nothing will happen to you here'. (Field notes—2022)

Rumours are what happens when denunciations fail to emerge due to the private dimension of both the complaint, still considered an intimate matter or an epiphenomenon (Ahmed, 2021), and the professional environment itself. This last point is particularly salient when read through a feminist lens: spaces coded as private are key locations of the reproduction of gender-based violence (Brown et al., 2020; Kelly, 1987).

'Washing the Dirty Linen in Private':[23] Internal Denunciation

Reputational Stigma Shifts from the Victim to the Denunciated

In some cases, rumours transform into 'internal denunciations' by gaining legitimacy within a network of peers. Firstly, for the rumour

---

23 Full quote: 'Ce linge-là ne saurait plus être lavé en famille' ('That kind of linen will no longer be washed privately'). This French expression was used in a collective and anonymous statement released on Facebook, following the denunciation (first

to overcome the various obstacles discussed above, it must concern cases of violence considered socially—but also criminally —as 'serious' and repeated. All the internal denunciations I observed concerned individuals who were denounced for sexual forms of violence and by several victims. Secondly, the denunciation gains greater traction when made by a man. As Luc Boltanski et al. (1984, p. 32) argue, 'To carry out a normal denunciation, characterised in particular [...] by the otherness of the denouncer and the victim, one must have the authority to stand up for another individual, to fly (symbolically) to his or her aid'. When men report violent individuals on behalf of women or gender minorities, they are much less likely to be suspected of feminist zeal or exaggerating the situation. Here, gender serves the purpose of 'otherness' required in the de-singularisation process, enhancing the legitimacy of the complaint.

When an individual is denounced internally, the stigma gradually shifts from the victim's reputation to that of the accused, now categorised in negative terms and no longer associated with sexuality but with violence:

> I'm still surprised to learn that some of my mates behaved badly towards girls. I'm really shocked to learn that someone I've met in my life is actually an abuser. Like [this DJ]: he was such a good guy, I loved him. But turns out he's a piece of shit. (Guillaume, DJ and producer, aged twenty-seven—2021)

Feelings of 'surprise' were frequent among male respondents recalling denunciations. They also materialise a moral boundary in terms of masculine behaviour—and more broadly, the associated practices in terms of masculinities (Connell, 2005)—which needs to be reaffirmed by clearly dissociating the 'good guys' from the 'bastards':

> [While discussing a denunciation of rape] But he was a guy—I thought he was *nice* [emphasised], you know! But he wasn't. And I've heard stories like that about people I knew when I was younger. I really felt they were people who wouldn't do that. But they did. (Bruno, producer and live performer, aged thirty—2022)

---

internal, then public) of the two co-founders and curators of an electronic music festival for sexual assault and rape.

Denunciations without a Public?

Denunciations can then be accompanied by sanctions. The most common response of interviewees was to cancel the artist from a forthcoming event. 'Given what I heard, we can't endorse it', says Marc (DJ and artistic director, aged thirty-four—2022) as he removes the name of an artist accused of sexual violence from the promotional poster he just received for an upcoming gig. Yet, no publicisation of this modification to the list of performers is made. Mathieu took similar action concerning a collaboration on his music label, which he cancelled:

> I've been really clear with him, saying that I absolutely don't want any weird business or problem, or any such thing. I just can't commit to an album project if there are things... I mean, I need to trust the person. (Mathieu, DJ, producer and label manager, aged thirty-three—2022)

The egalitarian norms that circulate at work (Bereni & Jacquemart, 2018) can act as a catalyst for individual action. Indeed, deciding to exclude an aggressor from spaces and networks that the victim still frequents is a way of 'acknowledging the existence of gender relations as power relations' and trying to 'reverse them by favouring the presence of the victim over the presence of the aggressor' (Duriez, 2009, as cited in Fourment, 2017, p. 115). Interestingly, who these male denunciators are intimately involved with seems to matter. I observed that most of the male artists who spoke out against such colleagues were, or had been, in conjugal relationships with feminist women.

Speaking out and taking action can also positively impact the whistleblower's professional reputation: 'It all started with us, and I'm pretty proud of it' (Marc, commenting on an internal denunciation, 2022). In other words, not only are men more likely to be heard when it comes to denouncing violence: by doing so, they gain a certain amount of professional recognition. This relative advantage male artists have in general—moreover, when they occupy positions of power in the hierarchies of the art world—can be perceived as an injustice by their peers, as Pascal (DJ and producer, aged twenty-nine—2022) recalls. One of his close friends, a DJ identifying as non-binary, refused to perform in a club where a member of the scene who had been spoken out against continued to work. Pascal suggested putting some pressure on the venue by using his own reputation as leverage: 'If they want me to continue to play there, then this guy can't be around'. His friend eventually asked him not to intervene, upset that Pascal might actually be listened to, unlike the victims or those lower down the professional hierarchy.

Generally, the electronic music world continues to be thought of as a world apart that has its own rules. Denunciations of violence should be dealt with as such. That is, between peers of a given professional network: the only recipients of the internal denunciation. During interviews and fieldwork, this sometimes means keeping the sociologist (a non-member of the art world) at bay:

> Yeah, I've heard a lot about [an internally accused DJ we had been discussing]. And I'm thinking of another story about a guy who runs a festival, but I promised I wouldn't talk about it. It goes a bit against what I was saying earlier, about denouncing and so on, but the person who told me was like 'You really shouldn't talk about it, it's dealt with internally'. So, I'm not going to talk about it. (Loic, DJ and producer, aged twenty-five—2021)

If the personal reputation of the accused is partly tarnished in the professional arena where the internal denunciation circulates, his artistic reputation is not. The general public does not hear about the denunciation and continues to listen to his work in spaces that still book him. The involvement of male artists and other practitioners, through relaying and speaking out, enables denunciations to 'grow' towards social legitimacy (Boltanski et al., 1984). In return, the denunciator is symbolically rewarded by peers, given that he embodies, by his actions, the egalitarian ethos of the art world. That is, denunciations of sexual violence also 'grow' the reputation of the selfless denunciator. Finally, by 'keeping it in the family', far from the scrutiny of the public, no major destabilisation of the taboo subject of sexual violence is at stake.

Involving the Public as a Moral Pledge

The Case Gone Public: 'Calling Out'

Unlike other art worlds, where forms of hierarchy can be the direct recipients of denunciations, the ways recruitment processes operate in electronic music impact publicisation practices. The recipient of the denunciation is the *public*—in the double sense of the audience and of the collective arena—as well as the support staff and artists ordinarily distant from the accused or the denunciator. Until then kept at bay, audiences and whole musical networks now become witnesses as well as actors in the organised boycott, becoming a form of 'external authority' (see Chapter 2 in this book). In all the cases I observed, the means by which denunciations are made public is through press releases posted on social media. The denunciators and signatories of statements are the artistic collectives to which the accused artists belong. The aim is to dissociate from the denounced to prevent any stigma tainting the group:

> We have decided to break the silence on important issues and we sincerely hope that speaking out will encourage others to do the same. Fear and shame must change sides. A few months ago, the collective was shaken by the news that one of our members, Puzupuzu, had committed serious acts against multiple victims. [...] This episode shook us all to the core: we realised that violence was present within our own communities and within our own collective, despite the values that have always underpinned it. (Extract of the statement posted by the *Qui Embrouille Qui* collective on their Facebook page, May 18, 2020)

A very similar rhetoric appears in other statements:

> At the end of August, we received a message alleging rape of F. by a member of the *Casual Gabberz* collective, CLUBKELLY, during a party among their mutual circle of friends. After several exchanges with F., via a third party whom we sincerely thank, there is absolutely no doubt as to the veracity of her statements, and the nature of the alleged offences is serious enough for us to share the following message with you. [...] The actions CLUBKELLY is accused of run completely counter to the values of the other members of the collective and therefore of the collective itself. CLUBKELLY is therefore no longer a part of *Casual Gabberz*. (Extract of the statement posted by the *Casual Gabberz* collective on their Instagram page, October 27, 2023)

In the comments section under these statements, the public congratulates the signatories for their 'honesty' in denouncing the actions of a close colleague. The accused is explicitly named, while the identities of the victims remain hidden. But contrary to the cautious anonymisation identified in rumours, this imprecision helps to socially validate the denunciation, distancing it from the individual level associated with complaints and bringing it up to the general level associated with political causes (Boltanski et al., 1984).

Public denunciations, like internal denunciations, are made possible by the fact that the fight against sexist and sexual violence has been established as a valid political problem in the electronic music world. They are followed by certain actions due to the nature of the denounced facts. As discussed, sexual violence is not 'supposed' to happen in such a festive, friendly, progressive and familial environment. Public denunciations thus endanger not only the individuals named but also the community as a whole, 'whose external credibility is diminished and also risks internal dissociation as a result of the polarisation inherent in the logic of such cases' (Boltanski et al., 1984, p. 15). Thus, public denunciations require drastic forms of alterisation of the accused.

The *Qui Embrouille Qui* case

This case of public denunciation was brought up by many interviewees during fieldwork. Its trajectory is exemplary of the different modalities and stages outlined in this chapter.

For several years, the violent nature of actions attributed to some members of this Parisian collective were the subject of rumours, circulating in a low-key way. As one interviewee close to the artistic group recollects: 'I tolerated it, we all tolerated it! Because we were having so much fun together. So yeah, from time to time [such and such member] would blow a fuse but overall we were happy to play [music] together' (Jérôme, DJ and producer, aged thirty-five—2022).

Over the course of 2019, the denunciation progressively gained legitimacy at an internal level. A festival removed from its programme, without publicisation, the appearance of one of the accused members. Finally, the affair became public in May 2020 through a statement published on the collective's official Facebook page, triggered in particular by a police investigation of one of the denounced members, Puzupuzu, for domestic violence. The fact that one of the denounced artists, DJ AZF, was the founder of the collective and a non-heterosexual woman accused of domestic violence was the cause of much discussion among interviewees. The case soon took on the artist's name, being referred to as the 'AZF case'.

The Effects of Public Denunciations

In the studied cases, all publicly exposed individuals suffered direct repercussions, including the end of their artistic careers.[24] After being called out,[25] they stopped receiving propositions for bookings in clubs and festivals and eventually left the scene. As frequently heard: 'You can destroy someone's career' (Justine, DJ and club employee, aged twenty-four—2022), and 'As soon as you're targeted, no matter what, it's over' (Jérémy, former DJ, aged thirty-two—2023). The stigma attached to the accused can then spread to those formerly close to him: 'We were caught in the act as accomplices. Well, not accomplices, but like "we knew"' (Jérôme, DJ and producer, aged thirty-five—2022). This stigma can also extend to professionals who continue to work with the exposed artist. 'We thought it sucked, we didn't understand why she continued to work with him', commented Justine, regarding a female colleague who released new productions with a DJ publicly accused of sexual harassment. Or as evoked by Apolline:

> With my agency, we decided to accept [a booking from an artistic group, soon after the public denunciation of one of its members]. As soon as it came out, loads of people around me were like 'No, don't play there, you can't play there'. So eventually I said, 'Oh, fuck it, I don't give a damn about this booking anyway, I'm going to cancel it'. (Apolline, DJ, aged thirty—2022)

The effectiveness of being banned was also mentioned by an interviewee who had been publicly called out. He points out how his case was used as an example, regretting how 'borderline guys' position themselves in the denunciation process:

> Guys who continued to call me for DJ sets would tell me that their headliners' agents were cancelling bookings, that they didn't want their artists' names to be next to mine on a line-up. So, they ended up cancelling my bookings after all [...] That was quite hard to deal with,

---

24 This occurs more or less progressively, with some denounced artists continuing to DJ in peripheral spaces of the art world before exiting completely. A longer ethnographical investigation might discern whether some manage to re-enter artistic networks, and if so, when and how.

25 During fieldwork, the expression 'cancelled' was occasionally used, though usually not directly referring to larger debates regarding 'cancel culture' as a political strategy.

when borderline guys tell you 'Oh no, we're not going to book you for gigs any more'. Because symbolically... yeah, you've become a symbol of sexist and sexual violence. (Jérémy, former DJ, aged thirty-two—2023)

Yet, in reaffirming a latent obstacle where the onus is placed on victims, the effectiveness of public denunciations can hinder the possibilities of speaking out: 'If he loses something, it'll be my fault and I'll be blamed' (Sarah, photographer and amateur DJ, female, aged twenty-nine—2023). Moreover, the accused are, in many cases, close acquaintances of the victims—either professionally, in the sense of a fellow 'community' member, or a partner or ex-partner. Take, for instance, Charlène, who explains why she hasn't publicly denounced another female artist:

> I haven't called her out because I don't want her to be excluded. And at the same time, I don't want to see her again, so I've isolated myself, I stopped going to events [...] But I don't want to put her out of her job. I would hate it if I had to. I mean, I would never send messages to collectives or promoters saying, 'You've booked the person who attacked me', you know? (Charlène, DJ, aged thirty—2022)

Here, Charlène is referring to a female colleague whom she has denounced only internally. While the vast majority of the denunciations I observed involved men accused of violent behaviours towards women, certainly not all gender-based violence is committed by males or in heterosexual relations. In the twenty-two cases under study here, two concern women accused of violence towards other women. Though the empirical data is not sufficient for a deep analysis, it does allow us to formulate a hypothesis regarding the intricate obstacles to speaking out in such cases. The euphemising of women's violence stems from sexism, while symmetrising male and female violence is simultaneously a masculinist theme (Cardi & Pruvost, 2011). Specifically, women denouncing female colleagues for such violence find themselves facing an additional double bind: a fear of fuelling masculinist or lesbophobic arguments[26] and a refusal to jeopardise the careers of peers already disadvantaged in this male-dominated environment.

---

26 This topic has been analysed by sociologists interested in female violence. See, for example, Vanessa Watremez (2012, p. 220), who writes: 'The debate, therefore, tends to be framed as such: if women are just as violent as men, and if there is just as much violence in homosexual relationships as in heterosexual ones, then gender and sexual orientation are not relevant factors in the study of violence'.

Public denunciations thus emerge at the end of a distinct process, and are received as socially valid because they are set forth by a group of peers. They concern acts of violence that are considered to be 'serious' (that is, when categorised as 'sexual' forms of violence), repeated and sometimes associated with police investigations. The denunciation thus leaves the private sphere, where it is partly ignored and partly managed, on a daily basis.

Conclusion

Ethnographic study of denunciations of gender-based violence in the French electronic music world brings to the fore three main observations. First, the rare public denunciations that emerge are not contradictory to the multiple untold or unheard rumours of gender-based violence. Public denunciation and the exclusion of the accused serve as an alterisation process, in a social world imagined as a close and closed community, somewhat comparable to a family where sexual forms of violence are not supposed to happen—or at least should be dealt with internally, out of the public eye.

Second, though denunciations of violence are evoked in the name of egalitarian principles, perpetrators face sanctions only if well-established and preferably male individuals or whole collectives act as whistle-blowers, thus giving accusations legitimacy. In this art world, individual reputations at the sexual, moral or political levels are entangled with professional reputations, and unequally distributed in terms of gendered power relations.

Finally, the fight against gender-based violence seems to have acquired the status of a recognised political cause, but this politicisation does not guarantee that each individual denunciation will be received as valid by peers. Moreover, 'exemplary' public accusations can paradoxically deter victims from speaking out, in addition to the other obstacles they encounter along the denunciation process. The egalitarian ethos, at least concerning the stance against gender-based violence, does not fundamentally disturb the gendered organisation of this art world.

References

Acker, J. (1990). Hierarchies, jobs, bodies: A theory of gendered organizations. *Gender and Society*, 4(2), 139–158. https://doi.org/10.1177/089124390004002002

Ahmed, S. (2010). Feminist killjoys (and other willful subjects). *The Scholar and Feminist Online*, 8(3). https://sfonline.barnard.edu/feminist-killjoys-and-other-willful-subjects

Ahmed, S. (2021). *Complaint!* Duke University Press. https://doi.org/10.1515/9781478022336

Attias, B. A., Gavanas, A., & Rietveld, H. (2013). *DJ culture in the mix. Power, technology and social change in electronic music.* Bloomsbury.

Becker, H. (1982). *Art worlds.* University of California Press.

Bereni, L., & Jacquemart, A. (2018). Diriger comme un homme moderne. Les élites masculines de l'administration française face à la norme d'égalité des sexes. *Actes de la recherche en sciences sociales*, 3(223), 72–87. https://doi.org/10.3917/arss.223.0072

Boltanski, L., Darré, Y., & Schiltz, M.-A. (1984). La dénonciation. *Actes de la Recherche en Sciences Sociales*, 51(1), 3–40. https://doi.org/10.3406/arss.1984.2212

Brown, E., Debauche, A., Hamel, C., Mazuy, M., & Bozon, M. (2020). *Violences et rapports de genre: Enquête sur les violences de genre en France.* INED. https://doi.org/10.4000/books.ined.14719

Buscatto, M. (2021). *Women in jazz. Musicality, femininity, marginalization.* Routledge. https://doi.org/10.4324/9781003177555 (Original work published 2007)

Cardi, C., Naudier, D., & Pruvost, G. (2005). Les rapports sociaux de sexe à l'université: Au cœur d'une triple dénégation. *L'Homme & la Société*, 4(158), 49–73. https://doi.org/10.3917/lhs.158.0049

Cardi, C., & Pruvost, G. (2011). La violence des femmes: Occultations et mises en récit. *Champ pénal*, 8. https://doi.org/10.4000/champpenal.8039

Cavalin, C., Da Silva, J., Delage, P., Despontin Lefèvre, I., Lacombe, D., & Pavard, B. (2022). *Les violences sexistes après #MeToo.* Presses des Mines. https://doi.org/10.4000/pressesmines.8223

Clair, I. (2011). La découverte de l'ennui conjugal. Les manifestations contrariées de l'idéal conjugal et de l'ethos égalitaire dans la vie quotidienne de jeunes de milieux populaires. *Sociétés contemporaines*, 3(83), 59–81. https://doi.org/10.3917/soco.083.0059

Clair, I. (2016). Faire du terrain en féministe. *Actes de la recherche en sciences sociales*, 3(213), 66–83. https://doi.org/10.3917/arss.213.0066

Connell, R. (1987). *Gender and power: Society, the person, and sexual politics.* Stanford University Press.

Connell, R. W. (2005). *Masculinities* (2nd ed.). Routledge. https://doi. org/10.4324/9781003116479 (Original work published 1995).

Dussy, D. (2013). *Le berceau des dominations. Anthropologie de l'inceste.* La Discussion. https://doi.org/10.3917/pock.dussy.2021.01

Fourment, É. (2017). Militantismes libertaire et féministe face aux violences sexuelles. Le cas de la gauche radicale de Göttingen. *Sociétés contemporaines,* 3(107), 109–130. https://doi.org/10.3917/soco.107.0109

Glaser, B., & Strauss, A. (1967). *The discovery of grounded theory: Strategies for qualitative research.* Sociology Press.

Hochschild, A. (2001). Emotional labour. In S. Jackson & S. Scott (Eds), *Gender: A sociological reader* (pp. 192–196). Routledge.

Jouvenet, M. (2006). *Rap, techno, électro... Le musicien entre travail artistique et critique sociale* (Éthnologie de la France). Éditions de la MSH. https://doi. org/10.4000/books.editionsehess.2541

Kelly, L. (1987). The continuum of sexual violence. In J. Hanmer & M. Maynard (Eds), *Women, violence and social control* (pp. 46–60). Palgrave Macmillan. https://doi.org/10.1007/978-1-349-18592-4_4

Perrenoud, M., & Bois, G. (2017). Artistes ordinaires: Du paradoxe au paradigme? *Biens Symboliques / Symbolic Goods,* 1. https://doi.org/10.4000/bssg.88

Picaud, M. (2020). Quand le genre entre en scène. Configurations professionnelles de la programmation musicale et inégalités des artistes dans deux capitales européennes. *Sociétés Contemporaines,* 3(119), 143–168. https://doi.org/10.3917/soco.119.0143

Picaud, M. (2023). La Nuit est morte, vive la Nuit? Action publique et transformations urbaines et économiques de la fête. *Terrains & travaux,* 2(43), 27–52. https://doi.org/10.3917/tt.043.0027

Rauh Ortega, A. (2018). *'Under-the-radar' electronic dance musicians: Opportunities and challenges with digital communication technologies* (Doctoral thesis, University of Leeds). http://etheses.whiterose.ac.uk/20632/

Thornton, S. (1995). *Club cultures: Music, media and subcultural capital.* Wesleyan University Press.

Watremez, V. (2012). La violence dans les relations lesbiennes: Recension des écrits. In C. Cardi, & G. Pruvost (Eds), *Penser la violence des femmes* (pp. 220–230). La Découverte. https://doi.org/10.3917/dec.cardi.2012.01.0220

Conclusion

Marie Buscatto, Sari Karttunen and Mathilde Provansal

As expressed in our general introduction, we chose an extensive definition of gender-based violence in order to describe all forms of violence and identify aggressors and victims beyond the men/women dichotomy, as well as the wealth of social processes which participate in producing, perpetuating, legitimising or challenging its existence. Using this robust epistemological stance, and through the development of in-depth case studies conducted in several artistic and cultural worlds—opera, visual arts, popular and electronic music, screen industries, photography and theatre—and a wide range of countries—Finland, France, Japan, the United Kingdom and the United States—this book identified several traits of gender-based violence experienced in artistic and cultural worlds.

First of all, artistic and cultural worlds fully operate as unequal and hierarchised gender regimes. These spheres not only maintain the binary division between men and women (both objectively and subjectively), but also reinforce this division as a 'natural' and dominant reality, upheld by heteronormative dynamics. While expressing themselves as open to non-binary, queer or transgender as well as homosexual, bisexual or asexual people—in other words as open to any kind of gender identity and sexuality—most people evolving in those worlds still identify themselves and others as either men or women, and participate in creating a heteronormative order. Moreover, aggressors tend to be men while victims tend to be women. And several social processes, embedded in daily professional practices, heavily participate in producing, perpetuating and legitimising such unequal, hierarchised and hurtful gender regimes.

Moreover, this book assesses the relevance of Liz Kelly's approach to gender-based violence as a *continuum*, from everyday sexism to criminal offences affecting women over their life course, whether it impacts their artistic education, their entry into the art world or their subsequent careers. The chapters constituting this book prove that this *continuum* of violence shapes how gender-based violence emerges, persists and ingrains itself in the dynamics that organise artistic and cultural worlds. This finding may inspire action for change to those artists, activists and professional intermediaries who are keen to reduce, or even to eliminate, gender-based violence in their professional worlds: start with combating everyday sexism, do not settle for repeated criminal sexual acts, as is still the case when gender-based violence is challenged in artistic and cultural worlds. While criminalising a few repeat offenders and excluding them from artistic and cultural worlds may seem like a first step towards the reduction of gender-based violence, our case studies do not seem to support this prevailing belief. Everyday sexism is at the heart of gender-based violence, allowing for its perpetuation and pervasiveness, even when repeat aggressors are condemned and excluded.

Last but not least, our book shows that those seeking to reduce gender-based violence, or even eliminate it, need to better document the social processes ingrained in professional practices in their specific artistic or cultural world that not only enable gender-based violence to occur but also make it difficult to combat. These include the sexualisation of female students and artists; the major role of male mentors in opening doors to young and experienced artists; the ideology of talent; the blurred boundaries between private and professional lives; the precariousness and high-level of competition; the lack of processes for denouncing gender-violence acts, even when criminal in essence. Our case studies on gender-based violence in artistic and cultural education and work contexts reveal that research on gender-based violence would greatly benefit from an expanded focus, examining the experiences of women, gender and sexual minorities beyond formal workplaces and educational settings, formal employment and paid work.

To conclude, it appears, through those different case studies conducted in several countries, that fighting gender-based violence is not only about creating safer educational and professional worlds, but also about creating equal access to training, to recruitment, to working and to recognition for women and gender and sexual minorities.

Despite its deep and rich findings, this book has limitations which we hope will inspire future research. The case studies' lack of coverage of lesbian, gay, bisexual, transgender and queer people calls for further investigation on gender-based violence targeting these groups. The limited number of cases encountered during fieldwork prevented authors from adequately studying the commonalities and specificities of gender-based violence against LGBTQ+ people. More research is needed to describe the forms of gender-based violence against people challenging the gender binary and heteronormativity in artistic and cultural worlds, to account for the contexts and the social processes driving the violence and to study its role in perpetuating gender and sexual hierarchies. Gender-based violence does not concern white heterosexual cis-men and cis-women only, even though marginalised voices were a minority in the case studies of this book.

Research is also warranted into gender-based violence experienced by people located at the intersection of several systems of inequality to understand how social class, race, age, sexuality, national origin or disability shape gender-based violence, its denunciation and challenges. Further attention to gender-based violence against minoritised people requires reflection on the best suited methodological approach to access and study their experiences. For example, collaborating with collectives fighting diverse forms of oppressions in the artistic and cultural fields may allow researchers to learn how best to recruit research participants.

Finally, this book offers an exploration of the pervasive issue of gender-based violence within a wide array of artistic and cultural sectors and across diverse global contexts. Despite this ambitious scope, its findings should be expanded to include voices from the Global South.

We hope that the important insights of *Gender-Based Violence in Arts and Culture: Perspectives on Education and Work* will spark discussions among students, artists, cultural intermediaries, activists, scholars, politicians and anyone concerned with ensuring creative freedom in work and education, untainted by gender-based violence.

Afterword

Paula-Irene Villa

Gender-based violence appears to be a paradox. Equally monotonous and highly variable, it is a universal phenomenon, yet it manifests in specific and context-dependent ways. Its repetitive patterns—rooted in entrenched practices, social justifications and systemic normalisation—coexist with significant variation in its specific expression. Harassment, sexual assault, inappropriate advances and coercion take different forms across settings, influenced by factors such as age, social norms, institutional structures, historical or regional contexts and legal framings. This interplay of specificity and uniformity highlights how gender-based violence is both structurally ingrained, and (re)shaped by embodied practices in specific sociocultural environments. In other words: gender-based violence happens everywhere all the time and it is always an element of an omnipresent heteropatriarchal culture—but it happens in a myriad of different ways. According to a vast amount of research, gender-based violence is globally pervasive but takes different forms depending on history, culture, law and economic structures (Alcalde & Villa, 2022; Fileborn & Loney-Howes, 2019; Gill & Orgad, 2018; Kelly, 1987; Merry, 2006; True, 2012).

This book brings together a wide range of diverse case studies from arts, culture and media industries, exploring how gender-based violence and sexism play out in different (national) regions and contexts. The presented studies align with the overall picture, adding depth and more specific evidence: while the specifics of gender-based violence vary depending on the industry, location and legal system, the broader patterns remain strikingly similar. The same harmful dynamics keep resurfacing, reinforcing and normalising these issues in professional spaces. Understanding both the unique details and the recurring

    https://doi.org/10.11647/OBP.0436.10

patterns is key to recognising why gendered violence persists—and what allows it to continue.

The tension between uniformity and specificity in gender-based violence necessitates empirical scrutiny—one of the key strengths of this anthology. The studies presented here make these dynamics tangible by revealing the prevalence of sexualised violence and everyday sexism alongside the distinct practices of institutions such as theatres, art academies, media organisations and informal music scenes. Moreover, they emphasise the lived realities of those affected, illustrating how gendered violence shapes educational trajectories, career opportunities, and workplace dynamics. At the same time, the book sheds light on the agency of individuals and collectives who resist these structures, forging alliances and transforming individual vulnerability into collective empowerment.

These essays situate gender-based violence within the *continuum* articulated by Liz Kelly (1987), asserting that such violence is not an accumulation of isolated incidents but rather a pattern embedded in professional and cultural hierarchies. Across diverse artistic and media sectors—whether in opera, theatre, film, photography or digital media— certain structural conditions create environments that facilitate and normalise sexualised violence. One key factor is the ambiguous nature of professional boundaries in the arts and cultural industries, where the division between personal and professional spheres is often blurred. The ethos of artistic genius—framed as an innate quality requiring cultivation by authoritative mentors—can legitimise hierarchical power imbalances. In this framework, transgressions, including physical and psychological violations, are often justified as part of artistic training or dismissed as necessary for creative expression. Many of the empirical studies in this collection highlight how these structural conditions impede the recognition of injustice, as victims often come to terms with their experiences only retrospectively. Even then, silence, minimisation and institutional inaction frequently prevail.

Additionally, the precarious nature of employment in the arts and cultural sectors heightens vulnerability to gender-based violence. The absence or limited applicability of labour protections—combined with freelance, unpaid, or informal working arrangements—creates an environment where individuals, particularly young or early-career professionals, lack structural safeguards. This precarity disproportionately concentrates power in the hands of a select few, exacerbating exploitative conditions.

Further compounding the issue is the deeply embedded sexist and sexualised cultural framework that has long shaped artistic representation. The objectification of women in the visual arts, the fetishisation of female roles in opera, and the gendered gaze in photography and film all reflect historical and ongoing structures of oppression. These dynamics extend beyond explicit portrayals to more subtle forms of gendered representation that reinforce hierarchical power relations. As the studies in this book demonstrate, representation is significant—but its impact is limited if structural change within institutions and production processes does not follow. As Bleuwenn Lechaux asserts, 'Making an issue visible does not automatically mean that it will be addressed'. Similarly, Anna Bull's research illustrates the persistent dissonance between progressive media portrayals and workplace realities, where the very industries producing critical content remain complicit in maintaining gendered power imbalances.

Ultimately, gender-based violence in the arts and cultural sectors cannot be understood in isolation from broader systems of gendered labour inequality, precarious working conditions, and heteropatriarchal cultural scripts. These intersecting structures sustain a *continuum* of gendered violence that spans diverse contexts, from the most affluent urban centres to marginalised rural communities, from progressive artistic subcultures to deeply conservative environments such as religious spaces (Alcalde & Villa, 2022). While specific manifestations differ, the underlying mechanisms remain strikingly consistent.

Crucially, the burden of change should not rest on individual victims, but on institutions and broader social structures. The imperative is to shift the focus from fixing those subjected to violence to transforming the systems that enable it. This lesson is underscored by the 2024 mass trial against Gisèle Pelicot's rapists in Avignon, which demonstrated the necessity of structural accountability: as much as 'shame must change sides', the responsibility for preventing gender-based violence must shift from the potential individual victims to the organisations. In the arts and cultural industries, this concretely means moving beyond expecting individuals—particularly women, young professionals, non-hegemonic men and those in precarious positions—to navigate inherently unsafe environments. Instead, institutions must implement structural protections, such as intimacy coordination in performance industries and proactive organisational accountability measures. As some studies in this book show, such emerging efforts, including initiatives like Intimacy Directors International, are promising steps toward institutional responsibility rather than individual endurance.

The power of collective action remains key in challenging gender-based violence, as evidenced by the #MeToo movement. While many contributions in this book engage with its impact, and rightly so, #MeToo did not emerge in isolation. It is part of a longstanding *continuum* of feminist, LGBTQ+ and broader social justice struggles against sexualised violence. Such movements go way back, they are a core element of feminist and Civil Rights Movements, of Labour Movements and of efforts to protect migrants and refugees (Bordin, 1981; Freedman, 2013; Tilly & Scott, 1978; Walkowitz, 1980). These movements have historically foregrounded the experiences of women as victims of gender-based violence, but have also often addressed gender-based and sexualised violence against children, disabled individuals, trans* people, queer people, people of colour and further groups 'othered' by hegemonic masculinity (Jewkes et al., 2015). #MeToo was and remains embedded in these wider struggles, acknowledging the multiplicity of potential victims:

> #MeToo reflects complex fights against sexualised and gendered violence, against everyday sexism and rape culture, and against the many shades of toxic masculinity and gendered ideologies. Although women remain a primary target of such violence, it is not limited to women and girls. Transgender, non-binary and queer people are at heightened risk for gender and sexual harassment and violence. In short, sexualised and gender-based violence serve as a display and reinforcement of institutionalised structures of power and as practices of forcing persons and entire groups into seemingly 'normal' gender and sexual scripts as well as into 'normal' power hierarchies. (Alcalde & Villa, 2022, p. 4)

Gender is itself a complex issue, a biosocial fact, a social construct and a societal structure; gender is a norm and experienced through myriads of vague, messy and ever-shifting embodied practices (Villa Braslavsky, 2023). Gender is also intersectional, i.e. inevitably linked to and co-

constituted by other social differences such as class, age, sexuality, etc. (Crenshaw, 1991). Gender is never quite only one immutable thing; thus, gender-based violence could not be one simple thing either. Rather, gender-based violence is one strategy used to keep women and all others than white, bourgeois, heterosexual, not disabled men in the places that social and political order assigns them.

In sum, gender-based violence as specific practices is enabled and sustained by social structures that normalise and reproduce its existence. Addressing it requires both recognising its systemic nature and implementing concrete institutional reforms. This book contributes to that endeavour by offering empirical insights, critical analysis and pathways toward structural transformation.

References

Alcalde, C. M., & Villa, P.-I. (2022). *#MeToo and beyond. Perspectives on a global movement.* University Press of Kentucky. https://doi.org/10.2307/j.ctv2mm210k

Bordin, R. (1981). *Woman and temperance: The quest for power and liberty, 1873–1900.* Temple University Press

Crenshaw, K. (1991). Mapping the margins: Intersectionality, identity politics, and violence against women of color. *Stanford Law Review,* 43(6), 1241–1299. https://doi.org/10.2307/1229039

Fileborn, B. & Loney-Howes R. (Eds) (2019). *#MeToo and the politics of social change.* Palgrave Macmillan. https://doi.org/10.1007/978-3-030-15213-0

Freedman, E. B. (2013). *Redefining rape: Sexual violence in the era of suffrage and segregation.* Harvard University Press. https://doi.org/10.2307/j.ctt6wpm5m

Gill, R., & Orgad, S. (2018). The shifting terrain of sex and power: From the 'sexualization of culture' to #MeToo. *Sexualities,* 21(8), 1313–1324. https://doi.org/10.1177/1363460718794647

Jewkes, R., Flood, M., & Lang, J. (2015). From work with men and boys to changes of social norms and reduction of inequities in gender relations: A conceptual shift in prevention of gender-based violence. *The Lancet,* 385(9977), 1580–1589. https://doi.org/10.1016/S0140-6736(14)61683-4

Kelly, L. (1987). The continuum of sexual violence. In J. Hanmer & M. Maynard (Eds), *Women, violence and social control* (pp. 46–60). Palgrave Macmillan. https://doi.org/10.1007/978-1-349-18592-4_4

Merry, S. E. (2006). *Human rights and gender violence: Translating international law into local justice.* University of Chicago Press. https://doi.org/10.7208/chicago/9780226520759.001.0001

Tilly, L. A., & Scott, J. W. (1978). *Women, work, and family.* Holt, Rinehart and Winston. https://doi.org/10.4324/9780203819395

True, J. (2012). *The political economy of violence against women.* Oxford University Press. https://doi.org/10.1093/acprof:oso/9780199755929.001.0001

Villa Braslavsky, P.-I. (2023, August 23). Je autoritärer die politische Haltung, desto größer die Ablehnung von Transgender und Queerness [Interview by T. Becker]. *DER SPIEGEL.* https://www.spiegel.de/kultur/lgbtq-interview-mit-der-soziologin-paula-irene-villa-braslavsky-zur-debatte-ueber-trans-a-ddda20e7-a577-4a3e-bee2-cf778935bedc

Walkowitz, J. R. (1980). *Prostitution and victorian society: Women, class, and the state.* Cambridge University Press. https://doi.org/10.1017/CBO9780511583605

Index

About the Team

Alessandra Tosi was the managing editor for this book.

Adèle Kreager proof-read this manuscript. Lucy Barnes compiled the index.

Jeevanjot Kaur Nagpal designed the cover. The cover was produced in InDesign using the Fontin font.

Jeremy Bowman typeset the book in InDesign and produced the paperback and hardback editions and created the EPUB. The main text font is Tex Gyre Pagella and the heading font is Californian FB. Jeremy also produced the PDF edition.

The conversion to the HTML edition was performed with epublius, an open-source software which is freely available on our GitHub page at https://github.com/OpenBookPublishers

Laura Rodríguez was in charge of marketing.

This book was peer-reviewed by Rachel Vogler, Nicoletta Mandolini and Ella Gonzales. Experts in their field, these readers give their time freely to help ensure the academic rigour of our books. We are grateful for their generous and invaluable contributions.

This book need not end here...

Share

All our books — including the one you have just read — are free to access online so that students, researchers and members of the public who can't afford a printed edition will have access to the same ideas. This title will be accessed online by hundreds of readers each month across the globe: why not share the link so that someone you know is one of them?

This book and additional content is available at
https://doi.org/10.11647/OBP.0436

Donate

Open Book Publishers is an award-winning, scholar-led, not-for-profit press making knowledge freely available one book at a time. We don't charge authors to publish with us: instead, our work is supported by our library members and by donations from people who believe that research shouldn't be locked behind paywalls.

Join the effort to free knowledge by supporting us at
https://www.openbookpublishers.com/support-us

We invite you to connect with us on our socials!

BLUESKY	MASTODON	LINKEDIN
@openbookpublish	@OpenBookPublish	open-book-publishers
.bsky.social	@hcommons.social	

Read more at the Open Book Publishers Blog

https://blogs.openbookpublishers.com

You may also be interested in:

Theatre and War

Notes from the Field

Nandita Dinesh

https://doi.org/10.11647/OBP.0099

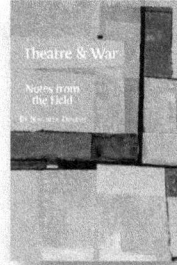

Active Speech

Critical Perspectives on Teresa Deevy

Úna Kealy & Kate McCarthy (eds)

https://doi.org/10.11647/OBP.0432

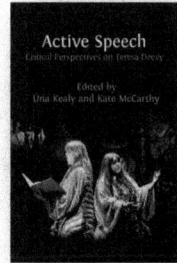

Women and Migration

Responses in Art and History

Deborah Willis, Ellyn Toscano & Kalia Brooks Nelson (eds)

https://doi.org/10.11647/OBP.0153

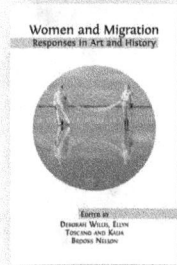

Women and Migration(s) II

Kalia Brooks, Cheryl Finley, Ellyn Toscano & Deborah Willis (eds)

https://doi.org/10.11647/OBP.0296